SUNJATA

A West African Epic of the Mande Peoples

SUNJATA

A West African Epic of the Mande Peoples

Recorded, Edited, and Translated by

DAVID C. CONRAD

Narrated by

DJANKA TASSEY CONDÉ

Hackett Publishing Company, Inc.
Indianapolis/Cambridge

10 09 08 07 06 05 04   1 2 3 4 5 6 7

For further information, please address:

Hackett Publishing Company, Inc.
P.O. Box 44937
Indianapolis, IN 46244-0937

www.hackettpublishing.com

Cover design by Abigail Coyle
Text design by Jennifer Plumley
Composition by Professional Book Compositors, Inc.
Printed at Sheridan Books, Inc.

Library of Congress Cataloging-in-Publication Data

Sunjata: a West African epic of the Mande peoples / recorded, edited, and translated by David C. Conrad; narrated by Djanka Tassey Condé.
    p. cm.
    Includes bibliographical references.
    ISBN 0-87220-697-1 (pbk.) — ISBN 0-87220-698-X (hardcover)
    1. Keita, Soundiata, d. 1255—Legends. 2. Mandingo (African people)—Folklore. 3. Legends—Mali. 4. Mali (Empire)—Folklore. I. Conrad, David C. II. Condé, Djanka Tassey.

GR352.82.M34S86   2004
398.2'089'96345—dc22   2004004260

The paper used in this publication meets the minimum requirements of
American National Standard for Information Sciences—
Permanence of Paper for Printed Library Materials,
ANSI Z39.48-1984

This book is dedicated to friends who
introduced me to the Condé bards of Fadama:

Djibril Tamsir Niane

and

Nanamoudou Condé of Baro

CONTENTS

CONTENTS

FOREWORD

This previously unpublished version of the great West African narrative popularly known as the "Sunjata epic" is being made available in response to a long-felt need for a text that is formatted in a reasonable approximation of the original performance values of the narrator, but which is at the same time readily comprehensible to readers previously unfamiliar with Manding cultures and their most definitive oral tradition. The narrative chosen for this book was recorded in five original sessions and several follow-ups in 1994 at Fadama, a village near the Niandan River in northeastern Guinea. The performer was the *jeli ngara* (master bard) Djanka Tassey Condé (d. 10/10/97), who was the last of the great Condé bards of Fadama. One of Tassey's brothers was the locally famous bard Mamadi Condé, who died in 1994. Tassey and Mamadi were sons of Babu Condé (d. 1964), one of the greatest bards who lived during the colonial era. Babu served as an informant for the historian Yves Person, and for the novelist Laye Camara. At the time of the Condé-Camara collaboration in 1963, Laye Camara described Babu as the most celebrated bard in upper Guinea.[1] Djibril Tamsir Niane (who first brought the Sunjata epic to the attention of the English-speaking world in his popular but reconstructed *Sundiata: An Epic of Old Mali* [Longman 1965]) was well acquainted with Babu and his sons Mamadi and Tassey, and it was Niane who introduced me to the Condé bards of Fadama in 1994.

The reservoir of knowledge from which the present text is drawn makes up part of the intellectual legacy left by Babu Condé and his forebears. One of Babu's ancestors, Frémori Condé, is said to have been the *jeli* of Imuraba Keita, who was a descendant of Sunjata's brother Manden Bori.[2] The Fadama Condé bards' perception of Mande history is influenced by a collective family belief that they are related to the Condé and Diarra of the ancient chiefdom, or *jamana*, of Dò ni Kiri (tr. "Dò and Kiri"), which was the homeland of three of the most important female characters in Mande epic tradition. Daughters of the ruling family of Dò ni Kiri, the Condé sisters are identified as Dò Kamissa the Buffalo Woman; Sogolon Condé, the mother of Sunjata;

---

[1] Camara 1984: 23.

[2] Camara 1984: 28.

and Tenenba Condé, the foster mother of Fakoli.[3] These women comprise the nexus of family alliances that form the basis of political power in the Mali Empire as it is portrayed in oral tradition.

The overall text that was performed by Tassey Condé is by far the most extraordinary that I have encountered since I began collecting Mande oral tradition in 1975. The parts that are excerpted for this book represent less than one-third of the overall narrative of more than 16,000 lines. Upon being approached with a proposal to produce a more reader-friendly edition than has heretofore been available, I felt reluctant to base it on the 1994 Tassey Condé recording because the comprehensive, fully annotated scholarly edition was still several years from publication. Alternative possibilities were weighed, one of which was to present a sequence of episodes from several different narrators. This would provide a variety of bardic perspectives and performance styles, but on the other hand such an approach would not only interfere with the narrative continuity, it would make it impossible to provide the consistent richness of detail available in the Fadama version. It ultimately became clear that, out of deference to the goal of producing a text that would engage the interest of nonspecialist readers and be easily understood by them, the best thing would be to employ the single most comprehensive, colorful, and dramatic version available. This means that until the complete, exhaustively annotated scholarly edition can be prepared for publication, Tassey Condé's narrative will be represented in print as a compromise between rigorous scholarly methodology and pedagogical expediency. It would have been preferable to do this in the reverse order, making the scholarly edition available before publishing this book. I have occasionally drawn on evidence from this text in various publications,[4] but I had not intended that the narrative itself would ever be printed in anything other than its most complete form.

The text presented in this book consists of a progressive narrative containing unusually detailed versions of all the best-known episodes of the Sunjata epic, in addition to some colorful and provocative passages that shed new light on the depth and complexity of the collective tradition. Readers who are previously acquainted with this narrative will find familiar heroes and heroines taking on new dimensions, secondary characters gaining in-

---

[3] Identification of the relationship between the Buffalo Woman and Sogolon varies from one version to another, but the testimony from the bards of Fadama is by far the most convincing in terms of internal consistency on details of kinship and political alliance in the tradition.

[4] For example, see Conrad 1999a: 199–215.

creased prominence, and previously unknown figures emerging from obscurity. At the same time, since the present offering does not include all the episodes of the recorded narrative and the annotations are kept to a minimum, it reveals only a fraction of what the bard has to say about lineage identities, ancestral relationships, ritual institutions, perceptions of power, and the spirit world, that are present in the overall body of material. In the interest of readability, the text presented here omits most of the esoteric details that appear in the narrator's digressions and spontaneous explanations, but care has been taken to insure that the episodes segue easily from one to another. Italicized insertions summarize the general contents of passages that are omitted from the episodes included here, and an epilogue outlines the broader range of topics covered over the entire scope of narrative from which the excerpts for this book are taken.

The manner of presentation here is driven at all levels by the goal of providing a reader-friendly text, and all editorial choices have been made accordingly. Strictly speaking, this material has been treated in a way that, according to my own standards, would be inappropriate and unacceptable in a scholarly edition. For research purposes, when we prepare the transcript of a performance like the one from which the present text was taken, we note every word and sound heard on the recording. When the scholarly edition is eventually published, in addition to the entire recorded narrative it will include, as much as possible, every flaw in the bard's speech, every idiosyncratic utterance, every misspoken or repeated word, and every interruption and comment from the audience. Most, though not all, of these things have been omitted from this text. A distinguishing characteristic of Tassey Condé's delivery is that he had the habit of frequently punctuating his narrative with a phrase that roughly translates as, "You heard it?" Sometimes he used it effectively to emphasize a dramatic turn of events, but at other times it sounded more like a habitual figure of speech with no apparent function (though it sometimes must have provided a brief pause for him to collect his thoughts). For this book I have retained the phrase when it served an immediately recognizable purpose, and omitted it when it did not.

The style of the Fadama *naamu*-sayers who encouraged the bard during these performances was unusually aggressive (for a complete explanation see the "Introduction"). The *naamu*-sayers voiced their interjections almost constantly, including in the middle of short phrases. In the scholarly edition, these will appear exactly as they are heard on the recording, but for present purposes the extremely short, fragmentary phrases formed by interjections are combined to form more complete lines, thus enhancing a narrative pace that is, in any case, quite fragmented by the frequency of the interjections.

Another means of smoothing the narrative path has been to shorten some of the names that are extremely long because they include titles or locations with which the character is associated as part of his or her identity. The bard also refers to these people by shorter, alternative names, which are employed once the character's identity is clearly established. Thus, for example, Tombonon Manjan Bereté becomes simply Manjan Bereté, Tabon Wana Faran Kamara is Kamanjan, and Farako Manko Farakonken is Maghan Konfara. An effort has also been made to minimize footnotes, partially through deletion of material that interrupts the narrative flow and that would require lengthy explanation and extensive annotation. All such details will be included in the complete, scholarly edition.

The first recording session with Tassey Condé at Fadama in 1994 was preceded by several hours of social formalities, explanations, and negotiations. When it was finally possible for the bard to begin his performance, he did so in an unusually abrupt fashion, without the usual Islamic blessing, introduction of family members, and genealogical references. Tassey commenced the next day's performance with all of these features, thus making it possible to provide this book with a classic Mande epic beginning. I have therefore violated one of the rules of handling oral tradition and borrowed our first sixty-seven lines from the opening of the second recording session.

Episodes from the overall performance of Tassey Condé that have been omitted, owing to the specific goals of the present volume, are not essential to the basic story line about the life and times of Sunjata and his contemporaries. All of the most standard episodes that are familiar from translations of other bards' versions are included in this book, along with some additional ones that are rarely heard. The quantity and quality of episodes in the repertoires of bards varies according to their individual knowledge and oral artistry. Each narrator makes choices about which episodes or parts of episodes to perform, depending on the occasion and audience. Formal division of the episodes and their contents becomes an issue only when transferring the epic from oral performance to printed transcript. The episodes from Tassey Condé's narrative that were selected for this book received their titles from the editor. An audio sample of Djanka Tassey Condé's performance of the Sunjata epic—the performance this translation is based on—is available for download at www.hackettpublishing.com.

ACKNOWLEDGMENTS

The 1994 research in Guinea that made this book possible was funded by a Fulbright Senior Research Grant administered by the Council for the International Exchange of Scholars, African Regional Research Program.

In West Africa the government of Guinea granted me research privileges, in a process that was facilitated by Mamadou Kodiougou Diallo of the University of Conakry. Djibril Tamsir Niane provided me with a written introduction to the elders of Baro and Fadama. Nanamoudou Condé of Baro personally introduced me in Fadama and accompanied me there on several occasions. The Condé family of Fadama have accepted me as an honorary member, and are always gracious with their cooperation and hospitality. Laura Arntson helped me in the first two recording sessions at Fadama, and Namankoumba Kouyaté of the Ministry of Foreign Affairs accompanied me on a later visit.

In Kissidougou, Guinea, where the text was translated, I received crucial support from Keri Giller of the U.S. Peace Corps and David Belle Isle of the CMS Mission. Through the several months of full-time work at that stage of the project, my translation assistants Djobba Kamara and Lansana Magasouba endured long, labor-intensive sessions to see the work through to its conclusion. Since 1994 my main research assistant in both Siguiri and Kankan, Guinea, has been Emmanuel Odoi Yemoson, and he has provided important information and support pertaining to this project.

In the United States during the preparation of this book, Kassim Koné contributed important, original information for several annotations and checked my accuracy on many others. Cheick M. Chérif Keita clarified some issues on lineage identity. Konrad Tuchscherer read the entire manuscript, corrected Manding terminology throughout, and rewrote technical parts of the "Notes on Nomenclature and Transcription." Valentin Vydrine advised on some of those corrections. Stephen Belcher was generous with his help in solving some difficult bibliographical problems. Jim Ford employed his technical expertise to help me with earlier versions of the maps. From beginning to end, this project had the best editorial oversight imaginable from Rick Todhunter of Hackett Publishing, and as project manager, Jennifer Plumley did a superb job of identifying details that required further attention in the copyediting stage. Throughout the entire period of work on this book, my wife Barbara Wechsberg kept it going with her daily support.

I am extremely grateful to all of these people for their contributions.

INTRODUCTION

The Cultural and Historical Context

The great African epic that is popularly known by the name of its central hero Sunjata is an essential part of the fabric of Mande culture. The heartland of Mande territory is located in what is now northeastern Guinea and southern Mali, but the Mande peoples are found in a much larger portion of sub-Saharan West Africa, speaking various related languages and dialects of the Mande family of languages. Mande-speaking peoples include the Maninka of northeastern Guinea and southern Mali, the Bamana of Mali, the Mandinka of Senegambia and Guinea-Bissau, and the Dyula of northern Côte d'Ivoire. There are many other culturally related groups located between southern Mauritania, western Burkina Faso, northern Liberia, and the Atlantic coast of Senegambia.[1]

Mande peoples are heirs to an extremely rich and vibrant historical legacy, the high point of which was the Mali Empire that flourished from roughly the mid-13th to the early 15th century. The epic narrative of Sunjata and his contemporaries illustrates the Mande peoples' own view of the glorious past, and it rightfully credits their ancestors with establishing one of the great empires of the medieval world.

Among the Bamana, Maninka, and related peoples of Manding culture, oral tradition is the domain of bards popularly known as griots, but as *jeliw* or *jelilu* (sing. *jeli*) to their own people.[2] They are the hereditary oral artists responsible for maintaining lively oral discourse that recalls the alleged deeds of the early ancestors, keeping them and their exploits alive in the community's collective memory. The *jeliw* are born into an occupationally defined group of oral artists and craft specialists whose families customarily inter-marry with one another, thereby helping to preserve monopolies on the areas of interest that account for their livelihood. For many centuries, the *jeliw* have served as genealogists, musicians, praise-singers, spokespersons,

---

[1] For more details, see "Notes on Nomenclature and Transcription."

[2] In this book the culturally specific term *jeli* is preferred to the very broadly used "griot," which describes bards of many cultures from the Senegambian coast to the Republic of Niger.

and diplomats.[3] As the principal narrators of oral tradition, the bards have been responsible for preserving narratives that express what peoples of the Mande cultural heartland believe to have happened in the distant past. Stories of the ancestors were passed from one generation of *jeliw* to the next, down through the centuries, and the principal Manding clans frame their own identities in terms of descent from the ancestors of epic tradition.

As specialists in maintaining the oral traditions of their culture, *jeliw* are known to their own people as guardians of "The Word." In early times they served as the spokespersons of chiefs (*dugutigiw*) and kings (*mansaw*), and were thus responsible for their patrons' reputations in the community. Generations of *jeli* families were permanently attached to leading households and ruling dynasties, from whom the bards received everything they required to support their families in exchange for their services in the oral arts. The *jeliw* fulfilled these responsibilities with praise-songs and narratives describing the great deeds of their patrons' ancestors. As advisors to distinguished personages, bards encouraged their patrons to achieve high goals by reminding them of the examples set by their heroic ancestors, as described in the epic narratives. The *jeliw* would point out mistakes, often through the use of proverbs, and admonish their patrons when they threatened to fail in their duties. At the same time, the bards' own security depended on their rulers' political power and social prestige, so the stories they told tended to be biased in favor of their own patrons' ancestors, at the expense of their rivals and enemies. This, among many other factors, doubtless contributed to distortion in the oral tradition, which is why many scholars refuse to take them seriously as sources of historical evidence.

While Manding peoples depend on their *jeliw* and the epic narratives for their perceptions of what happened in the distant past, many scholars from outside Manding society do not believe oral tradition is a useful source of historical information. Indeed, some have expressed disbelief that Sunjata ever really existed. This has been a fundamental difference between the local African point of view and the perspectives of some foreign academics. European scholarship relies most heavily on written sources, and for the great days of ancient Mali we have information recorded in Arabic, including the works of three especially prominent 14th-century Arab chroniclers, Al-'Umari, Ibn Battuta, and Ibn Khaldun.[4] However, where the Mali Empire is concerned, the Arabic sources speak mostly of people and events in times

[3] For details on *jeli* status and identity in Mande society, see Conrad and Frank 1995.

[4] Levtzion and Hopkins 1981: 262ff., 289ff., 322ff.

well after the founding of that great state. Al-'Umari did not begin writing about Mali until the year that the Malian ruler Mansa Musa died (1337). Ibn Battuta did not visit the royal court until 1352–53, during the reign of Mansa Sulayman. Ibn Khaldun did not record his information about Mali until 1393–94, when the power and influence of the great state had apparently begun to decline. Ibn Khaldun does say that Mari Jata (one of Sunjata's praise-names that is still in use) was "their greatest king, he who overcame the Susu . . .," and that he ruled for twenty-five years,[5] but aside from those brief remarks there is very little in the Arabic chronicles about people and events of Manden for times prior to and during the founding of the Mali Empire. The earlier period, which probably included the late 12th and early 13th centuries, is the one addressed by events described in the Sunjata epic. Therefore, despite the acknowledged problems involved in looking at oral tradition as a potential source of reliable information, Manding discourse has had great influence on what is generally thought about the founding of the Mali Empire.

When European scholars question the usefulness of Mande epic as a source of historical evidence, they are quite right to do so according to the accepted standards of methodology, because stories that have been passed on by word of mouth for some seven centuries are bound to be seriously flawed in terms of genuine historical content. The Sunjata epic includes detailed but obviously fanciful dialogue between characters, in addition to raw folklore, supernatural beings, improbable feats of magic, and mythological elements that clearly defy scientific credibility. Some historians do labor to analyze Manding oral sources in the belief that they can yield evidence that has at least a reasonable degree of historical probability, with many years spent scrutinizing every available version of the tradition in search of useful clues. Such endeavors require thorough knowledge of all aspects of the culture, including the social and spiritual values underlying the deeply ingrained sense of a shared history expressed through oral epic.

All things considered, the Mande oral epic demands our attention because we lack alternative sources of information. But even if we did have other options, it would be lamentably shortsighted to ignore the voices of Manding peoples themselves. The subjects that the *jeliw* favor as being of historical interest are representative of Manding cultural values. They are presented with consummate artistry and engaging perspectives that are expressed in one of the world's great epic narratives, and they provide richly textured insights into what one West African society feels is important in its distant past.

[5] Levtzion and Hopkins 1981: 333.

The Manding peoples' ideas of what is most important in the past are markedly different from the kinds of history that are studied and appreciated by people strictly adhering to European standards of scholarship. For one thing, in Manding societies all matters involving family, clan, and ethnic kinship are of supreme importance. People are identified by their *jamu*, which is the family name or patronymic associated with one or more famous ancestors who are remembered for important deeds that are alleged to have occurred around the beginning of the 13th century. Thanks to regular exposure to live or locally taped performances by *jeliw* that are played privately or heard regularly on local radio broadcasts, general awareness of the heroes and heroines of ancient times enters the people's consciousness in childhood and remains there throughout their lives. Memories of the ancestors are constantly evoked in praise-songs and narrative episodes that are sung or recited by the bards on virtually any occasion that calls for entertainment. In the elaborate greetings that are tendered during social encounters, friends, acquaintances, and strangers alike salute each other with reference to their respective *jamu*—that is to say family names that extend back to distinguished ancestors of the heroic past. When strangers meet, they quickly learn each other's *jamuw* or patronymics, thus establishing their relative places in the cultural landscape. Travelers meeting far from home soon establish relationships through their *jamuw* because of links that are believed to have formed between their ancestors during encounters that are described in the epic narrative. Strangers arriving in distant towns or villages establish immediate connections with "related" families and find comfort and security with their hosts. When elders meet in village council, the ancestral spirits are felt to be present because, according to tradition, it was they who established the relative statuses of everyone present, as well as the administrative protocols to be followed and the values underpinning every decision. It is no exaggeration to say that, regardless of gender, the ancestors who are described in *kuma koro*, or "ancient speech," define the identity of virtually everyone of Manding origin.

The Bard and His Narrative

Djanka Tassey Condé lived his entire life in the small village of Fadama near the Niandan River in northeastern Guinea. For most of his adult life, he lived in the shadow of his brother Djanka Mamadi, who, like Tassey, was identified by the name of their mother, Djanka. Their father, Babu Condé (d. 1964), was one of the most famous bards of the colonial era, when Guinea was part of French West Africa. Babu was descended from a lineage of Condé bards who trace their ancestry to forebears who lived in the land of Dò ni Kiri, as it is described in Mande epic. Even among other bardic families of Manden, the

Condé of Fadama are respected for their vast knowledge of Mande epic tradition. In the 1970s and 80s, when Mamadi Condé was *belentigi* (chief bard) of Fadama, he was one of the best-known orators in Manden, distinguished for the depth of knowledge that he displayed in his epic discourse. When Mamadi died in 1994, his brother Tassey became the *belentigi*. Several months later in that same year, the editor of this book arrived in Fadama to begin a collaborative relationship with Tassey Condé that lasted until that great bard's death in 1997.

To record the entire narrative from which the episodes in this book have been selected, a total of six full days were required, spread over a period of several weeks. Continuing work on the overall body of material required additional meetings over the course of several years. At the beginning of the first meeting, the Condé family elders held a lengthy discussion among themselves and with the newly arrived stranger, before they eventually consented to allow Tassey's epic discourse to be recorded. The recording sessions took place in one of the many round, thatch-roofed houses of mud brick in the Condé family compound. The previous occupant of this house was Tassey's brother Mamadi Condé, and a large portrait of him that hangs on the wall still overlooks the bed with its mosquito net and the room's other sparse furnishings.

Many *jeliw* accompany themselves on indigenous musical instruments such as the small lute (*nkoni*), the big twenty-one–string calabash harp (*kora*), or the *bala* (native xylophone). With or without music, the *jeliw* often recite their narratives accompanied by *naamu*-sayers,[6] and this was how Tassey Condé performed in his home village.[7] A *naamu*-sayer, or responding person, is a secondary performer whose job it is to reply to and encourage the main performer with short, interjected comments. The most common interjection is *naamu*, for which there is no very accurate translation, though it is what people also say when they hear their name called, and it can be rendered as "yes" or "I hear you." Among other expressions commonly heard from encouragers are *tinye* ("it's true"), *walahi* ("I swear"), and *amina* ("amen"), which is usually heard after a spoken blessing. Occasionally, when the encourager is especially excited by something the bard says, he will repeat the line or interject

---

[6] More specifically, *naamu namina*, or *naamutigiw* (*naamu* "owner"). The term probably originates from the Arabic *na'am*: Maurice Delafosse, *La langue mandingue et ses dialects (Malinké, Bambara, Dioula)*. Vol. 2. *Dictionnaire Mandingue-Française*. Paris: Librairie Orientaliste Paul Geuthner, 1955, p. 535.

[7] During the longer recording sessions with Tassey Condé, he was accompanied by the *naamu*-sayers Mamady Kouyaté, Mamady Douno, and Nandaman Doumbouya who took over from one another every fifteen or twenty minutes.

a comment of several words (e.g., l. 3773). The words of the *naamu*-sayers were an important part of Tassey Condé's performance, so they are included in the text just as they occurred, opposite most lines of the narrative.

The *jeliw* who tell the stories of the ancestors in the time of Sunjata think of the language employed on those occasions as *kuma koro* ("ancient speech"). Musical performances involving the singing of stories and praises about Sunjata are called *Sunjata fasa*, and the overall narrative is known as Manden *maana*, or Manden *tariku*.[8] The epic consists of a series of episodes that form a core narrative known by virtually any *jeli* performer. Details vary from one bard to the next, but the core episodes follow more or less the same basic outline, no matter who tells it. Nevertheless, some *jeliw* are more knowledgeable than others, and a few, as in the case of Tassey Condé, provide details or even entire episodes that are not heard from other performers. In the best-known episodes, as told by some bards, a particular character behaves in some odd, seemingly inexplicable way, or strange things happen for no apparent reason. For example, some *jeliw* describe how Dò Kamissa the Buffalo Woman gives away the secret of how she can be killed, without providing any explanation of why she would do so. Similarly, descriptions of the pregnancy of Sunjata's mother seem entirely mythological, owing to claims that it dragged on for seven years. In the present version, Tassey Condé provides reasonable motives and logical explanations for these and other elements that would previously be consigned to the realm of pure fantasy.

Through dozens of generations of storytelling, bards have doubtless forgotten much of the earliest discourse, distorted surviving parts, and created new elements, so it is impossible to know for sure what, if any, genuinely historical facts might have survived in reference to people and events of the Mali Empire. This book presents Tassey Condé's versions of the core episodes, along with a few less-common ones that are of particular interest. Parts of the general outline of the story of Sunjata and other epic heroes and heroines are more or less familiar to most ordinary citizens of traditional Manding societies, which is one of the characteristics that qualify it as an epic. Owing to what Manding peoples are repeatedly told by the *jeliw*, they think of the characters in the epic as their own ancestors, and those epic heroes and heroines serve as examples for ideal behavior.

Individual episodes of the Sunjata narrative highlight various themes that demonstrate the values and ideals of the society from which the epic evolved through many generations of professional storytellers. Tassey Condé reflects the Manding peoples' interest in questions of political power and authority

[8] Or *taliku*, Ar. *tarikh* = "chronicle."

early in his version of the epic, by listing seven kings (*mansaw*) who ruled autonomous chiefdoms prior to the time when Manden was unified into a single great state of the Western Sudan. In all versions of the epic, Sunjata Keita is the hero consistently acknowledged as the leader who liberates Manden from Soso oppression and becomes *mansa* of the unified chiefdoms (*jamanaw*) that subsequently expand into the Mali Empire. For that reason, in today's Manding societies the Keita *jamu* carries special distinction, even for those not directly connected to village chiefs whose claims to authority are based on alleged descent from Sunjata's lineage. However, at performances by modern-day *jeliw*, members of many other families bask in the reflected glory of early kings, because Tassey Condé and similarly knowledgeable bards identify other *mansaw* who ruled individual *jamanaw* in Manden during the period leading up to imperial unification. The *jeliw* do not always list the same *mansaw*, so all told there may be as many as a dozen charismatic leaders who are actually named, thus effectively increasing the opportunities for reflected glory available to their alleged descendants in latter-day audiences.

Some of the Maninka bards, including Tassey Condé, refer to Sumaworo Kanté of Soso as one of the "original" *mansaw* of Manden. A popular image has emerged of the Soso ruler as little more than a bloodthirsty "evil demon." This is traceable to a widely read novelette, D. T. Niane's *Sundiata* (1965), which was based on one version of the epic narrative. That book stresses Sumaworo's brutality with his beheading of enemies and his garments made of human skin. This conveys a false impression of how Sumaworo is actually perceived, because it fails to reveal that the alleged brutality is only one aspect of a multidimensional character portrayed by the Manding *jeliw*. Like other bards, Tassey Condé embellishes Sumaworo's reputation as a great sorcerer king through the attribution of appropriately terrifying deeds, including the wearing of human skin apparel (l. 4914–19), but he also credits him with being the provider of a great cultural legacy of fine musical instruments (l. 2786–92). Sumaworo is described as eventually seizing control of Manden and ruling as a tyrant, but at the same time he is perceived as having been one of the seven *mansaw* who laid the groundwork for one of the great civilizations of West Africa (l. 184). Indeed, had Sunjata and the armies of Manden not succeeded in bringing an end to Sumaworo's ambitions, the latter's southward expansion to incorporate the Mande *jamanaw* into Soso might have eventually led to an empire similar in scope to the one that emerged as Mali.

The earliest episodes of the epic are concerned with the hardships involved in conceiving the hero who will launch the Mali Empire. In accord with the Manding systems of belief, the quest for future glory is set in motion by diviners who foresee the coming of a hero and prescribe the steps needed to achieve the prophesied outcome. Sunjata's father, Maghan Konfara, is a relatively minor character whose problems, as related by the *jeliw*, do not compare to the severe hardships suffered by his female counterpart, Sogolon Condé. The father's problems consist of a series of frustrating failures to produce children with various wives as he follows the instructions of his diviners, trying to identify the woman destined to be Sunjata's mother. In oral tradition, everything involved in the conception of a hero of Sunjata's stature is characterized by hardships, endured by both mother and son, that set the hero apart from the rest of society. In the performance of a gifted bard like Tassey Condé, key phrases can succinctly define fundamental Manding values. Speaking of the father's difficulties in locating the future mother, the bard says, "It is hard to give birth to a child who will be famous" (l. 307). Once the correct woman is found and impregnated, Maghan Konfara recedes into the background, and in most versions of the epic the specific occasion of his death goes unnoticed. Quite the opposite is true of Sogolon Condé, who continues as a central figure in several episodes. She is gradually revealed to be one of the great heroines of Manding oral tradition, and her death is invariably noted as a significant event in the narrative.

In Manding epic tradition, the greatest heroes do not acquire their special powers from their fathers. It is the mothers who are perceived as the sources of their sons' greatness, and these women invariably suffer severe hardships before the hero is born. Such adversity is part of the formula for the future glory of a leader who initiates momentous change in the lives of his people. Sogolon Condé is the source of Sunjata's greatness, so the quest to locate her, and descriptions of her trials and tribulations, take up several episodes of the epic. In her first appearance Sogolon is the forgotten girl of her village, bypassed for years by all suitors because she is too ugly to marry. When the Buffalo Woman reveals certain secrets, we learn of childhood injuries that caused Sogolon's physical deformities. The hunters who select her according to their pact with the Buffalo Woman subsequently try to abandon her. Later, once Sogolon is pregnant, her rival co-wives cause her to suffer repeated miscarriages for several years before she can succeed in the painful and potentially life-threatening process of giving birth, or what the Bamana describe as "women's war."[9] When the long-awaited hero is finally born, Sogolon suffers the anguish of coping with her son's lameness, as well as additional abuse from her co-wives. As the narrator Tassey Condé remarks, "A source of greatness will not be acquired without hardship" (l. 1317).

---

[9] Brett-Smith 1994: 220–21; Koné 2002: 26.

According to values that are often reaffirmed in the general corpus of Manding oral tradition, it is imperative that Sunjata's iron resolve and other leadership qualities be forged on the anvil of both his and his mother's sufferings. In the mother's case, those ordeals comprise only one dimension of Sogolon's character. Many of the most important women in Manding oral traditions are described as sorceresses, and Sogolon is one of the most powerful of these. Sorcery, or the manipulation of occult power (*dalilu*), is an important part of a shared Manding cosmology. That belief system involves complex strategies for communicating with the supernatural world through sacrifice, masked ritual, incantation, divination, and healing with various kinds of medicine (*basi*), including herbs, powders, potions, and amulets. It also includes personal interaction with various kinds of spirits that dwell in bodies of water, in caves and large rock formations, and in forest groves. The spirits have individual identities and archaic, pre-Islamic terms to describe them, but in general they are simply referred to as *jinn* (genies), a word borrowed from Islamic tradition.

In Sogolon's case, it is her *dalilu*, or powers of sorcery, that enable her to survive and meet the series of challenges that mark her own path to greatness. Before delivering Sogolon to her future husband, the hunters each attempt to have sex with her and are pierced by porcupine quills or (in some versions) mauled as if they were trying to molest a lioness (l. 1515–66). Wounded and humiliated, the brothers try to abandon Sogolon, but find her waiting when they arrive at their destination (l. 1592–1621). Sogolon's initial encounter with her husband, Maghan Konfara, is characterized by a fierce sorcerer's contest in which she severely tests the defenses of Sunjata's future father (l. 1781–1804). But if Sogolon's occult powers see her through various difficulties and establish her credentials as the mother of a hero, they also initiate trouble. During her marriage celebration she reveals her formidable powers to her co-wives, who are also sorceresses (l. 1951–88), and this sets off their deadly rivalry: "They all dipped their hands into their *dalilu*" (l. 1996).

If the *jeliw* recall Sogolon Condé and her co-wives as having formidable powers of sorcery, the same can be said of most of the central characters in the Sunjata epic. Identifying archetypal figures of the distant past as masters of supernatural power is the bards' way of accounting for the ancestors' momentous contributions to Mande civilization. Availing himself of poetic license, the Maninka oral artist paints with a vocal brush on a broad canvas of colorful sound, producing larger-than-life heroes and heroines. Thus imprinted on the collective Manding consciousness, key ancestors who represent each of the principal families achieve the status of cultural icons, establishing legacies of which their descendants can be proud. According to the social ideal as conveyed in *jeli* performances, latter-day descendants should seek to emulate their illustrious forebears.

In addition to Sogolon, some of the most prominent female sorcerers include Sogolon's formidable elder sister, Kamissa of Dò, who transforms herself into a man-killing buffalo (l. 612–13). Sunjata's sister Kolonkan calls on her own *dalilu* when needed, as she does when seeking meat for the delegation that arrives to take Sunjata back to Manden. On that occasion Kolonkan removes the hearts and livers of wild game killed by her brothers, without leaving a mark on the carcasses (l. 3548–52). At first glance, women's feats of magic often seem to be limited to traditional domestic duties, but the political significance of their exploits should not be overlooked. Kolonkan's ritual hospitality to the search party from Manden heralds the impending return of her brother Sunjata to release his people from their bondage to Soso and establish the foundations of the Mali Empire. Similarly, when Fakoli's wife Keleya Konkon prepares hundreds of helpings of a half-dozen different meals simultaneously in a single cooking pot (l. 4471–4526), she is a central participant in sacrificial feasting as a prelude to war, and is subsequently detained as a political hostage. When Fakoli's mother Kosiya Kanté sacrifices herself to the genies so her brother Sumaworo can acquire the occult objects that he craves, Kosiya's co-wife Tenenba Condé assumes the outwardly mundane domestic responsibility of becoming Fakoli's foster mother (l. 3097–3105). However, as one of the three great Condé sisters of Dò ni Kiri, Tenenba is a sorceress in her own right, and it is she who sees to it that Fakoli acquires the protective medicines and supernatural might that will account for his legendary stature at the vortex of the Manding power structure.

Heroes and heroines alike tend to be endowed with occult powers by the *jeliw* who maintain the charismatic ancestors in a shared Manding consciousness. The magic of heroes is often associated with hunters and warriors who require supernatural gifts to survive their encounters with dangerous animals and deadly enemies. In the final episode of this book, the enemy King Jolofin Mansa transforms himself into a crocodile to escape Sunjata's soldiers (l. 5316–20), but Sitafa Diawara has the *dalilu* required to prevail over the beast after being swallowed by it (l. 5416–22). As a surviving contemporary of Sunjata's father, Kamanjan Kamara of Sibi is a link to an earlier generation of sorcerer kings. When Sunjata pays his respects to the Sibi *mansa*, Kamanjan warns the young hero that he will need all his *dalilu* to battle Sumaworo of Soso, making his point by causing a large tree to flip upside down onto its top branches (l. 4787–89). Sunjata occasionally demonstrates his own occult powers, as he does with the same river-crossing magic possessed by his mother (l. 2529–31), and he matches the tree-flipping magic of Kamanjan of

Sibi (l. 4790–91). However, sorcery is less central to Sunjata's image and accomplishments than it is to those of Sumaworo Kanté, the *mansa* of Soso. In Sumaworo's youth he negotiates with forest genies to acquire objects that form the basis of his occult powers (l. 2795–2803). As *mansa* of Soso, Sumaworo emerges as one of the great sorcerers of Manding epic, with abilities that are enhanced by a private oracle, Nènèba, which unerringly identifies future threats to its master's political power (l. 3287–3301).

If the indigenous system of belief, with its sorcery, sacred sites, initiation societies, medicines, masks, and arcane ritual, is the spiritual backbone of Manding epic tradition, Islam also plays a major role in the events described. In oral tradition, Muslim *moriw* are diviners who are frequently consulted for their wisdom. The primary identity of one of the central characters, Manjan Bereté, is that he is "the first Muslim leader of Manden" (l. 329) and an influential advisor to Sunjata's father. Events of the epic are alleged to have occurred in the second half of the 12th and first half of the 13th centuries, and by that time Islam had been present in the Western Sudan for at least two centuries. The kingdoms of Takrur, Ghana/Wagadu, and Gao all had resident Muslim merchants by at least 1000 to 1100 CE, and a chief of the Juddala tribe of the Sanhaja of the western Sahara went on the pilgrimage to Mecca in 1035.[10] As for the Mali Empire, Sunjata's own son Mansa Wali made the pilgrimage during the time of Sultan Zubayr of Egypt sometime between 1260 and 1277.[11] Within the Manding belief system, Islam was regarded as an additional source of spiritual power. At some point after the initial period of Islam's introduction from across the Sahara, when it's main impact was on urban populations, it began to be shaped and adapted to suit the inclinations of rural village inhabitants, and incorporated into their ritual practices. Sometime during the course of those developments, characters from Arab tradition and Muslim Prophets were appropriated and inserted into Manding genealogies and descent lists (e.g., l. 4170–4201).[12]

While the *jeliw* attribute formidable occult powers to many legendary ancestors of both genders, it is Fakoli Koroma who sets the standard for sorcery among those charismatic leaders of early times. In the epic tradition, Fakoli is still a child on his foster mother's back when he is carried to a series of important sacred sites and introduced to the principal rulers of the Mande territories (l. 3106–58). During the course of this journey, the infant acquires a

---

[10] Levtzion 1973: 33.

[11] Levtzion and Hopkins 1981: 333.

[12] For details on claims to ancestors from Arab tradition, see Conrad 1985.

wealth of protective medicines, blessings, and amulets that are necessary for his future life as one of the greatest battle commanders of his era, the most powerful of sorcerers, and the legendary patriarch of several blacksmith clans. The *jeliw* consistently portray the adult Fakoli as being dwarflike in stature, and the praise-songs refer to him as "Big-headed, big-mouthed Fakoli." When Fakoli marches to war he wears a medicine bonnet adorned with an array of potent objects, including dried birds' heads, horns, and amulets. The most famous occasion on which Fakoli reveals his enormous powers is a meeting among the elders, when this shortest of heroes bends low to pass through the council hall doorway that towers high over his head. Fakoli is ridiculed for this seemingly absurd pretense, but replies by demonstrating that a man's true size is not always exposed to view. He temporarily enlarges himself to such a size that he raises the roof of the council hall (in some versions he wears it like a hat), and the men who ridiculed him are squeezed against the walls by his magically expanded bulk (l. 4271–4324).

The ancestors' ongoing involvement with sorcery, divination, ritual sacrifice, and genies vividly reflects the Manding peoples' pervasive interest in the supernatural world, but that drama plays out in the natural world of human relationships. Where the temporal world is concerned, the *jeliw* like to describe how families, clans, and chiefdoms interacted with one another in ancient times. Local audiences find these descriptions to be intensely interesting, because in some cases they influence their own relationships with people in today's world. In the "joking relationships" called *senankuya*, a member of one family will humorously insult someone of another family because of something alleged to have happened between their ancestors. For example, when men of the Condé and Traoré clans meet for the first time, one will jokingly claim that the other is his slave, and the other will argue that the reverse is true.

As portrayed by *jeli* discourse, the relationships between key ancestral figures had far deeper significance than what is suggested by joking insults. The colorful, larger-than-life characters who orbit around Sunjata are participants in events that lead to the founding of the Mali Empire. In the process, the charismatic ancestors contribute to the establishment of a social framework kept so alive and vibrant by the *jeliw* that it has endured to modern times. According to the bards, many of the most important families of ancient times were somehow related to one another through marriage, and those liaisons still contribute to the prestige of families in contemporary Manding societies.

According to the reservoir of knowledge preserved by the Condé family of Fadama and passed down to Djanka Tassey, Sunjata was related, either directly or by marriage, to a surprising number of other major characters in Mande epic. Some of the family relationships are standard elements of the epic, while others are less often seen. Through his stepmother, Sansun Bereté, Sunjata was connected to Manjan Bereté, leader of the Muslim community. Sansun Bereté's daughter Nana Triban, Sunjata's half-sister, is married to the buffalo killer Danmansa Wulanni. Their offspring is Turama'an Traoré, so according to Fadama wisdom, both the buffalo killer and the great military leader are part of the central hero's extended family (l. 2039–48). Sunjata is also related to the buffalo killer's elder brother, Danmansa Wulanba (and therefore all his descendants among the Diabaté *jeliw*), because Wulanba married Tenenbajan, a daughter of the younger brother of Maghan Konfara, Sunjata's father. The son of Tenenbajan and Danmansa Wulanba was Kankejan, another of Sunjata's most famous generals, who was part of his family (l. 2049–50). Through Sogolon, Sunjata is related to the Buffalo Woman of Dò and her brother Donsamogo Diarra, the *mansa* of Dò ni Kiri. Kamanjan Kamara, the *mansa* of Sibi, becomes Sunjata's brother-in-law through marriage to Kolonkan (l. 4851).

One of the most politically significant extended kinship links conveyed by the Fadama bards involves two separate instances of family relationship between Sunjata and Fakoli. In the first instance, Fakoli's father's second wife is Sunjata's mother's sister Tenenba Condé, who becomes Fakoli's foster mother after Kosiya Kanté sacrifices herself to the genies. In this case the narrator Tassey Condé reveals his own sense of the enduring importance of such relationships in Maninka society, with his comment: "The Koroma *kamalenw* [male youth] call us Condé 'uncle,' although that Condé woman did not actually give birth to any Koroma" (l. 3180–81). In the second instance, when Fakoli returns to Manden after his wife Keleya Konkon is detained by Sumaworo, he asks Sunjata to replace her so it will not be said that his deeds in battle are only the result of his need to find a wife. Fakoli specifically requests Sunjata's "nephew wife," who according to custom was available to Sunjata from his uncle, the Diarra/Condé ruler of Dò ni Kiri. The result is Fakoli's marriage to Ma Sira Condé (l. 4671–79), which reinforces his connection to both his foster mother Tenenba Condé and to Sunjata. An intriguing consequence of these foster-parent and marriage alliances is that, with Fakoli being the nephew of the Soso *mansa* Sumaworo, Sunjata's arch enemy becomes a member of his own extended family.

Concerns with the relationships between Sunjata, Fakoli, Sumaworo, Turama'an, Kamanjan, the Condé sisters of Dò ni Kiri, and all the other major characters are present in most versions of the epic regardless of who tells the story. The importance of kinship, social intrigue, and political alliance is central to the spirit of the oral tradition. Individual narrators, following on earlier generations of family members who taught them their art, sometimes contribute unusual features to their versions, and this is true of the Fadama pool of knowledge from which our text is drawn. In Tassey Condé's version, there are other, less prominent faces in the exquisitely detailed crowd of characters who populate this epic panorama, contributing socially integrated additions to the great family web of which Sunjata is the center. During Maghan Konfara's search for the woman who will give birth to the child of heroic destiny, his diviners tap into various segments of the female population. They advise him to marry a light-skinned woman, so he marries nine of them, but none deliver the child in question. This process is repeated in turn with nine each of mulatto women, black women, slave girls, and female bards. In each case when the narrator announces that the desired child was not produced, he inserts a subtle contradiction by specifically naming one of the women, to the effect that "aside from Marabajan Tarawelé, none of them gave birth" (l. 258–59), or "aside from Nyuma Damba Magasuba, none of them bore any children" (l. 274–75). The easily overlooked "aside from" remarks convey the notion that other children resulted from the marriages to different groups of females. Thus, in this version of the story, the number and identity of Sunjata's half-siblings is augmented to include representatives of a wide spectrum of the social order, including a slave and a female bard (l. 284, 304).

Such liberal alleged integration into the royal bloodline could be interpreted to indicate a belief on the narrator's part that there were no social boundaries in the time of Maghan Konfara, and that a *mansa* would marry a slave or a female bard. The question of when class and occupational distinctions became part of Manding social organization is of great interest to scholars, and despite the risks of relying on oral tradition for historical information, they are interested in what it has to say on the subject. In this case, it seems most likely that the bard is merely embellishing his story and enhancing the prestige of Sunjata's father. Regarding the first group of women, he says Maghan Konfara married nine of them "because of his power . . ." (l. 234). Such things are subject to various interpretations by non-Manding outsiders, according to their individual literary, cultural, or historical interests. For present purposes, it is sufficient to note that in celebratory performances commissioned by prosperous community leaders of Manding towns and villages, the bards' descriptions of far-reaching family alliances contribute to the audience's sense of their own connections to great people of the distant past. People named Bereté, Condé, Diabaté, Diawara, Kamara, Keita, Koroma, Kouyaté, Kulubali, Magasuba, Traoré, and many others take pride in the distinguished ancestors of the same name, while awareness of those legendary people's association with Sunjata contributes to a general sense of political and cultural unity.

Stories of co-wife and sibling rivalry, such as the drama that plays out between Sogolon and Sunjata vs. Sansun Bereté and Dankaran Tuman, repeatedly highlight family strife as a favorite subject in Manding oral tradition. One of the most enduring consequences of family conflict pits sister against brother in an episode where Kolonkan seizes the initiative in a politically sensitive situation and exploits her social position as hostess to the extremely important delegation from Manden.[13] Finding herself with no meat in the house, Kolonkan goes into the bush and, using her *dalilu*, extracts the hearts and livers of wild game killed by her brothers. When the hunters retrieve their kill, Manden Bori is furious because he thinks Kolonkan is disrespecting her brothers and showing off for the guests by unnecessarily exercising her sorcery. In the presence of the delegates from Manden, he chases Kolonkan and causes her wrapper to come off. Despite a social convention that sisters are expected to have great influence over the fate of their brothers, Manden Bori further humiliates Kolonkan by using his own sorcery to cause fresh blood to flow from the meat that his sister had cooked for their guests. Kolonkan accuses Manden Bori of shaming her in front of the Mande people whom she was entertaining according to her customary duties and for the family benefit. She then places a curse on Manden Bori and his branch of the Keita royal lineage, declaring that the *mansaya* (kingship) would be passed down to them, but that they would never peacefully agree on who would hold the power (l. 3625–27). There is reasonably reliable evidence in the Arabic writings of Ibn Khaldun that, historically, the *mansaya* did pass from the line of Sunjata to that of his brother.[14] Manden Bori's descendants are said to live in the region of Hamana not far from Tassey Condé's home village. When the bard was asked about any enduring consequences of Kolonkan's curse, he said the people of Hamana have never done what was needed to lift the curse. He explained that every village in Hamana would need to sacrifice a cow. The tenderloin and internal organs of the cows must be given to the Keita women of Hamana to compensate for the meat that Manden Bori took back from Kolonkan. Each Keita woman must also receive a cloth wrapper to make up for the one that was stripped from Kolonkan in her struggle with Manden Bori. Tassey explained that if the people of Hamana do not make the sacrifice,

---

[13] For detailed discussion, see Conrad 1999a: 217.

[14] Levtzion and Hopkins 1981: 334.

the curse will never be removed. When he said that, all the elders of Fadama who were present chimed in together, saying, "The curse will be there!"[15]

In the conflict between Kolonkan and her brother, the portrayal of Manden Bori as brash and impetuous corresponds to many similar images of him to be found in a wide range of epic variants. If the *jeliw* are strikingly consistent in describing Manden Bori as a hotheaded youth, Tassey Condé adds an additional dimension to this character in another episode of intense family drama featuring the opposition of strong-willed siblings. In Sogolon's last important act before dying, she takes her three sons and her daughter Kolonkan outside of town for a private meeting. She reveals that before Maghan Konfara died, he entrusted to her powerful *dalilu* consisting of three things that he had not wanted to bequeath to his eldest son, Dankaran Tuman. Sogolon explains that the things are only effective if all three are in the same person's possession, and she asks her sons to agree that they should go to Sunjata, since he is the one who was sent for by the people of Manden. The second eldest son, who is called So'olon's Jamori, and whom many *jeliw* fail to mention in their performances, insists that the *dalilu* be divided among the three brothers. Sunjata, confident that he can accomplish his destined goals with the *dalilu* that he already possesses, tells Jamori to choose whatever he desires. However, Manden Bori has a bitter dispute with Jamori over his refusal to agree with their mother's wishes. Manden Bori insists that Sunjata take his share, and Sogolon is so grateful that she takes him aside and presents him with the legacy of her ancestors in Dò ni Kiri, a brass finger ring that is said to be the prototype of one of the protective devices still worn by Mande hunters.

Another dramatic case for illustrating the Manding peoples' fascination with family and clan relationships of the distant past is that of Fakoli as both nephew of Sumaworo, the *mansa* of Soso, and as progenitor of several of the most important blacksmith clans. In some parts of northeastern Guinea, Fakoli's primary family identity or *jamu* is Dumbia (Doumbya, Doumbouya, and so forth) and in others it is Koroma. Those families as well as the Sissoko and other blacksmith families of Manden, claim descent from Fakoli.[16] According to the Condé bards of Fadama, Fakoli's father was Mansa Yerelenko, the *mansa* of Negeboriya. This was apparently an important iron-producing region (*nègèbòriya* = "place where iron comes out"), and was therefore densely populated with blacksmith communities.

Fakoli's family blacksmith connection also extends northward to the kingdom of Soso, because the oral tradition identifies his uncle, Sumaworo the

---

[15] Conrad 1999a: 214.

[16] Conrad 1992: 175.

tyrannical *mansa*, as originating from a blacksmith lineage. In a passage not included in this book, Tassey Condé says Sumaworo's ancestors arrived in Manden from a place called Folonengbe in Ivory Coast to offer their services as ironworkers. Therefore, when Fakoli's father Mansa Yerelenko married Sumaworo's sister Kosiya Kanté, he made an advantageous economic and political alliance. Fakoli was the product of that union, and his fame as the most powerful of sorcerers, one of Sunjata's greatest generals, and heir to the power of two blacksmith-ruled kingdoms, helps to account for the fact that several different hereditary ironworking lineages claim him as ancestor.

Several of the most familiar episodes in the Sunjata epic highlight the Manding peoples' interest in all matters involving kinship patterns and family conflicts. One of the most dramatic of these is Tassey Condé's version of the confrontation between Fakoli and his formidable maternal uncle Sumaworo, which results in the nephew's loss of his wife, Keleya Konkon. This is a favorite tale of the *jeliw*, but they often provide only brief accounts, in which Keleya Konkon outshines several hundred of Sumaworo's wives, so he keeps her in Soso and Fakoli angrily returns to Manden. Some of the abbreviated versions are illogical and confusing, with suggestions of incest owing to the family relationship between uncle and nephew.[17] Tassey Condé offers details not usually heard, and he introduces a logical sequence of events that eliminate the apparent confusion found in many versions. According to Tassey's narrative, the fact that Fakoli's natural mother Kosiya Kanté is the sister of Sumaworo is the source of a vexing dilemma that confronts the hero as Manden and Soso prepare for war. Fakoli explains to the elders of Manden that he cannot join them in their attack on Soso, because that is his mother's homeland. Sunjata concurs, saying he would feel the same way if Manden were to attack his mother's homeland of Dò ni Kiri (l. 4342–50).

Arriving in Soso, Fakoli joins the forces of his uncle Sumaworo, and his wife Keleya Konkon works her magic to outshine Sumaworo's wives in preparing the sacrificial feast for war. The conflict between nephew and uncle arises not from their wives' competition, but from a misunderstanding purposely contrived by conspirators who are threatened by Fakoli's superior abilities and implicit claim to authority as Sumaworo's nephew. Convinced that his nephew has purposely ignored orders to attend a meeting, Sumaworo interprets this and Keleya Konkon's exploits as indications that Fakoli has ambitions to take over the power in Soso. Sumaworo reminds Fakoli that Keleya Konkon is his own cousin, and that he had received her from Sumaworo in

[17] Conrad 1992: 167.

the first place. When he takes Keleya away from Fakoli, the implication is that the woman is returned to her original family to punish and humiliate the nephew for his alleged disloyalty (l. 4611–18). This dramatic falling out within the ruling family of Soso contains the ingredients of classic tragedy and entertains Manding audiences with the delicious irony that the misunderstanding is a major factor in the eventual downfall of Soso, the triumph of Manden, and the founding of the Mali Empire.

Regardless of what ancestral deeds are described in individual episodes of the Sunjata epic, the narratives as recounted by the most erudite bards of Manden are sure to revolve around two principal themes: the complexity of relations between people, and those people's relations with the spirit world. Where human relations are concerned, the oral discourse addresses multiple levels of society as perceived in its most idealized traditional form. Within immediate families, the drama plays out according to partnerships and rivalries between individual wives and their husbands, between competitive co-wives, and between siblings of both genders. The wider village scene employs specifically named archetypal characters representing key occupational groups including the bards, warriors, hunters, blacksmiths, slaves, merchants, river boatmen, Muslims, and specialists in the occult arts of divination and sorcery. Relations between extended families or clans (*kabilaw*) throughout the lands of Manden feature intricately woven kinship patterns established through politically significant marriages. On the national stage of kingship (*mansaya*) and statehood, charismatic leaders of both genders establish frameworks of power and authority through political intrigue, negotiation with the spirit world, and, on occasion, forceful and potentially lethal action.

The outcome of events involving human activity at all levels is at least partly determined by the success or failure of strategies for negotiation with the spirit world, because in the Manding cosmos everything has a sacred dimension. Diviners draw on whatever sources of occult knowledge or skill are available to them, to identify the sources of their clients' problems and prescribe appropriate sacrifices and courses of action to reach desired solutions. The most prominent male and female ancestors are masters of magic and medicine who apply their secret knowledge to protect themselves and their people, and to cope with both human and supernatural enemies. As immortal cultural icons, these archetypal heroes and heroines negotiate with genies, render themselves invisible, appear in several places at the same time, and transform themselves into various kinds of living creatures. Such were the tools of the larger-than-life people of legend, who shaped the souls of their descendants and established the kind of history that is valued by traditional Manding societies.

NOTES ON NOMENCLATURE AND TRANSCRIPTION

Cultural Terminology[1]

In its broadest sense, "Mande" refers to a number of West African ethnic groups speaking languages belonging to the Mande family of the wider Niger-Congo phylum of languages.[2] Contemporary Mande languages are related in varying degrees to the language(s) spoken in the medieval Mali Empire founded in the 13th century.[3] Likewise, those people who today speak diverse Mande languages—from Mali to Liberia—often claim an ancestral link to the Mali Empire. As a result of the expansion and eventual breakup of

---

[1] The section "Cultural Terminology" was contributed by a specialist in ethnolinguistics, Dr. Konrad Tuchscherer of St. John's University.

[2] The earliest use of "Mande" as a linguistic classification—"the Mande family"—was made by S. W. Koelle, the German missionary philologist who worked out of Freetown, Sierra Leone, in the mid-19th century. See *Outlines of a Grammar of the Vei Language Together with a Vei-English Vocabulary, and an Account of the Discovery and Nature of the Vei Mode of Syllabic Writing* (London, 1853): 10–11; Koelle elaborates fully in his monumental *Polyglotta Africana* (London, 1854; reprinted, with introduction by P.E.H. Hair and David Dalby, Graz, 1963).

[3] Note that the relationship between contemporary Mande languages and the language(s) of the medieval Mali Empire has here been cautiously labeled as "related," but might be more emphatically described as "descended." For example, all Manding languages (e.g., Maninka, Bamana, and so forth) are direct descendants of a language or languages spoken in the Mali Empire. This obviously includes lesser known Manding languages, including (among others) the likes of Konyanka (Guinea) and Manya (Liberia); it also includes the more distant—but still directly descended—languages of Vai (Liberia) and Kono (Sierra Leone), neither of which are regarded today as Manding languages proper. The term "descended" is problematic for two reasons. First, languages such as Susu (and the related language Yalunka, also of Guinea) and Soninke (mostly Mali) are Mande languages and descended from languages spoken in the Mali Empire, but not from the language(s) that produced contemporary Manding languages. Susu and Soninke are not classified as Manding languages—they are examples (and there are others) of closely related extant cousins of Manding languages, which perhaps antedated the Mali Empire. The second point relates to some of the remaining Mande languages, which are not Manding languages and for which, unlike for Susu and Soninke, the historical and

the Mali Empire in the 15th century, Mande peoples spread throughout western Africa. This spreading out of Mande peoples from the Mali Empire into new territory is often referred to as the "Mande Diaspora." The story of this dispersion is expressed in oral traditions like one from the Vai of Liberia that tells of the famous trek of "Kamara the Younger" from the source of the Niger River through the forest to the sea. In other narratives, the Mande Diaspora takes a less benign form, as in the story of the overrunning of indigenous West Atlantic peoples by the so-called "Mani Invaders."

Today historians and linguists have identified the closest living languages descended from those spoken at the royal court of the Mali Empire. These constitute a branch of the Mande language family referred to as "Manding." This Manding group includes important languages such as Maninka (Fr. Malinké), Bamana (Fr. Bambara), Dyula, and Mandinka. These Manding languages have a high degree of interintelligibility, and some scholars prefer to characterize them as dialects or regional variations of a single language.[4] The Manding branch forms a continuum, with its epicenter in "Manden," the name given to the heartland of the old Mali Empire (see Map A), and radiates outward from Mali and Guinea as far as Senegal in the west and Ivory Coast to the southeast. There are perhaps as many as 20 million speakers of Manding languages, with about half of that number speaking a Manding language as

---

linguistic relationship to the languages of the Mali Empire is less clear. This includes, for example, the group of Mande languages commonly termed "Southwestern," which includes Mende, Loma, Kpelle, Bandi, and Loko. These languages are spoken in different parts of Sierra Leone, Liberia, and Guinea. Some might argue that it would be misleading to say that these languages are "directly descended" from the language(s) of the Mali Empire, no matter how much the speakers of such languages (many of whom have Manding names) insisted that this is the case, and despite certain linguistic similarities (perhaps the most obvious being the similar numeration systems that most Mande peoples share, which originally suggested to outside observers that the languages had a shared history). Whether "descended" or "related," these languages have certain roots in the languages of medieval Mali, even if only through more recent linguistic borrowing. Nonetheless, the Manding languages form a special core group among the wider subfamily of Mande languages.

[4] While the Manding language group is referred to here as a "branch" of Mande, some scholars have employed "dialect cluster," which suggests that, despite its existence under various regional names, there is really one language, "Manding" (or the relatively recently coined "Mandekan," introduced in the 1960s—a term that only adds to the confusion in terminology and should be avoided). The linguistic interintelligibility is certainly exaggerated in this latter designation. For example, despite a shared linguistic heritage, Mandinka (Senegal-Gambia) and Bamana (Mali) are significantly different, with less than 50 percent interintelligibility.

a first language. For linguists, the entire taxonomy of Mande languages in West Africa is based on levels of genetic interconnectedness to the core Mande languages known as "Manding."

In West Africa the names of ethnic groups and languages are often the same. For example, one can be a Mandinka and speak Mandinka, or be a Wolof and speak Wolof (a non-Mande language). It is also possible for a Mandinka to speak Wolof, just as an Englishman might speak French. Scholars speak of a "Mandinka people" just as they refer to a "Mandinka language." Likewise, scholars have found it useful to talk of "Manding peoples" (like the Mandinka or the Dyula) as a cultural subset of Mande language–speaking peoples, in the same way that "Manding languages" are a branch of a much larger Mande language family. It must be stressed, however, that there is no specific Mande or Manding *language*, but instead Mande and Manding *languages*. In the same way, we cannot talk of the Mande or Manding *people*, but rather Mande and Manding *peoples*.

The Sunjata epic has only slight meaning for those Mande peoples most distantly related to the Mali Empire. Such peripheral Mande peoples may claim linguistic and cultural heritage from the Mali Empire, and in this way Sunjata's founding of that great medieval state is an important part of their history even if they do not know the epic. Among such peoples, like the Mende of Sierra Leone, there are no *jeliw* and the Sunjata epic is not told. For all Manding peoples, however, no matter how distantly separated geographically from one another, the epic is central to their shared cultural consciousness and tradition of origin. This book presents the Sunjata epic as it features in the lives of Manding peoples, as told by Maninka bards of Manden, the Mande heartland.

Variations in Names

There are inconsistencies in the pronunciation of the names of some characters in the Sunjata epic. The inconsistencies are characteristic of a strikingly colorful and vibrant oral culture, and they reflect its inherent dynamism and creativity. Thorough exploration of this subject would involve lengthy discussion of historical, cultural, and linguistic issues that extend far beyond what is necessary here. What does need to be addressed is the fact that among the usages that appear in the text of this book, there are a few that require explanation, owing to conspicuous variations occurring in other published versions of the epic.

Due to regional differences and the speech of individual informants, when the names of some major characters in the Sunjata epic are rendered into print, they can appear in a variety of forms. The name of the prominent character, Fakoli, is among the most consistent, because its sound does not present much chance of variant pronunciation. However, the name of the central character, Sunjata, has been spelled in almost every conceivable way. It originated as a term of praise, referring to the hero as his mother's lion (*jara*): Sogolon's Jara (regional variants: Jata, Jala, Jada). In rapidly spoken Maninka or Bamana, this becomes So'olon Jara, Son-Jara, Sunjara, Sonjara, Sonjata, and so on. Transcription of the name from the *nko* script, invented by the Maninka scholar Souleymane Kanté, comes out as Sondiada. French orthography has contributed Sondyata, Soundjata, and Soundiata, among others. Distinctive regional pronunciations contribute additional variants, as in the Konyan of southeastern Guinea, where the name is pronounced Sonjala.

Similar to Sunjata, the name of the Soso ruler Sumaworo is seen in a wide variety of spellings. In texts recorded from Bamana informants of Mali, I have rendered it Sumanguru, but the sound from my Maninka informants in Guinea is more like Sumaworo, as I have it in the text of this book. The name is also seen as Sumamuru, Sumanworo, Soumaworo, Soumaoro, and Sumaoro, among others. In the Konyan region, he is known as Sumawolo.

The name of Sunjata's father also varies widely from one narrator to the next. Tassey Condé uses two forms, the shorter of which is Maghan Konfara, seen in other published variants as, for example, Maghan Kon Fatta and Fata Magan. Alternative short versions of the father's identity are Naré Famagan and Naré Maghan Konaté, among others, with Konaté being his family identity (patronymic, *jamu*). The longer form, which Tassey pronounces as Farako Manko Farakonken, corresponds to published variants such as Mankon Farakò Maan Kènyin and Fara-Koro Makan Kègni.

In the performance from which the text for this book was drawn, there was an unusual pronunciation of the name of a prominent bard in the story. He is usually known by some variation of the name Bala Fasaké (Fasséké, Faseke, and so forth), but Tassey Condé pronounces the name as Bala Fasali. It is clear that this variant did not originate with Tassey, because his father, the famous bard Babu Condé, pronounced it the same way when he narrated the Sunjata epic for Laye Camara (1984: 72).

The name of one of the most prominent chiefdoms, or *jamanaw*, of Mande epic tradition is referred to by virtually all bards as "Dò ni Kiri." This is usually translated as "Dò and Kri" (in usage, the retention or dropping of one vowel from Kiri to Kri varies, and sometimes seems to depend on the narrator's rhythm). The translation is technically correct because the name refers to individually named parts of the *jamana* that lie on opposite banks of the Niger River. However, the melodious sound of Dò ni Kiri is lost in translation, and "Dò and Kri" conveys a sense of division in the chiefdom of twenty-two villages in a way that is not consistent with the spirit of the text. Therefore, in order to more closely retain the sound and sense of the place, I have elected to leave the name untranslated, as Dò ni Kiri.

Untranslated Words

Owing to the uniqueness of cultural elements, there are always meanings that do not move easily from one language to another, regardless of what languages are involved. In the Manding languages spoken by most bards who narrate oral tradition that include the Sunjata epic (Bamana, Maninka, Mandinka), there are words for which there is no ideal translation into English. Within the narrative presented in this book, there are several terms that contain nuances of meaning about occupational and social status and identity, for which there are no equivalents in the English language. In those cases the Maninka language term has been retained, with a brief definition in the footnote and a more complete explanation in the Glossary.

NOTE ON THE MAP OF THE
MANDE HEARTLAND (MAP A)

The handmade map labeled "The Mande Heartland and Related *Jamanaw* According to Oral Tradition" is a work in progress that has gradually evolved from an inadequate and erroneous first effort (Conrad 1994: 356) through the more ambitious one included in *Epic Ancestors of the Sunjata Era* (Conrad 1999b: xvii). This map indicates the locations of pre-imperial chiefdoms (*jamanaw*) of the Mande heartland and their neighbors, according to the traditional bards who describe the legendary locations and travels of people active during the life and times of Sunjata.

The present edition of the map includes, for the first time, the location of the home of Sunjata's father, Maghan Konfara, according to the reservoir of traditional knowledge represented here by Tassey Condé. Tassey refers to the "land of Konfara" and speaks of the people being "in Farakoro" (or Farako); so, pending further clarification, on the map Farakoro is identified as the town, and Konfara as the *jamana*, or chiefdom.[1] Tassey specifies that Konfara was in a swampy region near the present-day town of Kourémalé, which is on the border between Guinea and Mali (l. 75–80), and that it extended up to the location now occupied by the town of Narena. The alleged location of Farakoro indicates that, according to the extremely knowledgeable bards of Fadama, Sunjata's birthplace was near the Kokoro River, not the Sankarani, which is the popular perception. However, the Sankarani's importance is not diminished in the perception of the Condé bards of Fadama. They believe that when Sunjata returned from exile, he crossed the Sankarani where Niani is located, and that councils were later held in that location.[2] The bard also says that once the issues with Soso were settled, Sunjata founded Maninkoura (New Mani), which is farther north, near where the Sankarani meets the Niger.

State boundaries that were imposed on Africa during the 19th-century European imperial "scramble" for territory have nothing to do with people

---

[1] Djibril Tamsir Niane, a leading exponent of Niani as the "capital" of the Mali Empire, transcribed the Mansa of Konfara's name as "Maghan Kon Fatta" (1965: 4).

[2] For discussion on the question of Niani as the town of Sunjata's childhood and the imperial capital, see Conrad 1994.

and events of the Sunjata era, and are not shown on this map. The largest portion of Mande territory represented here is in present-day Mali. Ivory Coast is at the bottom on the right half of the map, on a jagged line running east of Kankan beyond the Wasulu Balé River (not indicated on Map B, "West Africa and Area of Detail"). A section of the Sankarani River running northeast of Niani (Guinea) marks the border between Guinea and Mali for roughly 60 km. In Mali, the Bakoy River passes to the west of Kita before descending to the area of Niagassola in Guinea.

The prominence of rivers as presented on this map reflects the importance they would have always had for economic, strategic, and spiritual reasons. The rivers are located according to their modern-day positions, though in some cases their courses are probably no longer entirely true to what they were in the days of Sogolon and Sunjata. Moreover, the names of some rivers were changed at some time in the past. For example, the Mafou River, which lies southwest of Kouroussa just outside the lower left border of Map A, was, according to Tassey Condé, formerly known as the Balen.

Some towns and regional locations that did not exist in the Wagadu or Sunjata eras are included as useful points of reference on the basis of their importance to Manding traditional history in general. Kaarta, Massina, and Baté, for example, all belonged to later centuries, though Tassey Condé does mention them in the comprehensive version of his narrative. For orientation, some familiar modern towns and cities (e.g., Segu, Bamako, Sikasso, Siguiri, Kankan) are included in brackets. Identifiable regions from the Sunjata era, such as Wagadu (ancient Ghana), Soso (Sumaworo's kingdom), and Buré (the location of goldfields then and now), are marked in their known locations.

There has been some uncertainty about the location of Sunjata's place of exile with his host Faran Tunkara, because it has been named as both Nema and Mema by various bards. Nema is south of Walata in modern-day Mauritania and within the bounds of Wagadu's ancient location, while Mema is in Mali between Lake Debo and Nampala. Both places are north of old Manden in the sahel, so from the *jeliw* perspective they serve equally well as Sunjata's place of exile. One authoritative source acknowledges both places as part of the larger domain of the Tunkara ruling lineage,[3] which, along with the semantic similarity of the names, helps to account for this duality. Both Mema and Nema are on the map in their known sahelian locations, and Kuntunya is indicated as in the region of Nema because that is where our bard Tassey Condé places it.

---

[3] Youssouf Tata Cissé and Wâ Kamissoko, *Soundjata la gloire du Mali: La grande geste du Mali* Vol. 2 (Paris, 1991): 37.

The location of one of the most prominent places in the epic, the Kamara *jamana* of Tabon and Sibi, is as well known now as it was in the time of Sunjata, unmistakable owing to the great natural stone arch that towers above some of its villages. Other famous locations, such as the meeting ground of Kurukanfuwa, the battleground at Dakajalan (in some versions identified with nearby Kirina), Dò ni Kiri (the Condé/Diarra *jamana* said to have been in the general region of modern-day Segu), and Negeboriya ("place from which the iron flows"), the *jamana* of Mansa Yèrèlènko, are in approximate locations according to what can be understood from oral tradition.

Our narrator Tassey Condé claims the kingdom of Soso consisted of four *jamanaw* ruled by Sumaworo, the names of which are among the Soso ruler's standard praises: Kukuba, Bantamba, Nyemi-Nyemi, and Kambasiga. Some references to these four places tend to be ambiguous. In parts of his narrative, Tassey Condé specifically refers to them as *jamanaw*, but at other times they seem to be towns, and it may be that they are recalled as both in the way that Tabon and Sibi together signify the ancient Kamara *jamana*, though they are individual towns as well (in different locations than they are now, according to local informants). Kukuba, Bantamba, and Nyemi-Nyemi are placed on the map where Maninka *jeliw* of Guinea believe they were located when Sumaworo ruled Soso. The bards believe Kukuba included a powerful stronghold located where Koulouba is now, on the strategic high ground above Bamako, overlooking the Niger. They equate Bantamba with Banamba in the Beledougou region, and claim it was the home of Sumaworo's oracle. At the present stage of research, references to Nyemi-Nyemi seem to point to Niamina, located within the perceived Soso boundaries southeast of the alleged location of Bantamba, on the Niger River. The double utterance in the praising could derive from the fact that one of several Mande villages called "Niani" was near Niamina,[4] with the praise originating as something like "Niani-Niami." Based on textual evidence, the four Soso provinces appear on the map in their rough, general areas pending further research, with question marks to indicate the uncertainty about exact locations.

---

[4] Cissé and Kamissoko 1991: 12.

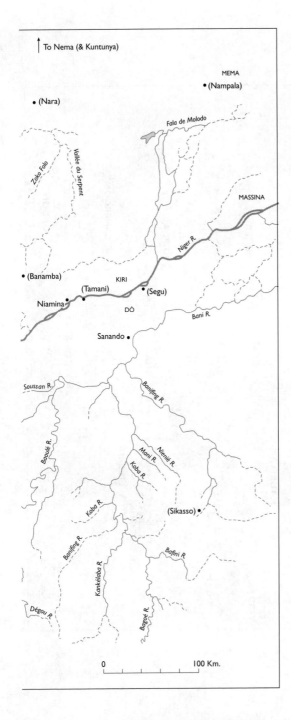

Map A. The Mande heartland and related *jamanaw* according to oral tradition.

Map B. Area detail in Map A.

NARRATIVE CONTENTS
BY LINE NUMBERS

BLESSINGS, INTRODUCTIONS, AND PROPHETS OF ISLAM

Allah ho ma salli Allah Muhammadu,
Walali Muhammadi salala Alehu salaamu.[1]
We spent the night in peace,
May God give us a peaceful day.   (Aminaaa)
5 Hatred and Satan,
May God save us from them.   (Aminaaa)
May God fulfill the hope with which our brother has
    come,
Who is Dauda Condé.[2]   (Naamu)
You have come to your ancestor,
10 And the people you meet here.   (Naamu)
May God fulfull your hope.   (Aminaaa)
The black-skins and the white-skins,   (Naamu)
We all descended from ancestor Adama.   (Na-amu)
Hawa is the mother of us all.[3]   (Naamu)
15 Our grandfather Kémo Poré's[4] son N'fa Namanjan,   (Naamu)
He should be performing this narrative,   (Naamu)
He is the master bard.[5]   (Naamu)

---

[1] Some Maninka bards (*jeliw*) begin their narratives with a Muslim blessing in local, nonstandard Arabic. The phrases invoke the names of God and the Prophet Muhammad, and partially derive from a common phrase used by pious Muslims whenever they mention the Prophet: *ṣallā'llāhu 'alayhi wa-sallama*, "may God bless him and grant him peace."

[2] Referring to the visiting researcher by his Maninka name.

[3] Adama and Hawa (Ar. Ḥawwā') = Adam and Eve.

[4] When the Condé patriarch Kémo Poré died at Fadama in October 2002, local radio in Kankan announced his age as 110.

[5] "Master bard": *jeli ngara*. With this customary formality, Tassey pays respect to Namanjan, who was senior to him. Interviews with Namanjan after Tassey's death have proven that while he can quote some mnemonic passages, he possesses virtually none of the vast knowledge that was passed on by Babu Condé to his sons Mamadi and Tassey.

He says I should narrate this speech,	(Naamu)
Though I am not endowed with that knowledge.	(Naamu)
20 You who boast that you know it,	(Naamu)
No matter how well you say it,	(Naamu)
There is always someone who knows it better than you,	(Naamu)
Because Manden is where everybody originated.	(Naamu)
I who have been designated to narrate,	(Naamu)
25 My name is Tassey Condé.	(Naamu)
Djanka Tassey Condé,[6]	(Naamu)
Younger brother of Laye Mamadi Condé,[7] who recently passed away,	(Naamu)
A son of Fadama Babu.[8]	(Naamu)
We are his sons.	(Naamu)
30 During the days of my father, a similar thing happened:	(Naamu)
People came to Fadama.[9]	
May the hope for which they came be fulfilled.	(Amina)
What you are asking about,	(Naamu)
If we should go by what you are speaking of,	(Naamu)
35 That would take the whole day.	(Naamu)
Between the black-skins and the white-skins,	(Naamu)
God made white men,	(Naamu)
God made three hundred and thirteen prophets,[10]	

---

[6] In keeping with local custom, Tassey is identified by the name of his mother, Djanka.

[7] "Laye" = Al-Hajj ("the pilgrim"). Either a given name, or signifying that Mamadi had made the pilgrimage to Mecca. This master bard died on January 16, 1994. For samples of his narratives, see Conrad 1999b: 95–154.

[8] Babu Condé of Fadama (d. 1964), one of the best-known and most respected *jeliw* of his time.

[9] Among those who consulted Babu Condé in Fadama were the French historian Yves Person in 1958, and the Guinean novelist Laye Camara in 1963.

[10] "Prophets": *alamusanda*. Though Tassey exaggerates the numbers for emphasis, this and the next line accurately reflect the Islamic division of the Prophets into two classes according to their missions. The first category is *Rasūl* (lit. "Messenger," "Envoy"), including Adam, Seth, Noah, Abraham, Ishmael, Moses, Lot, Ṣāliḥ, Hūd, Shu'ayb, Jesus, and Muhammad. These are also referred to in the Koran as *al-mursalun* ("those who are sent"), which is probably the source of Tassey's Maninka

	God made one hundred and twenty-four messengers.[11]	(Naamu)
40	All of them came from white men,	
	None of them came from black men.	(Naamu)
	All of the messengers came from the whites.	(Naamu)
	(You heard it?)	(Naamu)
	In those days the black world was not well known.	(Naamu)
45	After making whiteness, He made blackness.	(Naamu)
	The first of them,	(Naamu)
	Was Sedina Bilali.[12]	(Naamu)
	The Sunjata you are asking about was a descendant	
	of this Bilali.	(Naamu)
	It is that Sunjata.	(Naamu)
50	Up to the time that the blacks and whites separated,	(Naamu)
	Up to the separation of the whites into several nations,	(Naamu)
	And then came Paris,[13]	(Naamu)
	If we go into that, we are all the same people.	(Naamu)
	We are all descendants of ancestor Adama.	(Naamu)
55	Our own line of descent started with Ibrahima.[14]	(Naamu)
	(You heard it?)	(Naamu)
	Between us and the Americans,	(Naamu)
	There is no need to discuss the relationship.	(Naamu)
	We and the Americans are descendants of Isiaaka.	(Naamu)

---

term *alamusanda*. In the above list, four were sent specifically to the Arabs: Ṣāliḥ, Hūd, Shu'ayb, and Muhammad (*The New Encyclopedia of Islam*, ed. Cyril Glassé. New York: AltaMira Press, 2001: 364–65).

[11] For the second category of Prophets, called *Nabī* (lit. "Prophet," pl. *anbiyā*), Tassey used the Maninka term *seyibawulu* ("messengers"). The Koran mentions twenty-five of these by name, with possible references to at least five additional ones. (*The New Encyclopedia of Islam*, ed. Cyril Glassé. New York: AltaMira Press, 2001: 364–65).

[12] Bilāl ibn Rabāḥ, a freed black slave of Islamic tradition who became a companion of the Prophet Muhammad and the first caller to prayers. The Mande bards have appropriated him as the Muslim ancestor of Sunjata's Keita lineage. For details, see Conrad 1985: 35–39.

[13] A reference influenced by the French colonial occupation of Guinea, 1898–1958. For more about Paris, see l. 4213–28.

[14] Here Tassey refers to the prophets Abraham and Isaac (l. 59), to which he returns later (l. 4168 ff).

60 The Americans have as much power as any Condé
       kamalen.[15]   (Naamu)
    The only difference is that they have a *dalilu*[16] that we
       do not have.   (Naamu)
    Just as they have the power in America,
    We have the power here.   (Naamu)
    That is why if you go into detail about Condé worthiness,
65 You will cause the vain ones to become conceited.   (Naamu)
    We will not talk about our common descent from our
       ancestor Adama,   (Naamu)
    Because he is for all of us.   (Naamu)

SEVEN KINGS OF MANDEN

    You say you want to know about Manden.   (Naamu)
    For us to give you many details about Manden,   (Naamu)
70 With which part of Manden will we start?   (Naamu)
    We will start with Sunjata's father,   (Naamu)
    Who is Farako Manko Farakonken.   (Naamu)
    The name of Ma'an[17] Sunjata's father is   (Naamu)
    Manko Farakonken of Konfara.[18]   (Naamu)
75 Do you know where Konfara is?   (Naamu)
    It is on the frontier between Guinea and Mali,
    At a place now known as Kourémalé.   (Naamu)
    The swampy area,
    Where the Kourémalé people dig their gold mines,
80 Is known as Konfara.   (Naamu)

---

[15] Worthy, able young men in their prime (see Glossary).

[16] Magic, occult, or secret power; in everyday use, any means used to achieve a goal (see Glossary).

[17] "Ma'an" is the Maninka contraction of Maghan, an archaic title synonymous with *mansa*, meaning "ruler," or "king."

[18] The Condé *jeliw* believe Konfara was the *jamana* ruled by Sunjata's father.

The father of Simbon[19] was named after that,	(Naamu)
But his real name is Maghan.	(Naamu)
He is Maghan Konfara.[20]	
That land of Konfara was acquired from us, the Condé.	(Naamu)
85 This Maghan Konfara of whom I speak,	(Naamu)
His son's name is Sunjata,	
The last *mansa* of Manden.[21]	(Naamu)
He is the last of the Mande[22] *mansaw*.	(Naamu)
(You heard it?)	(Naamu)
90 When Sunjata was born,	(Naamu)
Who was the *mansa* of Manden?	(Naamu)
The first *mansa* of Manden, the very first!	(Naamu)
He is the ancestor of the Condé,	(Naamu)
He is Donsamogo Diarra.	(Naamu)
95 This Condé ancestor Donsamogo Diarra,	(Naamu)
The Ma'an Solonkan from whom he descended,	(Naamu)
It was this Ma'an Solonkan who sired four sons,	(Naamu)
And three daughters.	(Naamu)
Of the four sons,	(Naamu)
100 The first son was Donsamogo Diarra.	(Naamu)
The next to him was Seku Diarra.	(Naamu)
The next to that was Mafadu Diarra.	(Naamu)
The next to that was Kiri Diarra.	(Naamu)

[19] A title of honor carrying the sense of "Master Hunter," used to address any respected leader. The bard applies it to Sunjata, his father, and hunters or warriors at various times in the narrative (e.g., l. 226).

[20] The shortened version of the name of Sunjata's father is applied as both name and title; transcribed by D. T. Niane as "Maghan Kon Fatta" (1965: 4).

[21] Tassey Condé was aware that there were many kings (*mansaw*) after Sunjata. He means this in the sense of "the greatest of them all." The name "Sunjata" derives from the practice of identifying a male child by his mother's name (cf. n. 6), in this case "Sogolon." Through usage, So'olon Jara (Sogolon's Lion) evolved to various forms including Son-Jara and Sunjata.

[22] When a present-day Maninka bard speaks of "Mande" in the epic, he is referring to Manding peoples living in the heartland of Manden, rather than all Mande language-speaking peoples. For details on terminology, see the "Notes on Nomenclature and Transcription."

Those are the four sons.	(Naamu)
105 Of the three daughters,	(Naamu)
The first daughter is Dò Kamissa.	(Naamu)
Turama'an came here because of the killing of	
Dò Kamissa's buffalo wraith.	(Naamu)
Otherwise, the Turama'ans[23] are from Morocco.	(Naamu)
Turama'an's ancestor came from Morocco.	(Naamu)
110 The second daughter is Tenenba Condé.	(Naamu)
The Fakoli that we talk about,	(Naamu)
If you hear "Soma Tenenba's son Fakoli,"	(Naamu)
She reared Fakoli,	
She did not give birth to him.	(Naamu)
115 It was a Kanté woman who gave birth to Fakoli,	(Naamu)
But it was Tenenba Condé who brought him up.	(Naamu)
She said they should call him Soma Tenenba's son Fakoli,	(Naamu)
That she was his mother because she helped him with	
dalilu.	(Naamu)
That is the second daughter of our ancestor.	(Naamu)
120 The third daughter is Sogolon Wulen Condé.	(Naamu)
This woman gave birth to the Sunjata that you asked	
about.[24]	(Naamu)
After Sunjata was born,	(Naamu)
The father of that Sunjata,	(Naamu)
Maghan Konfara,	(Naamu)
125 Who were his ancestors?	(Naamu)
One of them was Mamadi Kani, who also sired four sons.	(Naamu)
He sired Kani Simbon,	(Naamu)
He sired Kani Nyogo Simbon,	(Naamu)
He sired Kabala Simbon,	(Naamu)
130 He sired Big Simbon Madi Tanyagati.	(Naamu)
He had four sons, and our Condé ancestor had four sons.	(Naamu)

[23] Turama'an Traoré's ancestors Abdu Karimi and Abdu Kassimu, later known as Danmansa Wulanni and Danmansa Wulanba.

[24] Here and elsewhere (e.g., l. 153), Tassey Condé refers to previous conversation with the researcher.

Kani Simbon's descendants are the people known as
    Kulubali.   (Naamu)
Kulubali is the first son of Manden.   (Naamu)
The next to that is Konaté.   (Naamu)
135   The next to that is Douno.   (Naamu)
The next to that came the Mansaré,[25] who are known as
    Keita.   (Naamu)

The seven Mande kings who ruled Manden,   (Naamu)
The first of those kings was the Condé ancestor,
Donsamogo Diarra.   (Naamu)
140   He fought to gain the Mande kingship.   (Naamu)
He loved Manden,   (Naamu)
He built Manden.   (Naamu)
Those of you who say you are Condé, you have power.   (Naamu)
The next in the leadership of Manden was the Kulubali's
    ancestor,
145   Kani Simbon.   (Naamu)
Kani Simbon ruled Manden and made it prosperous.   (Naamu)
He improved Manden without going to war.   (Naamu)
You cannot point to anyone who fought against Kulubali.   (Naamu)
He ruled and was able to improve Manden.   (Naamu)
150   To the end of his reign, he never fought with anyone.   (Naamu)
The next to that was the Kamara ancestor,
Tabon Wana Faran[26] Kamara of Sibi Mountain.   (Naamu)
That is the Kamanjan[27] you were talking about.   (Naamu)
(You heard it?)   (Naamu)

---

[25] From *mansa*, "king"—i.e., of royal lineage. An honorific for branches of the Keita lineage claiming descent from Sunjata, also applied to patronymics (*jamuw*) related to Sunjata, including the Konaté and Kulubali. Keita: The *jamu* of Sunjata's father was Konaté, but according to tradition, when Sunjata returned from exile to take over the power in Manden, he received the name "Keita" (for a popular etymology, see l. 4134). Sunjata is also called Konaté (e.g., in some songs from Gambia and elsewhere).

[26] A title, probably of Soninke origin, that was roughly the equivalent of "Mansa." In Mande epic, it is usually applied to the Kamara ruler of Sibi and Tabon, and to the ruler of Nema/Mema, Faran Tunkara (see l. 178).

[27] A nickname, "Tall Kamara," alternative to the ruler's formal title/praise name, Tabon Wana Faran Kamara.

155 He did well with Manden and made it prosper. (Naamu)
   Anyone who rebelled against his rule,
   Would be captured and brought back into line. (Naamu)
   He was never captured or defeated in war. (Naamu)
   No battle commander ever captured the Kulubali ancestor,
160 Kani Simbon. (Naamu)
   No war leader ever captured the Condé ancestor,
   Donsamogo Diarra. (Naamu)
   If you are narrating a history,
   Tell it the way it happened. (Naamu)
165 From the time my eyes were first open up to now, (Naamu)
   None of our elders has ever told us (Naamu)
   That these people were captured by any battle
      commander. (Naamu)
   The next to that is the ancestor of the Danaba,
   Tenen Mansa Konkon of Kirina. (Naamu)
170 He descended from the Kamissoko. (Naamu)
   He also did well with Manden. (Naamu)
   From beginning to end of his reign,
   He was the walking stick that Manden leaned on. (Naamu)
   (You heard it?)
175 The Kamissoko are in Kirina, (Naamu)
   The Kònò of Kirina are their descendants. (Naamu)
   Next to that is the Tunkara ancestor,
   Faran Tunkara of Kuntunya. (Naamu)
   When Ma'an Sunjata and Manden Bori disappeared, (Naamu)
180 During their exile that is where they were seen. (Naamu)
   Maybe we will soon come to that. (Naamu)
   The next one is the Kanté ancestor,
   Soso Bali Sumaworo. (Naamu)
   He is the sixth *mansa*. (Naamu)
185 (You heard it?)

   All those who I have just counted, (Naamu)
   No battle commander ever captured them. (Naamu)
   After they made their laws and decrees that brought
      progress to Manden, (Naamu)

	After they united so they could combine their strength,	(Naamu)
190	All of those kings,	(Naamu)
	When it was time for one of them to rule,	(Naamu)
	The seven regions would unite;	(Naamu)
	They would help him with his kingship,	(Naamu)
	Up to the end of his reign.	(Naamu)
195	But for war to break out,	(Naamu)
	It was because of Soso Bali Sumaworo.	(Naamu)
	(You heard it?)	
	Soso Bali Sumaworo is the sixth *mansa* of Manden.	(Naamu)
	The seventh *mansa* was Ma'an Sunjata.	(Naamu)
200	But if we had started with Ma'an Sunjata,	(Naamu)
	If we do not narrate some of the other episodes,	(Naamu)
	Then we have left out half of Manden.	(Naamu)
	If you hear that Sunjata was made *mansa*,	(Naamu)
	That Sunjata got power at the time those things happened,	(Naamu)
205	Ma'an Sunjata's father was a *mansa*.	(Naamu)
	After the reigns of all those other people,	
	It is God who chooses from among the people.	(Naamu)
	Now in the meeting that took place,	(Naamu)
	The country was put in the care of Maghan Konfara.	(Naamu)
210	This is about how Sunjata was born.	(Naamu)

THE SEARCH FOR A SPECIAL WIFE

	When Manden was put in the care of Maghan Konfara,	(Naamu)
	He had the power,	(Naamu)
	He had the wealth,	(Naamu)
	He was popular,	(Naamu)
215	He had *dalilu*,	(Naamu)
	But he had no child.	(Naamu)
	(You heard it?)	(Naamu)
	Simbon, Sunjata's father, had no child.	(Naamu)

	He craved a child.	(Naamu)
220	His friends had begun to have children,	(Naamu)
	But no child was had by Maghan Konfara.	(Naamu)
	But his *dalilu* had now shown,	(Naamu)
	His *moriw*[28] had said,	(Naamu)
	His sand diviners[29] had said,	(Naamu)
225	His pebble diviners had said,	(Naamu)
	"Simbon, you will sire a child who will be famous."	(Naamu)
	(You heard it?)	(Naamu)

	Everybody he consulted said the same thing.	(Naamu)
	"But try to marry a light-skinned woman,"	(Naamu)
230	They told him, "Maghan Konfara,	(Naamu)
	Marry a light-skinned woman.	(Naamu)
	If you marry a light-skinned woman,	(Naamu)
	She will give birth to the child that has been foreseen."	(Naamu)
	Because of his power, he married nine light-skinned women.	(Naamu)
235	Aside from Flaba Naabi,	
	He still did not sire a child.	(Naamu)
	He was perplexed.	(Naamu)
	If you say that you want to know about Sunjata,	(Naamu)
	What Sunjata's father had to endure,	(Naamu)
240	The people of Manden had to endure.	(Naamu)
	From the last Wednesday of the month of Jomènè[30]	(Naamu)
	To the same time the following year,	(Naamu)
	He did not sire a child.	(Naamu)

	He sent the *moriw* back into retreat.	(Naamu)

---

[28] A nominal Muslim who, in oral tradition, often performs divination (see Glossary).

[29] Seers and healers who identify the source of all kinds of problems by spreading a pile of sand and reading symbols in it, or casting multiple objects such as pebbles or cowrie shells and reading the configurations in which they land. Diviners then prescribe appropriate sacrifices to remedy the problem.

[30] The first month of the year.

245 He told them, "I am in need of a child,
So do your best.   (Naamu)
The child that has been foreseen,   (Naamu)
It is said that if I sire it,   (Naamu)
It will rule Manden.   (Naamu)
250 I must sire this child."   (Naamu)
They went back into retreat.   (Naamu)
All of the *moriw* were present.   (Naamu)
They came back and told him,   (Naamu)
They said, "Simbon,   (Naamu)
255 Marry somebody who is a mulatto."   (Naamu)
(You heard it?)   (Naamu)
He also married nine of those mulatto women.   (Naamu)
Aside from Marabajan Tarawelé,   (Naamu)
None of them gave birth.   (Naamu)
260 From that time of the year to the same time the
        following year,   (Naamu)
Those women were with him in the house,   (Naamu)
But they never bore any male children.   (Naamu)
Simbon was frustrated.   (Naamu)
(You heard it?)   (Naamu)

265 He sent the *moriw* back into retreat.
He said to them, "Tell me the truth.   (Naamu)
Ah! If you see that I will not have any children, tell me. (Naamu)
This is something that only God can provide;
It cannot be bought in the market."   (Naamu)
270 This time they told him,   (Naamu)
"Very well, marry a black woman.   (Naamu)
There is a woman who is black, but her heart is white."   (Naamu)
This time he married nine black women.   (Naamu)
Aside from Nyuma Damba Magasuba,   (Naamu)
275 None of them bore any children.   (Naamu)
It was difficult for Sunjata to be born.   (Naamu)
(You heard it?)   (Naamu)

Maghan Konfara was frustrated.   (Naamu)

	They told him again,	(Naamu)
280	"Very well, man,	(Naamu)
	Free one of your slave girls and marry her."	(Naamu)
	In those days they still practiced slavery.	(Naamu)
	He liberated nine slave girls.	(Naamu)
	Aside from Jonmusoni Manyan,	(Naamu)
285	None of them bore any children.	(Naamu)
	Simbon was frustrated.	(Naamu)
	When the last Wednesday of Jomènè arrived,	(Naamu)
	He gathered together the people of Konfara.	(Naamu)
	(You heard it?)	(Naamu)
290	When the people of Konfara had gathered,	(Naamu)
	He separated into groups the *moriw*,	
	The sand diviners, and the pebble diviners.	(Naamu)
	He sent them all into retreat.	(Naamu)
	He said, "I told you not to hesitate.	(Naamu)
295	If you see that I will have no child, tell me.	(Naamu)
	Go inside the house.	
	If you do not tell me the truth,	(Naamu)
	I will kill all of you and replace you."	(Naamu)
	When they came out of retreat, they told him,	(Naamu)
300	"Simbon, you will sire a child.	(Naamu)
	Make one of your *jelimusow*[31] happy.	
	Marry her so she will give birth."	(Naamu)
	He made nine *jelimusow* happy,	(Naamu)
	But aside from Tunku Manyan Diawara,	(Naamu)
305	None of them ever gave birth.	(Naamu)
	All of Manden became frustrated.	(Naamu)
	It is hard to give birth to a child who will be famous.	(Naamu)
	When all of Manden became frustrated,	(Naamu)
	The diviners became ashamed of themselves.	(Naamu)
310	They held a meeting themselves and swore an oath:	(Naamu)

[31] Female bards (sing. *jelimuso*).

"Anybody who has broken a taboo should confess it.   (Naamu)

Maybe this is our fault.   (Naamu)

If we do not get together and tell this man the truth,   (Naamu)

The feet of our descendants will not be able to even break

    an egg in Manden."   (Naamu)

315 (You heard it?)   (Naamu)

They went back into retreat and came back out.   (Naamu)

They told Simbon,   (Naamu)

They said, "Someone will come from the East.   (Naamu)

He will be coming from the land of the white-skinned

    people.   (Naamu)

320 That has been revealed to us.   (Naamu)

The problem of your childlessness,   (Naamu)

Let him pray to God for a solution to your problem.   (Naamu)

If you let him pray to God on the matter of your son,   (Naamu)

Anything he tells you will have been agreed upon by God.   (Naamu)

325 We will not be able to accomplish it.   (Naamu)

It is a good man that God has shown to us."

While they waited there in Farakoro,[32]   (Naamu)

Manjan Bereté arrived.   (Naamu)

Now the first Muslim leader of Manden,   (Naamu)

330 Who opened the door[33] on the people of Manden,   (Naamu)

He was Manjan Bereté.   (Naamu)

He is the ancestor of the Bereté in Manden.   (Naamu)

The home of the Bereté people is Farisini Hejaji,[34]   (Naamu)

In the land of Mecca.   (Naamu)

335 Farisi is the name of a region.   (Naamu)

It is the home of the Bereté,

---

[32] Sometimes shortened to "Farako." Evidently the hometown of Sunjata's father, located in the territory (*jamana*) of Konfara. Farakoro appears in the longer version of Maghan Konfara's name, as he was known to Tassey Condé and his ancestral bards of Fadama: Farako Manko Farakonken.

[33] That is, he was instrumental in the introduction of Islam.

[34] "Farisi," is from Fars, a region in Persia. Hejaji is from Hejaz, a region that was the ancient cradle of Islam, including the Red Sea coast of Arabia and the cities of Mecca, Medina, and others.

	They are Suraka.[35]	(Naamu)
	Manjan Bereté came;	(Naamu)
	He took his lodgings with Simbon.	(Naamu)
340	He said, "You need the religion practiced in my homeland.	(Naamu)
	The Prophet has said nobody should take up swords in the religion again,	(Naamu)
	That we should now be gentle with one another.	(Naamu)
	Let us win people over by kindness,	(Naamu)
	So we can awaken their minds and they can join the religion.	(Naamu)
345	For anyone who does that, the blessings will be great."	(Naamu)
	Bereté packed up some books and came from Farisi.	(Naamu)
	He would come to the land of Manden because it was a powerful place.	(Naamu)
	If he found someone who would join him in the land of Manden,	(Naamu)
	Who would work with the Koran,	(Naamu)
350	His blessings would be great.	(Naamu)
	When Manjan Bereté came and met Simbon,	(Naamu)
	He brought with him his little sister,	(Naamu)
	Because they could not adjust to the food here.	(Naamu)
	He brought his sister so she could prepare his food	
355	Until he became acquainted with the Mande people.	(Naamu)
	That is why Sansun Bereté came with him.	(Naamu)
	When they came and took up lodgings with Simbon,	
	He welcomed them.	(Naamu)
	After Simbon welcomed them,	(Naamu)
360	His wife Jonmusoni Manyan went to him and said, "Simbon,"	(Naamu)
	She said, "Aah, the man who was described by your diviners,	(Naamu)
	It seems to me that this is the man.	(Naamu)
	Because from the day of his arrival until today,	(Naamu)

[35] A Maninka and Bamana term for the local perception of "Arab," which includes Moors and North Africans in general.

When it was two o'clock he would wash his feet
    and pray. (Naamu)
365 When it was four o'clock he would wash his feet
    and pray. (Naamu)
When it was seven o'clock he would wash his feet
    and pray. (Naamu)
When it is eight o'clock I can hear him praying in his
    room. (Naamu)
Get closer to this man. (Naamu)
You see yourself sitting here idly. (Naamu)
370 Do not allow every stranger to flow past you like a river. (Naamu)
A citizen's well-being arrives in the form of a stranger."
Maghan Konfara went to the *Karamogo*[36] Bereté.
He observed that whenever the *karamogo* was drinking
    fresh milk, (Naamu)
He was so clean that the milk could be seen flowing down
    his throat. (Naamu)
375 He said to him, "Karamogo, forgive me. (Naamu)
It has been a long time since you arrived,
But I have now come to greet you. (Naamu)
You came and found me troubled." (Naamu)
Maghan Konfara said,
380 "Come here and I will show you the cause of my worry." (Naamu)
Taking the teacher by the hand,
He opened his gate and showed him all his barren wives. (Naamu)
He said, "You see this number of women? (Naamu)
Among them are light-skinned women,
385 There are black-skinned women, bards, and slaves. (Naamu)
Before you came, your arrival was foretold. (Naamu)
Pray to God for me, so that I can sire a son." (Naamu)

Bereté had come so that his kind[37] could be known. (Naamu)
He was devoted to his faith and he had never violated a
    taboo. (Naamu)

---

[36] "Teacher." As the proper noun "Karamogo," an honorific for a distinguished Muslim community leader, signifying a respected scholar, learned one, wise man.
[37] "His kind": Muslims.

390 Maghan Konfara was pleased.	(Naamu)
Bereté went into retreat and prayed to God.	(Naamu)
God replied to him,	
Saying the man should marry a woman with the same	
totem as the Bereté.	(Naamu)
If he marries a woman with the same totem as the	
Karamogo,	(Naamu)
395 He will sire a child.	(Naamu)
Oh! What was his totem?	(Naamu)
God said, "You came and saw them and they were not	
praying."	(Naamu)
They told him, "You must marry the daughter of someone	
who prays."	(Naamu)
When Simbon was told this,	(Naamu)
400 Once he had been told,	(Naamu)
Maghan Konfara said "Ha!	
Karamogo, I am very fortunate."	(Naamu)
(You heard it?)	(Naamu)
"The promise that I made to pray,	(Naamu)
405 Being occupied with my chiefly duties,	
That has resulted in lack of respect for that promise.	(Naamu)
From the time that you arrived up to now,	
You have prayed at every prayer time,	(Naamu)
But you did not meet me at prayer.	(Naamu)
410 Perhaps my totem wife[38] is among those now within	
the yard.	(Naamu)
Maybe we are related through marriage."[39]	(Naamu)
Maghan Konfara said,	
"Since you have come, you are my totem.	(Naamu)

---

[38] A woman with the same totem as the Bereté (l. 394). The "totem" (Maninka *tana*, Bamana *t'né, tènè*) is a sacred animal or plant that, according to legend, saved the life of an ancestor of a particular family, and thus must never be killed or eaten by a member of that family. Elsewhere in this narrative *tana* is translated as "taboo," where it refers to a sacred object that must not be touched or used by anyone but the owner.

[39] Suggesting they might be cousins.

Your little sister who accompanied you here,	(Naamu)
415 Please give her to me."	(Naamu)
The Karamogo said, "I cannot do that."	(Naamu)
Maghan Konfara said, "Why will you not do that?"	(Naamu)
He said, "We cannot come from white to black."	(Naamu)
(You heard it?)	(Naamu)
420 "We are Bereté.	(Naamu)
It was our ancestor who planted a date farm for the Prophet at Mecca.	(Naamu)
That was the beginning of our family identity.	(Naamu)
When the date farm was planted for the Prophet,	
He blessed our ancestor.	(Naamu)
425 He said everyone should leave us alone:	(Naamu)
Bè anu to yè, and that is why they call us Bereté.[40]	(Naamu)
No man of Manden will tell you	(Naamu)
That we originated the Bereté family identity.	(Naamu)
It was the Prophet who said we should be set apart,	(Naamu)
430 That nobody's foolishness should trouble us.	(Naamu)
Bè anu to yè, everyone should leave us alone.	(Naamu)
Thus we became the Bereté.	(Naamu)
From that time up to today,	(Naamu)
We have not done anything other than the Prophet's business.	(Naamu)
435 This place has already become impious	(Naamu)
Because of your lack of attention to Islam.	(Naamu)
So how can I give you my little sister?	(Naamu)
I did not come from Farisi for that purpose,	
So I will not give you my little sister."	(Naamu)
440 "Aaah," said Simbon, "Give her to me.	(Naamu)
If you want wealth, I will give you wealth."	(Naamu)
(You heard it?)	(Naamu)

[40] Such explanations for the origins of the names of people and places are based on folklore and are called popular etymologies (cf. l. 1397–98, 2574–76, 4101–03, 4134, 4843–44).

"If you do not give her to me, (Naamu)

I will take her for myself, (Naamu)

445 Because you are not in your home, you are in my home." (Naamu)

When Manjan Bereté was told this, he said, (Naamu)

"If you take my sister for yourself, I will go back to Farisi. (Naamu)

I will go and get Suraka warriors to come and destroy
    Manden (Naamu)

If you take my little sister by force." (Naamu)

450 Simbon said, "You just do that. (Naamu)

If you go back to Farisi to get warriors, (Naamu)

You might come and destroy Manden. (Naamu)

But by then your sister will be pregnant. (Naamu)

I will have a child by then. (Naamu)

455 Even if I die, it will still be my child." (Naamu)

(You heard it?) (Naamu)

He said, "I have taken her." (Naamu)

He took her. (Naamu)

"If you call for wealth, I will give you wealth. (Naamu)

460 If you call for the sword, I will agree to that. (Naamu)

I have the power, you have no power, you are in
    my place." (Naamu)

Manjan Bereté packed up his books and went back to
    Farisi. (Naamu)

He went and told his fathers and brothers, (Naamu)

"The Mande *mansa* that I went to visit, (Naamu)

465 He has used his chiefly power to take my little sister
    from me." (Naamu)

His fathers and brothers said, "Ah, Manjan Bereté, (Naamu)

Your youth has betrayed you. (Naamu)

You carry the sacred book. (Naamu)

You have been looking for someone (Naamu)

470 To help you with the work of the sacred book.

Go back and tell the Mande people, (Naamu)

Tell Simbon,

That if he is in love with your younger sister,

You will give him both her and the book. (Naamu)

475 Tell him, 'If you convert and become another like me, (Naamu)
So that we can proselytize together, (Naamu)
I will give you my younger sister. (Naamu)
But if you refuse to convert, I will go for my warriors.' (Naamu)
If he does not convert, come back and we will give you
    warriors. (Naamu)
480 If he agrees to convert, that is what you went for." (Naamu)

Manjan Bereté returned to Farakoro. (Naamu)
After he explained to Simbon, (Naamu)
Maghan Konfara said, "What your father said,
That your youth betrayed you, is true. (Naamu)
485 If you had done what he said in the first place,
You would not have returned to Farisi. (Naamu)
All I want is a child, no matter what the cost. (Naamu)
I agree to what you propose. (Naamu)
Since you have requested that I convert, (Naamu)
490 I agree." (Naamu)
They shaved his head,[41] and together they read the
    Koran. (Naamu)
After reading the Koran, (Naamu)
Manjan Bereté gave his little sister to Maghan Konfara. (Naamu)
His sister was called Sansun Bereté. (Naamu)
495 (You heard it?) (Naamu)
It was this Sansun Bereté (Naamu)
Who bore the first son, called Dankaran Tuman. (Naamu)
He was older than Ma'an Sunjata. (Naamu)
(You heard it?) (Naamu)
500 After she bore that one son,
She had a daughter who was called Nana Triban. (Naamu)
She only gave birth to that one son and that one
    daughter. (Naamu)

After siring those two children, Simbon became troubled
    again. (Naamu)

---

[41] Signifying that the person had become a Muslim.

Simbon said "Karamogo!   (Naamu)

505 Go back into retreat.   (Naamu)

The son that was foretold,   (Naamu)

If it is your nephew, let me know.   (Naamu)

If it is not him, let me know.   (Naamu)

We should not lie to one another."   (Naamu)

510 Manjan Bereté went into retreat.   (Naamu)

He prayed to God.   (Naamu)

God revealed to him that this was not the son that was
    foretold.   (Naamu)

He came out and told Simbon that the son who was
    foretold,

When he was born a trumpet would be blown,

515 And his name would never disappear.   (Naamu)

He said, "This is not the son."   (Naamu)

Simbon said, "How do I get that son?   (Naamu)

Pray to God for me to have this son.   (Naamu)

Will I get that son?"

520 "Yes, you will get that son."   (Naamu)

"Very well, pray to God for that."   (Naamu)

Manjan Bereté prayed to God.   (Naamu)

He said, "Simbon, you will get this child.   (Naamu)

What God revealed to me, when I was praying to him,   (Naamu)

525 Is that there are others like me who will come.   (Naamu)

They too will come from the land of the white-skins."   (Naamu)

Bereté said, "When those people come,

They will not bring any woman with them.   (Naamu)

But the place that they will name as their destination,   (Naamu)

530 If you give them a message they will bring you a woman
    from that place.   (Naamu)

She will bear that child."   (Naamu)

*[In an omitted passage, the narrator describes the Moroccan back-
ground of two brothers, Abdu Karimi and Abdu Kassimu, who will
travel to the land of Dò ni Kiri to hunt a buffalo that is devastating the
countryside, and will eventually become known as Danmansa Wulanni
and Danmansa Wulanba.]*

TWO HUNTERS ARRIVE IN MANDEN

Abdu Karimi and Abdu Kassimu came to Manden.	(Na-amu)
From Morocco they walked through the night.	(Naamu)
The following day they walked all day.	(Na-amu)
535 In the evening of that day,	(Naamu)
They were already under the three *nkiliki* trees[42] of Manden.	(Naamu)
Those three *nkiliki* trees—	(Na-amu)
When people used to come from Dò ni Kiri,	(Naamu)
From the home of the Condé,	(Naamu)
540 They used to rest there.	(Naamu)
Those who used to come from Manden,	(Naamu)
From the home of the Mansaré,	(Na-amu)
They used to rest there.	(Naamu)
Those who used to come from Negeboriya,	(Naamu)
545 From the home of the Koroma,	(Naamu)
They used to rest there.	(Na-amu)
Those who used to come from Soso,	(Naamu)
From the home of the Kanté,	(Naamu)
They used to rest there.	(Naamu)
550 People would get news of the world there.	(Naamu)
When Abdu Karimi and Abdu Kassimu came there,	(Na-amu)
They measured out their food,	(Naamu)
They cooked their meal,	(Naamu)
They ate and slept there.	(Na-amu)
555 They were worried.	(Naamu)
Abdu Karimi and Abdu Kassimu were Arab *kamalenw*.	(Na-amu)
They did not know where to go from there.	(Naamu)

[42] *Dichrostachys cinerea* or *Dichrostachys glomerata*, a tree of the mimosa genus, producing small flowers.

They went to where some traders had left their cooking
    pots. (Naamu)

After eating, the Arab *kamalenw* said, "Let us lie down
    here, (Na-amu)

560 Let us wait for these traders to return. (Naamu)

We will soon learn our next destination. (Naamu)

While they were sleeping,

Some traders who were on their way from Manden
    arrived. (Naamu)

Some also arrived from Negeboriya, home of the
    Koroma. (Na-amu)

565 They greeted one another. (Naamu)

The Arab *kamalenw* asked, "Is everything all right with the
    people of Manden?" (Na-amu)

The traders replied, "There is nothing wrong with them." (Naamu)

The *kamalenw* asked, "Is everything all right with the
    Koroma of Negeboriya?" (Na-amu)

The traders said, "Nothing is troubling them." (Naamu)

570 They too measured out their food; (Na-amu)

Then they went to sleep. (Naamu)

While they were lying there, (Naamu)

Some traders who were on their way from Soso arrived. (Na-amu)

The traders who had gone to Dò ni Kiri and found it in
    turmoil, (Naamu)

575 They came back. (Naamu)

They all met in that place. (Na-amu)

They said to Abdu Karimi and Abdu Kassimu, "Where are
    you from?" (Naamu)

The *kamalenw* said, "We are from Morocco." (Naamu)

They asked, "Where are you going?" (Na-amu)

580 The *kamalenw* replied, "We were on our way to the land
    of the Condé, (Naamu)

But we do not know the way." (Na-amu)

The traders said, "The *mansa* of Dò ni Kiri, (Naamu)

Donsamogo Diarra, (Naamu)

It is he and his sister who are quarrelling." (Naamu)

585 (You heard it?) (Naamu)

22

I just told you about the first daughter of Ma'an
    Solonkan,   (Na-amu)

Called Dò Kamissa.   (Naamu)

She and her brother,   (Naamu)

Donsamogo Diarra,   (Naamu)

590 They had quarreled over the issue of the legacy left by
    Ma'an Solonkan.   (Na-amu)

They did not agree.   (Naamu)

(You heard it?)   (Naamu)

Dò Kamissa said,   (Naamu)

"Donsamogo Diarra,   (Na-amu)

595 If you refuse to share the property with me,   (Naamu)

I will take it myself."   (Naamu)

The Condé elders said to her, "Go and try to take a share
    for yourself;

You are too headstrong."   (Na-amu)

She said, "Shall I take it for myself?"

600 They said, "Yes."   (Naamu)

She went out of the town.   (Naamu)

She went to stay in a farm hamlet.   (Na-amu)

They did not know that she had the power   (Naamu)

To transform herself into different things.   (Naaaamu)

605 The twelve towns of Dò,   (Naamu)

The four towns of Kiri,   (Naamu)

The six towns on the other side of the river,   (Naamu)

That is what is known as Dò ni Kiri.   (Na-amu)

(You heard it?)   (Na-amu)

610 At the break of day,   (Naamu)

The buffalo that she transformed herself into   (Naamu)

Would kill people in all of those places.   (Na-amu)

It had become a bad time.   (Naamu)

Donsamogo Diarra said,   (Na-amu)

615 "The buffalo has killed all of the hunters that I sent for
    from Manden."   (Naamu)

(You heard it?)   (Na-amu)

He sent a message to the Koroma of Negeboriya,
But the buffalo killed all of the hunters who came. (Naamu)
He sent for the hunters of Soso,
620 But when they came the buffalo killed them all. (Naamu)
Donsamogo Diarra was at a loss. (Na-amu)
He sent out the word from Dò ni Kiri. (Naamu)
Donsamogo Diarra said, "People have died because of me. (Na-amu)
Anyone who kills this buffalo, (Naamu)
625 Three age sets of the girls of Dò ni Kiri, (Na-amu)
I will display them to the person.
Any one of them chosen by that person will become his
wife." (Naamu)
Everybody who visited Dò ni Kiri was informed of this. (Na-amu)
When the traders returned to the camp under the
nkiliki tree,
630 They told the travelers about the turmoil in Dò ni Kiri. (Naamu)
They said, "The quarrel with their sister has resulted in
many deaths. (Na-amu)
Hunger has come to Kiri (Naamu)
Because no one can go in or out. (Naamu)
The paths to the village have been closed,
635 The paths to their farms have been closed. (Na-amu)
There is no way for farm crops to be brought home. (Naamu)
The buffalo is blocking the way. (Na-amu)
The Condé say that anyone who kills this buffalo, (Naamu)
They will bring out three sets of their girls to you, (Naamu)
640 That any one you choose will become your wife." (Naamu)
(You heard it?) (Na-amu)

The traders said, "Things in Dò ni Kiri have become very
bad." (Naamu)
The Arab *kamalenw* were still camped there. (Naamu)
The younger brother, Abdu Karimi, said, "Big brother, (Naamu)
645 Do you hear what they are saying?" (Naamu)
Abdu Kassimu replied, "I hear it." (Na-amu)
They said, "Let us go to Dò ni Kiri." (Naamu)
The elder brother said, "Eh, little brother, (Naamu)

24

	What about these things they are talking about?	(Na-amu)
650	Suppose the buffalo kills us?"	(Naamu)
	Abdu Karimi replied,	
	"If the buffalo kills us, it will be for the sake of	
	the Condé."	(Naamu)
	He said, "They are having a bad time in Dò ni Kiri.	(Na-amu)
	I feel sympathy for them.	(Na-amu)
655	The ancestor of those Condé,	(Naamu)
	Their ancestor Samasuna,[43]	(Na-amu)
	Our fathers told us,	
	That before the Prophet could make any progress,	(Na-amu)
	God told him to fight at Kaïbara.[44]	(Naamu)
660	No matter how difficult the fight at Dò ni Kiri will be,	
	The battle at Kaïbara was more difficult than that.	(Na-amu)
	The Condé we are talking about,	(Naamu)
	Their ancestor Samasuna,	(Na-amu)
	He took one thousand of his sons	(Naamu)
665	To go and help our ancestors fight at the battle of	
	Kaïbara.	(Na-amu)
	He lost all one thousand of his sons."	(Naamu)
	Still speaking, Abdu Karimi said, "Those Condé,	(Na-amu)
	The one thousand sons that the ancestor Samasuna gave,	(Naamu)
	They all remained on the battleground of our ancestors'	
	war at Kaïbara.	(Na-naamu)
670	But if the two of us should die for the sake of	
	the Condé,	(Na-amu)
	Will that equal one thousand men?	(Naamu)
	If death approaches,	(Na-amu)
	Die for a good cause.	(Naamu)
	We do not equal one thousand men.	(Naamu)

[43] Samson (Ar. Shamsūn) is not mentioned in the Koran, but according to other sources of Muslim tradition (e.g., al-Tha'labi and al-Tabari), he dedicated his life to God and continually fought against idolators.

[44] Maninka usage of Khaybar, an oasis 95 miles from Medina, Arabia, the site of a famous battle fought by the Prophet Muhammad and his army.

675 But if we should die for the sake of the Condé, (Naamu)
We will do what the one thousand men did. (Na-amu)
Let us go to Dò ni Kiri.
If we should retreat after hearing that the Condé are
    suffering, (Naamu)
And those ancestors suffered at Kaïbara for our sake, (Na-amu)
680 Then we are bastards." (Naamu)
Abdu Karimi encouraged his elder brother. (Na-amu)
Abdu Kassimu now had the courage to go to Dò ni Kiri. (Naamu)
They packed their belongings and went straight to
    Konfara. (Na-amu)
They bypassed Dò ni Kiri and went straight to Manden. (Naamu)

[In an omitted passage, the narrator introduces the buffalo's female genie companion, who advises the brothers on how to respond to abusive women they will meet, and how to approach Dò Kamissa, the Buffalo Woman, and avoid being killed by her.]

685 When they arrived, Manjan Bereté was sitting (Naamu)
In a circle near Maghan Konfara. (Naamu)
They were playing *wari*.[45] (Na-amu)
Manjan Bereté was sitting in the circle near Simbon,
With prayer beads in his hands. (Naamu)
690 He was praying to God:
"May God not let me be embarrassed by my prediction." (Naamu)
They remained sitting when they saw the two men
    coming. (Naamu)
When those people arrived, (Naamu)
They met in that same circle. (Naamu)
695 They stopped playing *wari*. (Na-amu)
Abdu Karimi said, "My respected *karamogo*, (Naamu)
I have come to God and I have come to you.
What makes one walk fast will make one talk fast. (Na-amu)

---

[45] Or *wali*, a popular game played with two rows of shallow holes, usually in a carved wooden board, with small stones or cowrie shells used as counters.

We have come to God,

700 We have come to the Mande people,

We have come to Simbon."   (Naamuuu)

After the greetings,

The Mande people asked them, "Where did you
    come from?"

The Arab *kamalenw* said, "We come from Morocco."   (Na-amuuu)

705 The Mande people asked them, "What is your family?"   (Naamu)

"We are Sharifu."[46]   (Na-amu)

The Mande people saluted them, "You Haidara."[47]   (Naamu)

The *kamalenw* replied, "Marahaba."[48]   (Naamu)

The Mande people said, "The honor is yours,

710 The honor is Simbon's."   (Na-amu)

The Arab *kamalenw* said, "We come from Morocco,

We are children of Abdu Sharifu.

We are descendants of Saïdina Ali."[49]   (Na-amu)

(You heard it?)   (Naamu)

715 The *kamalenw* explained, "We have heard that the Condé
    are suffering,   (Naamu)

That they are quarreling with their sister.

She has transformed herself into a buffalo.

Every morning in the twelve towns of Dò,   (Naamu)

The four towns of Kiri,   (Naamu)

720 And the six towns across the river,   (Naamu)

The buffalo has been killing people in all of them."   (Na-amuuu)

They said, "That is why we have come.   (Naamu)

[46] Contraction of the longer plural form Sharifulu (l. 1665) from the Arabic Shurafa' (sing. Sharīf), a lineage claiming descent from the family of the Prophet Muhammad.

[47] A prestigious Muslim family name in Manden, here used in a greeting as the equivalent of Sharifu.

[48] A standard response to a greeting directly honoring one's ancestors by mentioning their *jamu* (patronymic, identity).

[49] 'Alī ibn Abī Ṭālib, cousin and son-in-law of the Prophet Muhammad, one of the first converts to Islam; renowned as a warrior during Islam's struggle for survival, he took part in most of the Prophet's expeditions and displayed legendary courage at the battles of Badr and Khaybar.

We want to go to Dò ni Kiri.	(Naamu)
We want to go and help the Condé with their trouble.	(Na-amu)
725 We want you to perform the sand divination for us.	(Naamu)
If our sand is sweet,	(Na-amu)
We will go to Dò ni Kiri.	(Naamu)
And if our sand is not sweet,	(Naamu)
We will go to Dò ni Kiri."	(Naamu)
730 Simbon chuckled.	(Naamu)
He said, "Ah, my men!"	
He said, "Manhood is in the mouth.	(Naamu)
If a man does not notice what you are saying,	
He might attack you.	(Na-amu)
735 Eyòòò, if the sand is sweet you will go!	(Naamu)
If the sand is not sweet you will go."	(Naamu)
They said, "Ah huh, we will still go."	(Naamu)
Simbon said, "Ah, blessings upon you."	(Na-amu)

He gave them lodgings in a house.	(Naamu)
740 Simbon left the strangers in their house;	
He went into his room and spread the sand.[50]	(Na-amu)
He spread and spread and spread, and said the words over it.	(Naamu)
He said, "If these boys are the source I have been told about,	(Naamu)
If they go to Dò ni Kiri, will they kill the buffalo?	(Naamu)
745 Let the sand be sweet."	(Na-amu)
When he spread the sand, he saw that the sand was sweet for them.	(Naamu)
Alone in his room, he spread the sand three times.	(Naamu)
When the sand was sweet,	(Na-amu)
He sent for the boys.	(Naamu)
750 He said, "Come here.	(Na-amu)
Come and let me spread the sand in your presence."	(Naamu)
When the sand was spread,	(Na-amu)
Abdu Karimi was pleased.	(Naamu)

[50] Preparing for sand divination (see n. 29).

Simbon told them,	(Na-amu)
755 "You Sharifu,"	(Naamu)
He said, "Your sand is good."	(Na-amu)
He said, "Your sand is sweet,	
But there are some sacrifices to be made."	(Na-amu)
They said, "What sacrifice is it?"	
760 He said, "There is a sacrifice,	
And the sacrifice is a complicated one."	(Naamu)

They asked, "What is the sacrifice?"	(Na-amu)
He said, "Offer three piles of peanuts.	(Naamu)
Go and pick some old straw out of a roof,	(Naamu)
765 Light it on fire, and roast the peanuts,	(Naamu)
Call the little children to come.	(Na-amu)
While the children are eating them,	(Naamu)
You should be standing nearby with your quiver of arrows.	(Naamu)
When the children are finished eating the peanuts,	(Na-amu)
770 Let them stand up and say, 'May God answer this sacrifice.'	
You respond to that with 'Amina.'	(Na . . .)
By the grace of God, the sand will be sweet."	(Na-amu)
"I will offer the peanuts."	(Naamu)
He made the peanut offering.	(Naamu)
775 He set them out in three piles.	(Naamu)
He went to his wives' cook house,	(Naamu)
He picked some old thatch out of the roof,	(Naamu)
He lit it on fire.	(Naamu)

As the peanuts were roasting,	(Naamu)
780 The hunters were preparing themselves.	(Na-amu)
(People of early times did not carry much baggage.)	(Naamu)
When they were finished dressing,	(Naamu)
They went and stood near the little children.	(Naamu)
When the children were finished eating the peanuts,	(Naaaam')
785 As the children were about to disperse,	(Na-amu)
The hunters said, "May God answer this sacrifice."	

As the hunters were leaving,   (Naamu)

Maghan Konfara said, "You Sharifu,"   (Na-amu)

He said, "The Condé foresee that anybody who kills this

    buffalo,   (Naamu)

790   That they will present three sets of girls to that person.   (Na-amu)

Any one you choose will be your wife.   (Naamu)

When you go, you will kill the buffalo.   (Naamu)

When they bring the young girls to you,   (Naamu)

You should present me with a wife."   (Naamuuu)

795   (What if you said that to someone and they did not bring

    the wife?)   (Na-amu)

The arrogant younger brother Abdu Karimi said,   (Naamu)

"I will not answer him;

I am looking for a wife for my elder brother."   (Naamu)

(You heard it?)   (Na-amu)

800   They departed.   (Naamu)

DO KAMISSA THE BUFFALO WOMAN

When they had passed through the land of Konfara,   (Na-amu)

When they crossed into the land of the Condé,   (Naamu)

After they had walked for one kilometer,   (Naamu)

They met a woman who had borne one child,   (Naamu)

805   Just as the female genie had told them.   (Naamuuu)

She had said, "You will not see me again.   (Na-amu)

But the advice I give you,   (Naamu)

If you do not heed it, the buffalo will kill you."   (Na-amuuu)

When they met this woman who had borne one child,   (Naamu)

810   After they greeted her,   (Naamu)

She spoke abusively to them.   (Na-amu)

She said, "Eh!

Is it the woman who should greet first,

	Or is it the man?	(Naamu)
815	You do not pass by a beautiful woman without greeting	
	her!"	(Na-amu)
	She said every possible bad word to them.	(Naamu)
	They said, "Mba."	(Naamu)
	They said, "We are children of the road.	(Na-amu)
	We do not know anything about women,	
820	We do not know anything about men.	(Naamu)
	We have never been to this country.	
	We speak to everyone we meet, so they can give	
	us help."	(Na-amu)
	She said, "Am I the one who is supposed to give	
	you help?"	(Naamu)
	Huh! They passed on by her.	(Na-amu)
825	They did not quarrel with her.	(Naamu)
	After they passed that one,	(Naamu)
	After walking one kilometer,	(Naamu)
	They met the full-breasted girl.	(Naamu)
	When they met this one,	(Naamu)
830	They said, "Lady, we greet you,	(Naamu)
	God is great,"	(Naamu)
	Ah! She abused them.	(Naamu)
	She said every bad word to them.	(Na-amu)
	The younger brother said,	(Naamu)
835	"Aaah, you do not understand.	(Na-amu)
	A beautiful woman like you will pass by a man like that?	(Naamu)
	You do not know what is happening."	(Naamu)
	(No matter how proud a girl is,	
	Once you call her "beautiful," she will soften.)	(Na-amu)
840	They went on their way.	(Na-amu)
	Humility really comes only with death,	
	But men act humble until they get what they want.	(Naamu)
	After they passed by her,	(Na-amu)
	She went on her way.	(Naamu)
845	After walking on for another kilometer,	(Naamu)

When they heard the pounding of the mortars and
    pestles[51] of Dò ni Kiri,   (Naamu)

They met Dò Kamissa herself.   (Na-amu)

She carried a hoe on her shoulder;   (Naamu)

A walking staff served as her third leg.   (Na-amu)

850 When they said, "Greetings mother,"   (Naamu)

Heeeh! She cursed their father.   (Naamu)

After that, she cursed their grandfather.   (Na-amu)

Then she cursed their mother.   (Naamu)

"You are calling me mother?   (Naamu)

855 Was I the one who gave birth to your father or your
    mother?"   (Na-amu)

She said every bad word to them.   (Naamu)

Abdu Karimi said, "Big brother,   (Naaaam')

Don't you think this lady resembles our mother?"   (Naamu)

Abdu Kassimu replied, "Heeh, this lady does resemble
    our mother.   (Na-amu)

860 Everything she is doing to us seems familiar."   (Naamu)

Abdu Karimi said, "The manner in which our own
    mother abuses us,   (Naamu)

That is the same way she abuses us.   (Na-amu)

Hey! Look at the way she walks,

As if she were our mother."   (Naamu)

865 Abdu Kassimu said, "Ma, where are you going?"   (Naamu)

She said, "Do I have to explain anything to you?   (Na-amu)

I am going to look for termites to feed my chickens."   (Naamu)

Abdu Karimi said, "Ah, big brother, hold my bag.   (Naamu)

He reached out to take the hoe from the old woman.   (Naamu)

870 He said, "Give me your hoe;

I will dig termites for your chickens."   (Naamu)

She replied, "When I look for termites,

Are you the one who always feeds my chickens?   (Na-amu)

If you don't let go of my hoe,   (Naamu)

---

[51] The mortar is a large wooden receptacle in which women pound grain with a heavy wooden, club-shaped pestle that can be as long as five feet.

875 What you are looking for from me, you will get soon."   (Na-amu)
   (You heard it?)   (Naamu)
   They scuffled over the hoe until he took it from the old
       lady.   (Naamu)
   When he got the hoe from her he dug for termites,   (Naamu)
   Put them in a bag, and loaded them on his head.   (Naamu)
880 The older brother, Abdu Kassimu, had his baggage.   (Naamu)
   He said, "Let us go."   (Naamu)

   When they got some distance ahead of the woman,   (Naamu)
   Abdu Karimi said, "Big brother,   (Naamuuu)
   The thing that the female genie told us,   (Na-amu)
885 Let us be careful because she said this is the buffalo.   (Naamu)
   The way the old woman looks,   (Naamu)
   Let us watch her carefully.   (Naamu)
   Let us walk briskly.   (Na-amu)
   If we leave her behind,   (Naamu)
890 It will mean that the person we are looking for is still
       ahead of us.   (Naamu)
   If we do not leave her behind,   (Naamu)
   Then we can believe that this is the buffalo we were told
       about."   (Naamu)
   The two men walked very briskly.   (Naamu)
   The old woman was still behind them.   (Na-amu)
895 As they walked, *chu, chu, chu!*
   They would look back and see the old woman behind
       them.   (Naamu)
   The younger brother said, "Didn't I tell you she is the
       one?"   (Na-amu)
   (You heard it?)   (Naamu)

   When they reached the road to Dò ni Kiri,   (Naamu)
900 The road leading to her hamlet branched off to the
       right.   (Naamu)
   The road to Dò ni Kiri branched off to the left.   (Naamu)
   When they started to take the big road to Dò ni Kiri,   (Naamu)
   She said, "Where are you going with my termites?"   (Naamuuu)

33

Then they knew for sure. (Naamu)

905 She said, "Don't you know what happened,

Between me and the men of Dò ni Kiri? (Na-amu)

So why did you take my hoe from me? (Naamu)

If the termites belong to me, why are you taking that road? (Naamu)

Don't you see my road?" (Naamuuu)

910 They went on that road.

[In omitted passages, the narrator names various groups of genies that support the Buffalo Woman, describes the Kulubali regime when Dò ni Kiri became known as Bambarana, and explains how Maninka warriors distinguished between themselves and the enemy in early times.]

When they arrived there,

God caused Ma Sogolon's sister Dò Kamissa to soften

toward them. (Naamu)

They were now in Dò ni Kiri. (Na-amu)

Everybody who had come to kill the buffalo was dead, (Naamu)

915 Every hunter who came. (Naamu)

A bird that was near the swamp, (Naamu)

Would call, *tumè-tumè.* (Naamu)

That was the buffalo woman's spy. (Naamuuu)

Even up to tomorrow, it is still acting as her spy. (Na-amu)

920 Even if you go into the swamp in the middle of the night,

You will hear it saying, "Someone is here." (Naamu)

As soon as the bird called *tumè-tumè,*

The buffalo would go out and kill them. (Naamu)

(You heard it?) (Na-amu)

925 Many wild creatures were on her side. (Naamu)

She had a wild cat. (Naamu)

The wild cat and the tree squirrel, (Na-amu)

They were stealing the Condé's chickens. (Naamu)

(You heard it?) (Na-amuuu)

930 The leopard and the hyena, (Na-amu)

They were stealing the Condé's cattle. (Naamu)

They attacked all of our[52] livestock.	(Na-amu)
The quarrel had now reached a critical stage.	(Naaaam')
Dò Kamissa and the genies were also attacking the people of Dò ni Kiri.	(Naamuuu)
935 This buffalo had now made widows of many women.	(Naamu)
This buffalo had now caused many men to lose their wives.	(Naamu)
This buffalo had caused many family heads to lose their children.	(Na-amu)
This buffalo had killed all the sisters.	(Na-amu)
(You heard it?)	(Naaaam')

940 While that was happening, the Arab *kamalenw* arrived.	(Naamu)
After they greeted our ancestor Donsamogo Diarra,	(Naamu)
He asked them, "How did you get here?"	(Na-amu)
They said, "Thanks to God."	(Naamu)
"Ah!" He said, "Where did you come from?"	(Na-amu)
945 "We come from Morocco."	(Naamu)
Donsamogo Diarra asked them, "What is your family name?"	(Naamu)
The *kamalenw* replied, "We are Sharifu."	(Na-amu)
Donsamogo Diarra saluted them, "You Haidara."	(Naamu)
They replied, "Marahaba."	(Naamu)
950 Donsamogo Diarra said, "Why have you come here?	(Na-amu)
Have you not heard about the trouble here?"	(Naamu)
(You heard it?)	(Na-amu)
He said, "Have you not heard that my sister Dò Kamissa has killed my people?	(Naamu)
Should it be said that Sharifu wasted their blood in the land of the Condé?[53]	(Na-amu)
955 Huh! You Sharifu,	

[52] The narrator proudly thinks of his own people, the Condé of Fadama, as part of the ancient Condé/Diarra family of Dò ni Kiri, (cf. l. 941).

[53] As descendants of the prophet Muhammad (see n. 46), they are Muslim elite, so he wants them to stay out of danger and give his children Koranic lessons (l. 963–65).

I am not pleased with you coming here.   (Naaaam')

I am not pleased to see you here."   (Na-amu)

They said, "Allah!"   (Naamu)

Donsamogo Diarra said, "Very well,

960 If it is God who has sent you,   (Naamu)

Do not go into the bush.   (Naamu)

Stay in town and I will assemble my children.   (Naamu)

I will give them to you so you can teach them.   (Na-amuuu)

Do not go into the bush.   (Naamu)

965 I do not want this country cursed because a Sharif dies

    on my land.   (Na-amu)

Dò ni Kiri must not be cursed."   (Naamu)

The Arab *kamalenw* said, "Very well."   (Na-amu)

They were given lodgings in a house.   (Naamu)

The buffalo woman was somewhere else,   (Na-amu)

970 Praise be to God.   (Naamu)

After the *kamalenw* were settled in a house,   (Naamu)

After one day, two days, their hosts killed a chicken for

    them.   (Naamu)

When the chicken was killed for them,   (Na-amu)

They put the sauce on the rice.   (Naamu)

975 They took a thigh of the chicken,   (Naamu)

And the backbone,   (Naamu)

And put that in the saucepan.   (Naamu)

They went out the back door and took them to the bad

    old lady in the bush.   (Naamu)

She was the buffalo.   (Na-amu)

980 When they got there they said, "Ma,   (Naamu)

Did we not both tell you that you resemble our

    mother?"   (Na-amu)

They said, "For God's sake,

We cannot contradict ourselves;

You do resemble our mother.   (Naamu)

985 Heh, when we separated from you, we didn't want to.   (Naamu)

We came to town and your brother killed a chicken

    for us.   (Naamu)

When we are in Morocco and kill a chicken,	(Naamu)
What we give to our mother is the back.	(Naamu)
What goes to our father is the thigh.	(Naamuuu)
990 Our mother, our father,	(Naamu)
You are all.	(Na-amu)
What goes to our father,	(Naamu)
What goes to our mother,	(Naamu)
It is all yours."	(Naamuuu)
995 She reached out her hand and took that and the sauce,	(Naamu)
And then she threw it at them.	(Naamu)
She said, "For what reason did you bring the termites?	(Na-amu)
When you brought the termites, was it not for the chickens?	(Naamu)
When you left, did I tell you I had a craving for chicken meat?	(Na-amu)
1000 Sharifu, stop trying to get what you want from me.	(Naamu)
You are being stubborn.	(Na-amu)
What you are doing to me now,	(Naamu)
If it had not been for the relations between the Sharifu and the Condé,	(Naamu)
What I have done to the others, I would have done to you.	(Naamu)
1005 Won't you leave me alone?	(Na-amuuu)
I am talking to you."	(Naamuuu)
The *kamalenw* took the sauce and returned to town.	(Naamu)
One day, two days,	(Naamu)
Another chicken was killed for them.	(Naamu)
1010 They did the same thing as before and took the pieces to her.	(Naamu)
She took them and gave them to the dogs,	(Na-amu)
And repeated the same words that she said before.	(Naamu)
They went back to town.	(Na-amu)
One day, two days,	(Naamu)
1015 The Condé killed another chicken.	(Naamu)
The *kamalenw* repeated the deed.	(Naamu)
When they came and met her,	(Naamuuu)

She took the chicken pieces and put them on the shelf.	(Na-amu)
She spoke to them the words that were in her mouth.	(Naamu)
1020 (You heard it?)	(Na-amu)
She said, "I know you are strangers.	(Naaaam')
Have you not yet spoken with some local people?"	(Naamuuu)
"Ah!" They said, "Old woman,	
We have talked with some natives."	(Na-amu)
1025 She herself was reluctant to tell them that she had killed	
local people.	(Naamu)
But if they had talked to some local people,	(Na-amu)
They would have told them about the mayhem she had	
caused.	(Naamu)
But the *kamalenw* did not let her know this.	(Na-amu)
They just said, "Old woman,	
1030 We have spoken with some local people."	(Naamu)
"Ah!" She said, "Didn't they tell you anything?"	(Naamu)
"Ah! They told us that the old woman has gone away,	(Naamu)
That she is their sister.	(Naamu)
They did not tell us anything else."	(Na-amu)
1035 (You heard it?)	(Naamu)
"They said their sister who is out of town,	(Naamu)
That the person from whom they seek blessings,	(Naamu)
That she is the one.	(Naamuuu)
They did not tell us anything else.	(Na-amu)
1040 We come from Morocco,	
We don't know anything.	(Naamu)
We are looking for blessings from our mothers.	
Do whatever you want to us."	(Naamu)
They went on their way.	(Naaaam')
1045 (You heard it?)	(Naamu)
If they had said to her,	(Naamu)
"Your brothers say that you have caused them suffering,	(Naamu)
You have killed off their people,"	(Naamuuu)
She would have thought that they were reproaching	
her.	(Na-amu)
1050 They did not say that.	(Naamuuu)

That is why when you go to some people, (Naamu)

The place where you came from, (Naamu)

What was being done there, (Naamu)

Do not report it. (Naamuuu)

1055 If you report what is being discussed,

You will not be able to accomplish your mission. (Na-amu)

The next time a chicken was killed, (Naamu)

The Arab *kamalenw* took the road and went back. (Naamu)

When they met the old lady, they said, "Ma, didn't we

tell you? (Naamu)

1060 As long as you are here, (Na-amu)

Until we finish with our visit here and return home, (Naamu)

We will not eat our mother's share, (Naamu)

We will not eat our father's share. (Naamu)

There is nobody in this town who will eat your share. (Naamu)

1065 Therefore, to whom should we give these shares?" (Na-amu)

When she took it from them, they started to leave, (Naamu)

But she said, "Sharifu take your seats." (Na-amu)

They sat down. (Naamu)

DO KAMISSA'S REVELATIONS

Dò Kamissa the Buffalo Woman said, "You have outdone

me. (Na-amu)

1070 No one can get the better of people like you." (Naamu)

She said, "You are polite. (Na-amu)

You were brought up well. (Naamu)

Eh! Despite everything you were told, (Naamu)

You were not discouraged. (Na-amu)

1075 You favor me? (Naamu)

Now I will cooperate with you." (Naamu)

(You heard it?) (Na-amu)

She said, "Had it not been for that,

	We would have wiped out Dò ni Kiri.	(Naamu)
1080	My brother Donsamogo Diarra,	(Na-amu)
	I was the first born of my father's children.	(Naamu)
	After I was born, when I reached puberty,	(Naamu)
	I said, 'My Lord God,	(Naamu)
	If my father sires a son,	(Naamu)
1085	When anyone tells me that my father has sired a son,	(Naamu)
	The two gold earrings that are on my ears,	(Naamu)
	I will give the largest of them to the person who brings	
	me the news.	(Naamu)
	My Lord God, if my father sires a son,	(Naamu)
	The first person who brings the news to me,	(Naamu)
1090	Of the two wrappers I am wearing,	(Naamu)
	I will give the beautiful outer one to that person.'	(Na-amu)
	I was the first to offer a sacrifice for my brother.	(Naamu)
	Therefore, should he tell me that women do not	
	receive property?	(Naamuuu)
	Huh!	(Na-amu)
1095	I would have wiped out their lineage.	(Naamu)
	But you Sharifu,	(Naamu)
	You have outdone me.	(Naaaam')
	I will cooperate with you,	(Naamu)
	I will give you my life.	(Na-amu)
1100	For I know that if you kill me,	(Naamu)
	You will bury me.	(Na-amu)
	If you kill me,	(Naamu)
	My body will not go to God as a bad body."	(Naamuuu)
	(You heard it?)	(Naamu)
1105	She said, "Before I give myself up to you,	(Na-amu)
	I will tell you three things.	(Naamu)
	If you agree to those three things,	(Na-amu)
	Then I will cooperate with you.	(Naamu)
	If you do not agree to those three things,	(Naamu)
1110	I will keep after you until you do agree to those things."	(Na-amu)
	The kamalenw said, "Ma, tell us the three things."	(Naamu)
	She said, "The first of those things,	(Na-amuuu)

	When you kill the buffalo,	(Naamu)
	Do not go to town immediately.	(Na-amu)
1115	Come to this hamlet.	(Naamu)
	You will come and find me dead.	(Naamu)
	My brother must not see my corpse,	(Na-amu)
	Because I am the only one who knows what I have done.[54]	(Naaaam')
	Come to this hamlet where you will find me dead.	(Naamu)
1120	You will come and see that I have poured water on the fire.	(Naamu)
	There will be a hoe;	(Naamu)
	There will also be an axe.	(Naamu)
	Take the axe and cut down a *toro* tree.[55]	(Naamu)
	Take the hoe and dig the grave.	(Naamu)
1125	After you have laid me in it, fire the musket.	(Naamu)
	My brother must never see my body.	(Na-amu)
	They must not carry my body to Dò ni Kiri.	(Naaaamuu)
	He is my father's son.	(Na-amuuu)
	I have not been doing good to them.	(Naaaam')
1130	I have wiped out their children,	(Naamu)
	I have wiped out their wives.	(Naamu)
	There are many widows there today.	(Na-amu)
	I am responsible for that."	(Naamu)
	(You heard it?)	(Na-amu)
1135	"That is the first thing.	(Naamu)
	The second thing is that they had promised	(Na-amu)
	That anyone who kills me,	(Naamu)
	They said they will present three sets of girls from Dò ni Kiri,	(Naamu)
	And that the one chosen by that person will become his wife.	(Naamu)
1140	My second thing is,	(Na-amu)

---

[54] Contrary to what the narrator has indicated in l. 953.

[55] The sycamore, *Ficus capensis*.

When they bring out their fine young daughters,	(Naamu)
Do not accept any of them.	(Naamuuu)
Refuse all of them,	(Na-amuuu)
Because my father's lastborn is still in the house.	(Naamu)
1145 Five age sets[56] of girls have gone to their husbands,	(Naamu)
But she has not married.	(Naamu)
If you do not marry her,	
She will never be married.	(Naamuuu)
Anyone who marries her,	
1150 Something special will be at her breast.	(Naamu)
You must marry her, you the Sharifu.	(Naamu)
She is very ugly.	(Naamu)
Have you not heared that Sogolon is short?	(Naamuuu)
The 'Short Sogolon' that you have heard about,	(Na-amu)
1155 Have you not heard that Sogolon is ugly?	(Naamu)
The ugliness of Sogolon that you keep hearing about,	(Naamu)
She is very ugly.	(Naamuuu)
The duct in her eye is injured and the tears run down,	(Naamu)
And I am responsible for that.	(Naamu)
1160 Her head is bald.	(Na-amu)
She has a humped back.	(Naamu)
I, Dò Kamissa, did that.	(Na-amu)
Her feet are twisted.	(Naamu)
When she walks, she limps this way and that,	(Naamu)
1165 And I am the cause of that.	(Na-amu)
How was I the cause?	(Naamuuu)
If you see her damaged tear duct,	(Na-amu)
Her bald head,	(Naamu)
A hump on her back,	(Naamu)
1170 I put my far-seeing mask[57] on her face,	(Naamu)

---

[56] Children born within the same span of about three years are identified as a single group that grows up together, going through the various initiation rituals into adulthood.

[57] A magic object allowing the wearer to see unimaginable distances. The concept might have entered oral tradition when Europeans were observed using telescopes

	Because of my love for her,	(Na-amu)
	Before she was old enough to wear it.	(Naamu)
	That is what cut her tear duct.	(Na-amu)
	That is why her hair fell out.	(Naamu)
1175	That is what put a hump on her back.	(Naamu)
	I am responsible.	(Na-amu)
	If she does not get married,	(Naamu)
	It will be my curse."	(Naamuuu)
	(You heard it?)	(Na-amu)
1180	She said, "If you see that her feet are twisted,	(Na-amu)
	And she is knock-kneed,	(Naamu)
	I was the cause of that.	(Naamu)
	I set her on my sorcery horse	(Naamu)
	When she was too young.	(Naamu)
1185	That is what caused her tendons to be stretched,	(Na-amu)
	And her feet to be twisted.	(Naamu)
	If she does not get married,	(Naamu)
	It will be my curse."	(Na-amu)
	She said, "I was the cause of all that.	(Naamu)
1190	If my sister does not get married,	
	I take the blame for it.	(Na-amu)
	Therefore, when you Sharifu come,	(Naamu)
	And they bring those beautiful Condé women to you,	(Na-amu)
	Do not accept any of them.	(Naamu)
1195	Choose my father's last-born.	(Na-amu)
	The name of that last-born is Sogolon Wulen Condé.	(Naamu)
	Some call her Humpbacked Sogolon.	(Naamu)
	Some call her Ugly Sogolon.	(Naamu)
	Everybody used to call her whatever they felt like.	(Na-amu)
1200	But her real name is Sogolon Wulen Condé."	(Naamuuu)
	(That is who will be the mother of Ma'an Sunjata.)	(Na-amu)
	She said, "If you choose her,	

---

and binoculars, but there also could have been an indigenous mask imbued with
such power.

There will be something special at her breast,

Because it will have all the *dalilu*.[58] (Naamu)

1205 The beautiful daughters that they are talking about, (Na-amu)

If you take her and are not satisfied with the way she

looks, (Naamu)

When you kill the buffalo, cut off its tail. (Naamu)

It is laden with gold and silver, (Naamu)

Because for every woman of Dò ni Kiri that I killed, (Na-amu)

1210 If they had gold on their ears, (Naamu)

I would take out the gold earrings (Naamu)

And attach them to the hair of my tail. (Naamuuu)

For every woman of Dò ni Kiri that I killed, (Na-amu)

Those who had silver rings in their ears, (Naamu)

1215 I would take out the silver earrings,

And attach them to the hair of my tail. (Naamu)

I have a lot of tail hair and it is laden with gold, (Na-amuuu)

The ear jewelry of Dò ni Kiri women. (Naaaam')

Exchange some of that gold, (Naamu)

1220 So you can go and marry a beautiful woman somewhere

else. (Naamu)

You can add her to Sogolon Condé,

But do not refuse to take her. (Na-amu)

That will be no problem. (Naamu)

Will you accept that, or not?" (Naamu)

1225 The Sharifu said, "We agree to that." (Na-amu)

She said, "That is the second thing. (Naamu)

The third one! (Na-amu)

When you kill the buffalo, (Naamu)

The buffalo's carcass must not be taken to the town." (Na-amu)

1230 They said, "Eh, Condé woman! (Naamuuu)

We have agreed to the other ones, (Naamu)

But the one that you just said, (Na-amu)

[58] The mother's physical deformities signal her possession of special occult powers
that she will pass on to her child.

We may not be able to convince your people about that.	(Naamu)
We have no power to fight them off,	(Naamu)
1235 To take the carcass from them.	(Naamu)
What if they force us?	(Na-amu)
We might not be able to convince them."	(Naamuuu)
The Condé woman said, "Oh,	
You will do your best to heed what I have said.	(Na-amu)
1240 If you can do the other things,	(Naamu)
Leave that one.	(Naamuuu)
But the other two things,	(Naamu)
You must respect them."	(Na-amu)
They said, "Very well."	(Naamu)

1245 As they were about to leave,	(Na-amu)
She said to them, "Sit down."	(Naamu)
When they took their seats,	(Naamu)
She said, "I control my own life.	(Naamu)
The weapons you brought,	(Na-amu)
1250 They will not do anything to me.	(Naamu)
The arrows and quivers you brought,	(Naamu)
Those will not do anything.	(Naamu)
I am in control of my own life."	(Naamu)
She put her hand in her basket of cleaned cotton.	(Naamu)
1255 She pulled out the spindle and handed it to them.	(Naamu)
She put her hand in the storage basket,	(Naamu)
She took out the small distaff,	(Naamu)
She took out the small staff that usually holds the thread.	(Naamu)
She took it and gave it to them.	(Naamu)
1260 She said, "When you go and find the buffalo,	(Naamu)
Put this in your bow and shoot the buffalo with it.	(Naamu)
That will stop the buffalo.	(Na-amuuu)
If you do not shoot the buffalo with that,	(Naamu)
If you shoot at it with your big arrow,	(Naamu)
1265 The buffalo will kill you."	(Naamuuu)

[In an omitted passage, Dò Kamissa provides the brothers with various enchanted objects that will help them kill her buffalo wraith.]

DEATH OF THE BUFFALO

They left the town and went to the bush, past the lake of Dò ni Kiri.	(Na-amu)
When they passed by the lake, they entered the forest.	(Naamu)
They crossed an open space and passed through more forest.	(Naamu)
Before they had crossed the next open space, they saw the buffalo.	(Naamuu)
1270 Now if you hear people say the name Diabaté,	(Naamu)
If they say the name Tarawelé,	(Na-amu)
Saying those names all started in the bush that day.	(Naamu)
Before that, the brothers' name was Sharifu.	(Na-amuu)
When they came to our land of Manden, they left their Sharifu identity;[59]	(Na-amu)
1275 They came to be known as Tarawelé and Diabaté.	(Na-amu)
We will soon come to the reason for that.	(Naamu)
The buffalo was there.	(Naamu)
The younger brother said to the elder brother,	(Naamu)
Abdu Karimi told Abdu Kassimu,	(Na-amu)
1280 He said, "Big brother!	
You take the magic dart and shoot it at the buffalo,	(Na-amu)
Because the killing of this buffalo will make history.	(Naamu)
The person who kills this one,	(Naamu)

[59] Only after the buffalo is mortally wounded does Tassey begin to use the names by which the brothers are usually known, Danmansa Wulanni and Danmansa Wulanba (l. 1362). These probably originated as praise names based on the brothers' exploits, e.g., Danmansa Wulanba can be roughly translated as "Big Lord of the Solitary Forest Buffalo" (for further details, see Major Characters).

Up to the time when the trumpet is blown on
    Judgment Day, (Naamu)
1285 This will be told in all the histories of future
    generations." (Na-amu)
He said, "You kill the buffalo." (Naamu)
Abdu Kassimu said, "Little brother, (Na-amu)
When somebody knows something, let him do it." (Naamu)
He said, "I was the first to be born,
1290 But I know what *dalilu* you have, (Naamu)
And I know you must kill the buffalo." (Na-amuuu)
He handed the magic dart to his younger brother. (Naamu)
Abdu Karimi told his elder brother to go on ahead. (Na-amu)
He lay down in the grass and began to crawl. (Naamu)
1295 He went ever closer to the buffalo,
Remembering what the old woman had told him, (Naamu)
That he should not try to kill the buffalo until he
    was in its shadow. (Na-amu)
She had said, "Do not miss me! (Naamu)
If you miss the buffalo, I will kill you." (Naamu)
1300 (You heard it?) (Na-amu)

The younger brother crawled until he reached the
    buffalo's shadow. (Naamuu)
He took out the distaff and put it on the spindle. (Naamu)
He pulled it back and back, (Naamu)
He pulled it still harder, (Naamu)
1305 And he could feel that he had something very
    powerful in his hand. (Naamuuu)
(You heard it?) (Na-amu)
When he had pulled it until his hand was back to his
    shoulder, (Naamu)
He let it go, *paa!* (Naamu)
It went and pierced the buffalo here, it went into the
    chest. (Naamuuu)
1310 (You heard it?) (Na-amu)
When the thing pierced its chest, the buffalo
    was shaken. (Naamuu)

When the buffalo shook, it raised its head and saw him.	(Naamu)
It bellowed, *hrrr!*	(Naamu)
Even while he was still right beside the buffalo,	(Naamu)
1315 He told his elder brother, "Keep going!"	(Na-amuu)
The buffalo had been pierced and the struggle	
between them had begun.	(Naaaam')
A source of greatness will not be acquired without	
hardship.	(Na-amuu)
Before peace could return to Manden,	(Naamu)
The hardship that it experienced up to the time that	
Sunjata was born,	(Naamu)
1320 That is what we are narrating.	(Naamuuu)
If this had not taken place,	
Sunjata would not have been born.	(Na-amu)
If Sunjata had not been born,	
Manden would not have been sweet.	(Naamu)
1325 If Manden had not been sweet,	
The Mande people would not have known	
themselves.	(Na-amuu)
(You heard it?)	(Naamuu)
The buffalo began to chase the *kamalenw*.	(Naamu)
Before Abdu Karimi could catch up with his elder	
brother,	
1330 The buffalo came closer.	(Na-amu)
When the buffalo caught up to him and bellowed,	(Naamu)
He dropped the bamboo stick,	
Which instantly sprouted into a grove of bamboo.	(Naamu)
Before the buffalo could get through it,	
1335 The *kamalenw* had gone far ahead.	(Na-amu)
When the buffalo passed the first obstacle,	
It began chasing them again.	(Naamu)
When it caught up with them again and bellowed,	(Naamuu)
They dropped the hot charcoal.	(Naamu)
1340 In those days the Mande bush had been there a	
long time.	(Naamu)
It had never been burned, so the bush caught on fire.	(Naamu)

When the buffalo tried to get through,

It was stopped by the fire. (Naamu)

It was forced to go back while they were dashing through

    the grass. (Naamu)

1345 (You heard it?) (Na-amu)

When the fire subsided,

The buffalo jumped into the ashes and chased them

    again. (Naamuu)

When it got close to them again,

They were already at the lake of Dò ni Kiri. (Na-amu)

1350 By the time it arrived at the lake and began to bellow, (Mmmm)

Abdu Karimi dropped the egg, which turned the ground

    into deep mud. (Naamu)

(You heard it?) (Na-amu)

The buffalo got stuck in the mud. (Naamu)

That is what is referred to in the Condé song,

1355 "Dala Kombo Kamba": (Naamu)

"Condé drinker of big lake water, (Naamu)

Those who drank the big lake water, (Naamu)

They did not stop to clean it. (Naamu)

Those who clean the big lake, (Naamu)

1360 They did not drink its big water." (Naamuuu)

(You heard it?) (Na-amu)

It was Danmansa Wulanba and Danmansa Wulanni[60] (Naamu)

Who cleaned the water of the big lake. (Naamu)

By the time they finished with that, (Na-amu)

1365 Water had penetrated the spindel wounds into the

    buffalo's intestines. (Naamu)

When the buffalo got to that place, it fell down. (Na-amu)

When the buffalo fell, Danmansa Wulanni said to his

    elder brother, (Naamu)

He said, "Big brother, look behind you! (Naamu)

The buffalo has fallen." (Naamuuu)

[60] The elder brother is Wulanba, the younger Wulanni.

49

1370 (You heard it?) (Na-amu)

When the brother looked back and saw that the buffalo
    had fallen, (Naamuuu)
A family lineage was created then. (Na-amu)
When the elder brother went back,
He put his foot on the buffalo's body. (Na-amu)
1375 He said "Ah, little brother! (Naamu)
You have given me a name. (Na-amu)
Ah, little brother! (Naamuuu)
You were sired by Abdu Mutulu Budulaye, (Naamu)
Abdu Mutulu Babatali. (Naamuuu)
1380 Aba Alibi's own son is Sedina Alia. (Naamu)
It was you who were sired by Alia. (Naamu)
It was to him that God gave a sword. (Na-amu)
Sedina Alia's son is Hassana Lonsani. (Naamu)
You were sired by him. (Naamuuu)
1385 Hassana Lonsani's son is Sissi. (Naamu)
Sissi's son is Kèmo. (Naamu)
Kèmo's son is Kèmomo Tènè. (Naamu)
Kèmo Tènè's son is Sharifu. (Naamu)
You were sired by Sharifu. (Naamu)
1390 Aah, Karimi! (Naamu)
You have given us names." (Na-amu)
After he praised his younger brother, (Naamu)
The younger brother said to him, "Eh, big brother! (Naamu)
If you were to be a praise-singer, (Naamu)
1395 No one could surpass you. (Naamu)
If you were to be a *jeli*, (Naamu)
No one could surpass you (*i jèmba tè*)." (Naamu)
That was the beginning of the *jeli* family known as
    Diabaté.[61] (Na-amu)
That became his lineage. (Naamuuu)

---

[61] With the previous line, a popular etymology (see n. 40). The singing or chanting of praises is one of the occupational specialties of *jeliw*.

1400	If you hear Diabaté in Manden,	(Naamu)
	It was first said when the buffalo was killed in the bush.	(Naamu)
	That is in the Mande language.	(Na-amu)
	(You heard it?)	(Naamu)

	After they finished killing the buffalo,	(Naamu)
1405	They saw that the tail was laden with gold and silver.	(Na-amu)
	That was when they first started cutting off the tails of	
	dead game.	(Naamu)
	When you hear that a young hunter kills an animal and	
	cuts off its tail,	(Naamu)
	This was the beginning of that custom.	(Na-amu)
	Cutting off the buffalo's tail accomplished two things	
	for them.	(Naamuu)
1410	It was laden with gold and silver in its tail hairs.	(Naamu)
	The second thing was that anybody who would deny	
	that they killed it,	(Naamu)
	Since it was a buffalo,	
	They knew that the tail could not be cut from a live	
	one.	(Naamu)
	As soon as they showed the tail,	
1415	People would know that the business was finished.	(Naamu)
	Ahuh!	
	Because they knew that Dò Kamissa's buffalo wraith,	(Naamu)
	Could only have its tail cut off if it had been finished.	(Na-amu)
	That proved to Dò ni Kiri that the *kamalenw* had really	
	killed the buffalo.	(Naamuu)

[In an omitted passage, Danmansa Wulanba nad Danmansa Wulanni try to respect Dò Kamissa's wish that her wraith be buried in the bush, but the townspeople insist on retrieving the buffalo carcass and dragging it into town to be desecrated.]

SOGOLON WULEN CONDE OF DO NI KIRI

1420	After finishing with the buffalo, they started beating	
	the ceremonial drum.	(Naamu)
	The twelve towns of Dò,	(Naamu)
	The four towns of Kiri,	(Naamu)
	The six towns across the river,	(Naamuu)
	All of the people were expected to attend.	(Na-amu)
1425	They all came.	(Naamu)
	When the twenty-two towns were all present, they said,	
	"What did we say?	(Naamuu)
	We said any hunter who kills this one,	(Naamu)
	We will bring out three age sets of girls,	(Naamu)
1430	And any girl he chooses from among them will become	
	his wife."	(Naamu)
	They said, "Bring your daughters forward."	(Naamuu)
	Huh!	
	If you bring out three age sets of daughters from	
	twenty-two towns,	(Na-amu)
	Bring the older set first,	(Naamu)
1435	Then the next one to those,	(Naamu)
	Then the youngest set.	(Naamuu)
	They brought out the beautiful Condé girls, who	
	formed three circles.	(Naamuu)
	They told the boys to choose.	(Na-amu)
	They said, "Even if you choose ten, they are your	
	wives.	(Naamu)
1440	Even if you choose twenty, they are your wives.	(Naamu)
	Even if you choose only one, that is your wife.	(Naamu)
	You have delivered us from disaster.	(Na-amu)
	It is the wish of everyone to have their daughter	
	married to these two."	(Naamu)

	When the girls were brought out,	(Na-amu)
1445	They said to them, "You the Sharifu,	(Naamu)
	We do not go back on our promise.	(Naamu)
	Take a look at these people.	
	Anyone that pleases you, take her.	(Naamu)
	The two men followed one another.	(Naamu)
1450	They went around the circle,	(Naamu)
	They went around the circle,	(Naamu)
	They went around the circle.	(Naamu)
	They came back to where they had started and said,	
	"Where are the rest of the girls?"	(Naamuu)
1455	(You heard it?)	(Na-amu)
	The Condé ancestor said, "You young men search every house,	(Naamuu)
	So that no one can hide his daughter."	(Naamu)
	They searched through the town and no one was found.	(Naamu)
	Everybody was wishing for them to marry their daughter.	(Naamuu)
1460	(You heard it?)	(Naamu)
	When the searchers returned they said, "There is nobody left."	(Naamuu)
	A bystander said, "What about the bad old woman who was just killed?	(Naamu)
	She has her father's last-born still in the house."	(Naamu)
	Somebody said, "Eeh, man!	(Naamu)
1465	Heeeye, can we show that one to the strangers?"	(Na-amu)
	(You heard it?)	(Naamu)
	Danmansa Wulanni said, "The exact one you are talking about,	(Naamu)
	Go and get her.	(Na-amu)
	Has she been married to another man?"	
1470	They said, "No."	(Naamu)
	"Has she been married before?"	
	They said, "No."	(Naamu)
	The brothers said, "If she is unmarried, go and get her."	(Naamu)

The people said, "Five age sets of girls have found
    husbands,

1475 But she has remained unmarried."   (Naamu)

They said, "Go and get her if she is an unmarried girl."   (Naamu)

Ma Dò Kamissa had told them that when they went to
    choose her,   (Naamu)

The door of her father's house was the one facing the
    town's meeting ground.   (Naamuu)

She had told them, "When she is coming from my
    father's house   (Naamu)

1480 To go into the town meeting ground,   (Naamu)

A little black cat will come from behind her and pass in
    front of her;   (Naamu)

The little black cat will go from in front of her and pass
    behind her.   (Naamu)

If you see that happening to anyone,

That is the girl I am talking about."   (Naamu)

1485 (You heard it?)   (Na-amu)

When she was sent for,

As she was being brought out of the house,   (Naamu)

When she got to the edge of the town meeting ground, (Naamu)

A black cat came from behind her and passed in front
    of her;   (Naamu)

1490 It went from in front of her and passed behind her. (Naamu)

As soon as the brothers saw her, they said,

"This is the one we have been talking about."   (Naamu)

They heard people go, "Wooo!"

They were asked, "Is this the one you were talking
    about?"   (Naamu)

1495 The brothers said, "Yes, this is the one we have been
    talking about."   (Na-amu)

(You heard it?)

She is the one who was taken and given to them,   (Naamu)

The mother of Simbon.   (Na-amu)

The birth of Simbon and the organizing of Manden, (Naamu)

1500 The person about whom it was foretold   (Naamu)

	Is the one who is about to be born.	(Naamu)
	We speak of Turama'an,	(Naamu)
	We speak of Kankejan,	(Naamu)
	We speak of Tombonon Sitafa Diawara,	(Naamuu)
1505	We speak of Fakoli,	(Naamu)
	We speak of Sumaworo,	(Na-amu)
	We speak of Tabon Wana Faran Kamara;	(Naamu)
	But the one who organized them all,	(Naamu)
	United them into one and called the place Manden,	(Naamu)
1510	The person who did it was Sunjata.	(Naamu)
	This is how his mother was married.	
	When she was given to them,	(Naamu)
	The younger brother, Danmansa Wulanni, said, "This is my brother's wife.	
	Give her to him."	(Naamu)

	When night fell and they went to bed,	(Naamu)
1515	As men normally approach their brides,	(Naamu)
	When the elder brother, Danmansa Wulanba, got close to her,	(Naamu)
	She ejected two porcupine quills from her chest and they stuck in him.	(Naamu)
	He jumped up and fell on the ground.	(Naamuu)
1520	He spent the rest of the night sleeping on the opposite side of the room,	(Naamuu)
	Because of her sorcery.	(Na-amu)
	Ancestor Donsamogo Diarra had said to them,	(Naamu)
	He said, "You the Sharifu,	(Naamu)
	Is this the one you want?"	(Naamu)
1525	They replied, "This is the one we want."	(Naamu)
	"Are you sure this is the one you want?"	(Naamu)
	They said, "This is the one we want."	(Naamu)
	He said, "My sister whom you killed,	(Naamu)
	All the *dalilu* that she had,	(Naamu)
1530	This one's is even more powerful.	(Naamuu)
	But if you say that you want her, I am giving her to you.	(Naamu)
	Take her with you.	(Na-amu)

If you are not compatible, (Naamu)

Bring her back so I can put her where you took her
from, (Naamu)

1535 And I will give you another one. (Naamuu)

She has powerful *dalilu*. (Na-amuu)

I don't want to contradict myself, but take a look at
this group of girls. (Naamu)

These people will wait for you up to three months. (Naamuu)

If you are not compatible with my sister, (Naamu)

1540 Come back and I will give you one of these. (Naamu)

I will put her back where she came from." (Naamuu)

They said, "Very well." (Na-amu)

She did not accept Danmansa Wulanba's advances. (Naamu)

In the morning when Danmansa Wulanni came
to him, (Naamu)

1545 He said, "Little brother, (Naamu)

Was I not the one who told you yesterday that you
should kill the buffalo?" (Naamu)

He said, "Uh huuh." (Naamu)

"Did I not say that you are more knowledgeable than I? (Naamu)

Ahuh, you should marry this woman yourself. (Na-amu)

1550 You should accept that. (Naamu)

The God who made it possible for you to kill the
buffalo (Naamu)

Has made me unable to take this woman. (Na-amu)

When we leave from here, we will exchange this gold
and silver, (Naamu)

We will marry another woman who I will keep. (Naamu)

1555 Do not say anything to the Condé, (Na-amu)

So they cannot say '*wooo*' to us the way they did
yesterday. (Naamu)

Therefore, you take her without letting anybody here
know about it." (Naamu)

When night fell,

Danmansa Wulanba was in a hurry for them to finish
eating supper. (Naamu)

1560	He took his blanket and went out to spend the night	
	with his friends.	(Naamu)
	By then Danmansa Wulanni and Sogolon Condé were	
	in the house.	(Na-amu)
	When they went to bed,	
	That was the one she really did something to,	(Naamu)
	Something she did not do to the elder brother.	(Na-amu)
1565	Danmansa Wulanba had spent the night on the other	
	side of the room,	(Naamu)
	But Danmansa Wulanni slept outside.	(Na-amu)
	The next morning,	
	As soon as he saw Danmansa Wulanba coming,	
	he said, "*Pah!*"	(Naamu)
	He said, "Big brother!	(Naamu)
1570	I am not going to tell you anything.	(Naamu)
	Let us beg to take our leave.	(Naamu)
	There is no way that we can explain this.	(Na-amu)
	We rejected all those beautiful Condé women.	(Naamu)
	Eh! The old woman has really caused problems for us.	(Naamu)
1575	Eh! That old woman!	(Na-amu)
	She killed the men of Manden, but she sent us straight	
	into decay.	(Naamuu)
	If we don't get another wife here,	(Na-amu)
	They will say we are too proud, that we look too	
	high.	(Naamu)
	We were given a group of women to choose from.	
1580	We declined them, but the one we took,	(Naamu)
	We cannot keep her.	(Naamu)
	Let us beg to take our leave.	(Na-amu)
	We should not say that we don't want her.	(Naamuu)
	When we have gone,	(Naamu)
1585	When we see a river in flood,	(Naamu)
	When we get to it, we will leave her there.	(Na-amu)
	We will cross the river and go on.	(Naamu)
	If she waits there long enough,	
	She will go back because she will not be able to cross."	(Naamu)

1590 When the boys arrived at the river, the water was in flood.	(Naamuu)
(You heard it?)	(Na-amu)
Danmansa Wulanni said, "Sister-in-law,"	(Naamu)
He said, "Wait here for us.	(Na-amu)
You can see the water yourself.	(Naamuu)
1595 We want to go upstream.	(Na-amu)
If we see any tree that has fallen across the river,	(Naamu)
We will come to get you so we can cross together."	(Naamu)
She said, "All right."	(Na-amu)
She waited for them there with her baggage.	(Naamu)
1600 Everything was in her bundle.	(Naamuu)
When they went upstream, they went farther and farther,	(Naamu)
They went until they saw a *sèbè* tree[62] that had fallen across the river.	(Naamuu)
Aah, the Sharifu now had their way.	(Na-amu)
They went across on it.	(Naamu)
1605 As they were crossing the river, they said,	
"Eh heh, we have done the right thing.	(Na-amu)
Don't you see, she has attached herself to us.	(Naamu)
She has slowed us down.	(Na-amu)
Who would want to take her along?	(Naamu)
1610 Hey! Look at my chest."	(Naamuu)
The elder brother said, "You don't even know what you're talking about.	(Na-amu)
I won't even show you mine.	(Naamu)
Sorceress!	(Na-amu)
Who would want to take a sorceress and bring her to his father's house?"	(Naamu)
1615 (You heard it?)	(Naamu)
While they were chatting, they arrived at Konfara.	(Naamu)
At the outskirts of Konfara,	(Na-amu)

---

[62] French *rônier, Borassus aethiopum.*

They met the Condé woman sitting and waiting
    ahead of them.   (Naamuu)
She said to them, "You the Sharifu,   (Naamu)
1620 Is this how you behave?"   (Naamu)
They said, "Ah, Ma, please forgive."   (Na-amu)

A NEW SORCERESS WIFE FOR THE MANSA OF KONFARA

When they arrived in the town,   (Naamu)
They went straight to Simbon's house.   (Naamu)
They had arrived in Konfara.   (Naamu)
1625 It was in Konfara that Sunjata was born.   (Naamu)
We should tell you that.   (Na-amu)
At the place of Maghan Konfara in Konfara. (Naamu)
When they arrived there in Konfara,
Danmansa Wulanba began to speak.   (Naamu)
1630 He said, "Nuru Soma,[63]   (Naamu)
Jidan Soma,   (Naamu)
Kalabali Soma,   (Naamu)
The first sorcerer of Manden,   (Naamu)
And the last sorcerer of Manden,   (Naamu)
1635 You, Latali Kalabi,   (Naamu)
Kalabi the younger,   (Naamu)
And Kalabi the elder,   (Naamu)
And Mamadi Kani,   (Naamu)
And Kani Simbon,   (Naamu)
1640 And Kani Nyogo Simbon,   (Naamu)
And Kabala Simbon,   (Naamu)

---

[63] Danmansa Wulanba, now functioning as a *jeli*, begins to praise the *mansa* of Konfara, thus affirming his own identity as ancestor of the Diabaté lineage of bards.

	And Big Simbon Madi Tanyagati,	(Naamu)
	And M'balinene,	(Naamu)
	And Bele,	(Naamu)
1645	And Belebakon,	(Naamu)
	And Farako Manko Farakonken.	(Naamu)
	I swear to God, you are a real king of diviners.	(Na-amuu)
	What you told us is what happened to us.	(Naamu)
	We went to Dò ni Kiri,	(Naamu)
1650	We killed the buffalo,	(Naamu)
	The people of Dò ni Kiri honored us,	(Naamuu)
	And the woman they gave us,	(Na-amu)
	Because of the way you foresaw things,	(Naamu)
	And because of your forthrightness,	(Naamu)
1655	And because of the way you help travelers,	(Naamu)
	We did not accept any other woman.	(Naamu)
	That is the one we have brought to you."	(Naamu)

	Simbon laughed.	(Naamu)
	"Aheh, where is the woman in question?"	(Naamu)
1660	They said, "She is outside."	(Na-amu)
	Simbon got up, took his elephant-tail fly whisk, and looked around.	(Naamu)
	He went and saw the sorceress sitting beside her bundle.	(Naamu)
	When he saw her beside it,	(Na-amu)
	When he looked at her, he said, "Heeee,	
1665	Sharifulu, oh father!	(Naamu)
	Take this one back.	(Naamu)
	I am not refusing her, I still want her.	(Naamu)
	But take her out of the town and let me prepare myself.	(Naamu)
	If you bring her to my house right now,	
1670	She will take my house from me.	(Na-amu)
	But you brought me a gift that I want to keep."	(Naamu)
	(You heard it?)	(Na-amu)
	"Go back outside the town."	(Naamu)
	They took her out of the town and waited there.	(Naamuu)

1675 Manjan Bereté,	(Naamu)
Who became the first *karamogo* in Manden,	(Naamu)
The one who worked to find the wife who would be	
the mother of Sunjata,	(Naamu)
Maghan Konfara gave him the ten kola.[64]	(Naamu)
He said, "Go and greet the Sharifu.	(Naamu)
1680 Tell them to come in."	(Naamu)
He said, "This is their town."	(Naamu)
(You heard it?)	(Na-amu)

It was Manjan Bereté who went,	
Who took the ten marriage kola of Sogolon Condé,	(Naamu)
1685 And used them to welcome the Sharifu.	(Naamuu)
If you see the Maninka carrying kola nut like that,	
It is to welcome those who are bringing a bride.	(Naamu)
That was the first marriage kola of Manden.	(Na-amu)
Today, that is a custom we pass on to the next	
generation.	(Na-amu)
1690 The kola was given to Manjan Bereté.	(Naamu)
Maghan Konfara said, "I have gotten a wife."	(Naaaam')
He said, "The Sharifu have brought me a wife.	(Naamu)
The prayer that you, Manjan Bereté, made to God,	(Na-amu)
Your request has been granted.	(Naamu)
1695 They have brought the woman,	(Naamu)
But they are still outside the town.	(Naamu)
Go and meet them,	(Naamu)
Greet them, and welcome them into the town.	(Naamu)
Tell them this is their home."	(Naamuu)
1700 Manjan Bereté was happy to see the strangers.	(Na-amu)
He said, "Karimi,	(Naamu)
Danmansa Wulanni,	(Naamu)
I give it to you,	(Naamuu)
I give it to your brother.	(Na-amu)

[64] Large, segmented, yellow or red nuts containing a mild stimulant like caffeine, which are ritually sacrificed or presented upon, among other occasions, the arrival of a bride.

1705	For the deed that you accomplished,	(Naamu)
	From Dò ni Kiri up to Manden,	(Na-amu)
	Simbon says that you are welcome,	(Naamu)
	That you have freed us from the suffering.	(Na-amu)
	When your brother is suffering,	(Naamu)
1710	As long as he has not been delivered from that suffering,	(Naamu)
	You will also share part of the suffering.	(Na-amu)
	The disaster that faced the Condé at the hands of the sister's buffalo wraith,	(Naamu)
	You have gone and succeeded in killing that buffalo,	(Naamu)
	And then returned to Manden with this beautiful woman.	(Naamu)
1715	Simbon says he is very pleased.	(Naamu)
	He says you are welcome.	(Naamu)
	Heh! This is the kola to welcome you.	(Na-amu)
	He says you should enter the town now.	(Naamu)
	He says the town is yours.	(Na-amu)
1720	He says the honor is God's and it is yours.	(Naamu)
	But he has put me in charge of you strangers."	(Naamu)
	When they had been thus honored,	(Naamu)
	He accompanied the strangers to town.	(Naamu)
	When the co-wives were told, "You have your wife,"[65]	(Naamu)
1725	They took their places behind the bride.	(Naamu)
	They said, "Sister-in-law, get up and let us go home."	(Na-amu)
	When they lifted her up, she had a twisted foot.	(Na-amu)
	Her feet were twisted and she could not walk without raising dust.	(Na-amu)
	When they lifted her up then,	(Naamu)
1730	The dust went this way,	(Na-amu)
	The dust went that way.	(Naamu)

[65] The bride is thought of as the collective possession of the family and the village into which she marries.

	The first song for welcoming brides in Manden was	
	sung then.	(Naamu)
	How did they sing this first bride-escorting song?	(Na-amu)
	The sisters said:	
1735	"Walk well,	(Naamu)
	Bride of my brother,	(Na-amu)
	Walk well.	(Naamu)
	Do not put us in the dust."	(Na-amuu)
	That became the first bride-escorting song of Manden.	(Naamu)
1740	(You heard it?)	(Na-amu)
	They saw that her walk could not improve,	(Naamu)
	That it was beyond her power.	(Naamu)
	The sisters said, "Let us carry her."	(Na-amu)
	That is how carrying the bride originated.	(Naamu)
1745	If you see that when the bride arrives at the outskirts	
	of the town,	(Naamu)
	The women pick up the bride and run with her,	(Naamu)
	That was done because of the condition of Sogolon	
	Condé's feet.	(Na-amu)
	The sisters said, "Let us carry her."	(Naamu)
	At that time men were not considered to be the	
	closest relatives.	(Na-amu)
1750	It was women who were the closest relatives.	(Naamu)
	As the women were carrying her, they saw other	
	women on the road.	(Naamu)
	If those women had not shouted encouragement,	(Naamu)
	They would not have arrived at their destination.	(Naamu)
	They were carrying a mature woman.	(Naamu)
1755	Five age sets had found husbands, but she had not been	
	married.	(Naamu)
	She was a mature woman.	(Na-amu)
	The sisters then said, "Are you not seeing the horse?"	(Naamu)
	When they said, "Are you not seeing the horse?"	
	The co-wives looked back and said, "Which horse is	
	that?"	(Naamu)
1760	They said, "That is the horse of Manden."	(Na-amu)

Before the co-wives could turn around,
They were already running past them saying,
   "Horse of Manden." (Naamu)
While they were running,
Ma Sogolon Condé's headscarf fell off, (Naamu)
1765 And her bald head was exposed. (Naamu)
The co-wives made a new song. (Na-amu)
What did they say in this song of the co-wives? (Na-amu)
They had not known that her head was bald. (Naamu)
What did they sing? (Naamu)
1770 They sang:
"The heron-head oooh. (Naamu)
Our heron-head has come this year,
Heron-head. (Naamu)
The woman's heron-head has come this year with
   her crest." (Naamu)
1775 This offended Sogolon Condé. (Na-amu)
She looked back at the women of Manden (Naamu)
And said, "Are you calling me a heron-head? (Naamu)
Huh! (Na-amu)
Am I the one you are calling heron-head? (Naamu)
1780 Well, I have arrived." (Na-amu)

Feeling angry, she was carried to her husband's door. (Naamu)
The husband had been sitting in his lounge chair at the
   back of his room. (Na-amu)
He had prepared himself with his own *dabali*.[66] (Naamu)
He had taken out his sorcerer's whip and laid it at
   his side, (Naamu)
1785 Because he knew that what was coming to him would
   show him her *dalilu*. (Na-amu)
If you see that when a Mande bride arrives at the door, (Naamu)
The sisters will put their heads inside and then pull
   them back out, (Naamu)

---

[66] A scheme or plan (pl. *dabaliw*). As a verb, secret power sometimes associated with evil (see Glossary).

Put their heads inside and pull them back out,	(Naamu)
The third time, they send the bride in to her husband.	(Na-amu)
1790 That's how it all started.	(Naamu)
The first time they held the back of Sogolon's head,	
To push her inside to her husband,	(Naamu)
She ejected a sorcerer's dart from her eye,	
And tried to pierce her husband's eye.	(Na-amu)
1795 It went *srrrrrr*!	(Naamuu)
(You heard it?)	(Naamu)
Maghan Konfara caught it.	(Naamu)
He said, "Condé woman, you have brought me a present.	(Na-amu)
This is my seventh year	(Naamu)
1800 That I have had the meat of Mande sorcery in my teeth.	(Naamu)
An ordinary piece of straw will not be able to pick it from my teeth,	(Naamu)
Only a sorcerer's dart will do that.	(Naamu)
You have brought me a dart for a toothpick."	(Naamu)
He caught it and laid it beside him.	(Naamu)
1805 He took his sorcerer's whip and lashed her on the head.	(Naamu)
She pulled back for the first time,	(Naamu)
And when she put her head in again,	(Naamuu)
She shot out her scalding breast milk,	(Naamu)
Trying to splash it on Simbon to blister his skin,	(Naamu)
1810 To let him know that a real woman was coming.	(Naamu)
Simbon repelled it.	
He said, "Condé woman, you have really brought me a gift.	(Naamu)
Ordinary Mande water does not clean our faces as well as warm breast milk.	(Na-amu)
You have brought me face-washing water."	(Naamu)
1815 He washed his face with that and again picked up his sorcerer's whip.	(Naamu)
He lashed her on the head, *cho*!	(Naamu)

	She pulled back her head a second time.	(Naamuu)
	The third time when the women tried to push her in,	(Naamu)
	If you see old men of Manden carrying a staff,	
1820	One with a small metal point on the end,	(Naamu)
	It was Sogolon Condé who brought it from Dò ni Kiri.	
	It belongs to the Condé.	(Naamu)
	It was this staff that Sogolon Condé now took out,	(Naamu)
	Trying to spear Simbon in the chest,	(Naamuu)
1825	Because she could see that she was up against a	
	real man.	(Naamu)
	She had sent two things and both were repelled.	(Naamu)
	But if this one went, it would pierce his chest.	(Naamuu)
	When this was thrown, Simbon caught it.	(Naamu)
	He merely praised it.	(Naamu)
1830	He said, "We walk with the *sunsun*[67] stick with	
	nothing on it,	(Naamu)
	But the Condé have sent us a *sunsun* stick wearing	
	a hat."[68]	(Naamu)
	That is the staff in question.	(Na-amu)
	It was not an ordinary spear.	(Naamu)
	It was your new bride's spear.	(Naamu)
1835	(You heard it?)	(Na-amu)
	Simbon said, "We have received a protective spear."	(Naamu)
	He laid it beside him and picked up his sorcerer's	
	whip,	(Naamu)
	And lashed her, *cho!*	(Naamu)
	Sogolon had used up her sorcery.	(Naamu)
1840	They pushed her in to him.	(Naamuu)
	When she was pushed inside to him,	(Na-amu)
	She reached for her bundle and took out her drinking	
	ladle.	(Naamu)

---

[67] *Diospyros mespiliformis*, an extremely hard wood called "false ebony" or "West African ebony."

[68] A metaphorical reference to the staff's metal tip.

	The ten kola nuts that are given to the women,	(Na-amu)
	It was Sogolon Condé who first put them into water.	(Naamu)
1845	It is the woman who is supposed to put the kola in water,	
	And then hand it to her husband,	(Naamuu)
	But many people were asking to do it.	(Na-amu)
	She was told to put them in the water	(Naamu)
	Instead of handing them to her husband.	(Naamu)
1850	Sogolon Condé put them in her cup.	(Naamu)
	She went and knelt in front of Maghan Konfara.	(Naamu)
	(You heard it?)	(Na-amu)
	She said, "You, Latali Kalabi,	
	Kalabi Doman and Kalabi Bomba,	
1855	God and Mamadi Kani.	(Naamuu)
	God and Kani Simbon,	
	God and Kani Nyogo Simbon,	
	God and Kabala Simbon.	(Naamuu)
	God and Big Simbon Madi Tanyagati.	(Naamu)
1860	God and M'balinene,	
	God and Bele and Belebakon,	
	God and Farako Manko Farakonken.	(Naamu)
	If you were not among the husbands of the world,	(Naamu)
	I would have gone to the other world unmarried.	(Naamu)
1865	I have now come to my husband.	(Na-amu)
	He is my married husband,	
	My husband who will take care of me,	
	My husband by whom I will give birth.	(Naamu)
	I have gotten my husband.	(Na-amu)
1870	It is the crocodile of the stream that leads one to the crocodile of the river.	(Nam-naamu)
	I have come to Simbon.	(Naamu)
	Drink."	(Naamuu)
	Simbon drank.	(Naamu)
	He accepted the ten kola nuts and set them down.	(Naamu)
1875	Alone, she went and sat on her husband's bed.	(Naamuu)
	If they had not finished with the sorcery,	(Naamu)

	That is why when a new bride is brought,	(Naamu)
	If you see her sitting in a chair,	(Naamu)
	If she does not sit on her husband's bed, she has something on her mind.	(Naamuu)
1880	She does not want to marry this man;	
	She has another man's name to confess.	(Naamu)
	(You heard it?)	(Na-amu)
	It is good for a new bride to want to be with her husband.	(Naamu)
	When she sat on the bed she said,	
1885	"The women called me heron-head.	(Naamu)
	I have not forgotten that."	(Naamu)
	The women of Manden had wanted to have fun.	(Naamu)
	Ah, *gba*!	(Naamu)
	Big sister,	(Na-amu)
1890	Jelimuso Tunku Manyan Diawara,	(Naamu)
	Jonmusoni Manyan,	(Na-amu)
	Tassisi Gbandimina,	(Naamu)
	Maramajan Tarawelé,	(Naamu)
	Mama Damba Magasuba.	(Naamu)
1895	[They said] "Who could be jealous of such a person?	(Na-amu)
	It is better to compete with one's equal.	(Naamu)
	She is bald-headed,	(Naamu)
	She has a humped back,	(Naamu)
	She has a weeping tear duct,	(Naamu)
1900	Her feet are twisted.	(Naamuuu)
	Why should we be jealous of this woman?	(Na-amu)
	Let us welcome her to begin with.	(Naamu)
	Let us tell the men of Manden	(Naamu)
	That each of us will have a day to cook for the strangers."	(Naamu)
1905	If you see that the Mande bride-welcoming ceremony lasts for eight days,	(Naamu)
	It is because of that.	(Na-amu)
	Each of those women chose her day to cook, killing a chicken.	(Naamu)
	On the eighth day, the men of the town said, "Eh!	(Naamu)

	Why should we just sit here watching our women get	
	all the recognition?	(Na-amu)
1910	We men must seize this day for ourselves.	(Naamu)
	If the women have killed chickens, we will kill a goat."	(Naamu)
	That is how the goat-slaughtering began.	(Na-amu)
	That is what they refer to as the day of killing the	
	stranger's goat.	(Naamu)

	When the bridal drum was played in the town circle,	
1915	The celebration was at its peak.	(Na-amu)
	The celebration with the bridal drum surpassed the	
	one of circumcision.	(Naamu)
	(You heard it?)	(Naamu)
	When they came to the town circle, all the women	
	were there in force.	(Na-amu)
	Sogolon Condé said to her husband, "Simbon,	(Naamu)
1920	If you agree,	
	I would like to go and see the people,	(Naamu)
	As they dance for the bride in the town circle."	(Na-amuu)
	She said, "I would like to go and see the people,	
	While they dance in the circle for the bride."	(Na-amu)
1925	Maghan Konfara said, "Eh!"	(Naamu)
	He said, "Condé woman,	(Naamu)
	That might be what they do in Dò ni Kiri,	
	The home of the Condé,	(Mmm)
	But here in Manden,	
1930	Women do not see the bride's dance circle."	(Na-amu)
	She said, "Un un, I will not go in person.	(Na-amu)
	If you agree,	(Naamu)
	I will stay here behind you and see them in the circle."	(Naamu)
	That is how sorcery was used.	(Na-amu)
1935	(You heard it?)	(Naamu)
	If you should be told	(Naamu)
	That Sunjata's mother was pregnant for seven years,	(Naamu)
	That she did not deliver for seven years,	(Naamu)
	That when he was finally born he did not walk,	(Naamu)
1940	It was all the result of that one night.	(Naamuuu)

	She said, "I will stay behind you,	(Na-amu)
	But I will go and see them."	(Naamu)
	Simbon said, "Ah, if you will not go there in person,	(Naamu)
	You and I are finished with what we were doing.	(Naamu)
1945	There is no sorcery you can show me,	
	That will be worse than that with which you started.	(Na-amu)
	If you keep your body here but can still see them,	
	I will not say 'no.'"	(Naamu)
	She said, "Very well."	(Naamu)
1950	(You heard it?)	(Na-amu)
	She put her left hand on her husband.	(Naamu)
	She was lying behind him on the bed.	(Naaaam')
	She stretched her right arm,	(Na-amu)
	She stretched her right hand,	(Naamu)
1955	It passed through the straw of the roof.	(Naamu)
	She stretched her arm,	(Naamu)
	She stretched her hand to reach the dance circle,	(Naamu)
	She laid her hand up in the *dubalen* tree.[69]	(Naamu)
	She pointed two fingers down;	(Naamu)
1960	Light was coming out of them.	(Na-amu)
	The circle was suddenly full of light, *wa*!	(Naamuu)
	And she was still lying behind her husband.	(Naamu)
	From behind her husband she said, "Heeeh,	
	Mande people know how to do it.	(Naamu)
1965	Heeeh," she said.	
	"Jonmusoni Manyan really knows how to dance!	(Naamu)
	Heeeh, Tunku Manyan Diawara has a good voice!	(Na-amu)
	Heeh, Tassisi Gbandimina knows how to dance!	(Naamu)
	Heeh, Maramajan Tarawelé is dancing!	(Naam . . .)
1970	Heeh, Flaba Naabi, heeya, she knows!"	(Naamuu)
	While they were dancing,	(Na-amu)
	Jonmusoni Manyan raised her head.	(Naamu)

---

[69] *Ficus thonningii*, called the "palaver tree," because village meetings, dances, and other social occasions are conducted in its shade.

	She saw that the inner circle was all lit up,	(Na-amu)
	But there were no torches.	(Naamu)
1975	When she saw it was lit up,	(Naamu)
	She looked up and saw the two fingers hanging down.	(Naamu)
	They were shedding light like a pressure lamp.	(Na-amu)
	She said, "Big sister Sansun Bereté,	(Na-amu)
	Big sister Maramajan Tarawelé,	(Naamu)
1980	Lift up your eyes.	(Naamu)
	This is the one about whom we said	(Na-amu)
	That we would not need to be jealous of her.	(Naamu)
	This is a sprouting tree,[70]	
	And when it grows to extend its branches,	
1985	It will take Manden away from us.	(Na-amu)
	Hee! The new bride is lying behind her husband,	(Naamu)
	But she is watching us with her two fingers, look!	(Naamu)
	Do you see the two fingers with eyes?	(Na-amuu)
	Mande women, if you are real women,	(Naamu)
1990	You had better get ready.	(Naamu)
	This one must not be successful here."	(Na-amu)
	(You heard it?)	(Naaaam')
	They suddenly stopped the wedding dance.	(Naamuu)
	All the women felt chilled.	(Na-amu)
1995	They all went home.	(Naamuu)
	They all dipped their hands into their *dalilu*.	(Na-amu)
	When Sogolon came to Maghan Konfara, she was still a virgin.	(Naamuu)
	After three days her bloody virgin cloth was taken out.	(Naamu)
	The following month, she became pregnant with Sunjata.	(Na-amu)
2000	That is how Sunjata was conceived.	(Naamu)
	(You heard it?)	(Na-amu)
	The co-wives said, "We will not be able to do anything against this woman."	(Naamuu)

---

[70] A metaphorical allusion to Sogolon.

She had gone to her husband almost at the end of the
    lunar month. (Naamu)

For the rest of that month, she did not see the other
    moon. (Naamu)

2005   She had conceived. (Naamu)

When the women of Manden heard this, (Na-amu)

They went outside the town and held a meeting under
    a baobab tree.[71] (Naamu)

They said, "Getting pregant is one thing, delivering
    is another." (Na-amu)

They said, "Make miscarriage medicine, (Naamu)

2010   Anything that will spoil the belly once it touches it. (Na . . .)

Everyone must prepare her own." (Naamu)

Sogolon Condé also had very powerful *dalilu*. (Na-amu)

When the belly wanted to expand, (Naamu)

They would come and say, "Younger sister," (Naamu)

2015   They would say, "This is the medicine for pregnant
    women here in Manden. (Naamu)

Aah, we wanted to get a child, (Naamu)

With all of us women here, (Naamu)

But we have not had any children. (Naamu)

Therefore, if one person should bring luck to our
    husband, (Naamu)

2020   Heh, you are the one bearing it, but it is a child for
    all of us. (Naamu)

Heh, M'ma, dilute this medicine in water and drink it." (Naamu)

Heh, the Condé woman would dilute that medicine in
    water and drink it. (Na-amu)

She would drink it. (Naamu)

After drinking it, the belly would shrink. (Naamu)

2025   It would shrink away, *jè*! (Na-amu)

(You heard it?) (Naamu)

This went on for seven years. (Na-amu)

---

[71] Maninka *sira* or *sida*: *Adansonia digitata*. The leaves are used as a condiment for cooked sauces.

When the seventh year arrived,	(Naamu)
Sogolon Condé left the town.	(Naamu)
2030 She prayed to God.	(Na-amu)
She said, "M'mari!	(Naamu)
That is enough!	(Naamuu)
The Mande people have done enough.	(Na-amu)
But I have come to you, God.	(Naamu)
2035 I am only a stranger here.	(Naaaam')
Those who brought me,	(Na-amu)
This is beyond their power to help."	(Naamu)

After the brothers had given Sogolon to Maghan Konfara,	(Naamu)
He took two of his daughters.	(Naamu)
2040 His daughter known as Nana Triban,	(Naamu)
The one who had the same mother as Dankaran Tuman,	(Naamu)
He took that Nana Triban,	(Naamu)
And Tenenbajan, daughter of his younger brother.	(Naamu)
He put the two together,	(Naamu)
2045 And gave them to Danmansa Wulanni and Danmansa Wulanba.	(Naamuu)
(You heard it?)	(Na-amu)
Nana Triban,	(Naamu)
It was she who gave birth to Turama'an.	(Na-amu)
Tenenbajan,	(Naamu)
2050 It was she who gave birth to Kankejan.	(Naamu)
(You heard it?)	(Na-amu)
Danmansa Wulanni and Danmansa Wulanba's children,	(Naamu)
Turama'an and Kankejan.	(Na-amu)
(You heard it?)	(Naamu)
2055 Those are their children.	(Na-amu)
Turama'an and Kankejan's fathers,	(Naamu)
Danmansa Wulanni and Danmansa Wulanba,	(Naamu)
It was they who killed the buffalo.	(Na-amu)

[In an omitted passage, the narrator describes his own family's relationship with characters in the narrative, and with ancestors from Arab tradition.]

THE CHILDHOOD OF MA'AN SUNJATA

That Ma'an Sunjata,	(Naamu)
2060 God made him into a person,	(Naamu)
Made him into a human fetus and he was born.	(Naamu)
After this son was born,	(Naamu)
When the Mande women were told about it,	(Naamu)
They gathered together again under the Mande baobab tree.	(Naamu)
2065 They said, "It is one thing to give birth to a son,	(Naamu)
And another thing for him to survive."	(Naamuu)
What did they do again?	(Naamu)
Through sorcery they stretched the tendons of his two feet.	(Naamu)
They confined him to the ground.	(Na-amu)
2070 (You heard it?)	(Naamu)
His lameness forced him to remain on the ground.	(Na-amu)
One year!	(Naamu)
Two years!	(Na-amu)
Three years!	(Naamu)
2075 Four years!	(Naamu)
Five years!	(Naamu)
Six years!	(Naamu)
The seventh year!	(Naamu)
The co-wives provoked Sogolon to anger.	(Naamuu)
2080 One day—	(Na-amu)
(Because we are walking on a straight path,	(Naamu)
We cannot wander from one side to the other,	(Naamu)
We have to take the main road,	(Naamuu)

74

So we will know how Manden was built,	(Naamu)
2085 You heard it?)	(Na-amu)
In the seventh year there came a day	(Na-amu)
When Maramajan Tarawelé went and picked some	
baobab leaves	(Naamu)
From the same baobab tree that was already	
mentioned.	(Na-amu)
While on her way back, Ma Sogolon Wulen Condé	
said,	(Naamu)
2090 She said, "Big sister Maramajan Tarawelé,	(Na-amu)
Won't you give me a few of your baobab leaves?"	(Naamu)
The house in which Ma'an Sunjata was lodged,	(Na-amu)
This was said under its eaves.	(Naamu)
Maramajan Tarawelé said, "Ah!"	(Na-amu)
2095 She said, "Younger sister,	(Naamu)
You who are the owner of sons,	(Naamu)
If you ask us for baobab leaves, what are we supposed	
to do?	(Na-amu)
Your lame son is sitting right there inside the house.	(Naamu)
You are alone in your search for baobab leaves.	
2100 Why don't you tell your son to get up and walk?"	(Na-amu)
Ma'an Sogolon Wulen Condé said, "Ah, that is not	
what I meant.	(Naamu)
I thought I could depend on sisterhood.	(Naamu)
But I did not know you were upset because I	
had this child."	(Naamuu)
They didn't know Sunjata was listening to them.	(Na-amu)
2105 After that was said,	(Naamu)
When Ma Sogolon Condé was passing by,	(Naamu)
Sunjata said, "Mother!	(Naamuu)
Mother!"	(Na-amu)
She did not answer because she knew he had overheard	
them.	(Na-amu)
2110 He said, "Mother, what are they saying?"	(Naamu)
She said, "Ah, forget about that talk."	(Naamu)
He said, "Ah, how can I ignore that?"	

He said, "Mother, I will walk today."   (Na-amu)
(You heard it?)   (Na-amu)

2115 He said, "What they are talking about,   (Naamu)
That you have a lame person in the house,   (Na-amu)
That you should beg them for a baobab leaf,"   (Naamu)
He said, "I will walk today."   (Na-amu)
He said, "Go and get my father's *sunsun* staff,   (Naamu)
2120 And bring it to me."   (Naamuu)
He said, "I will walk today."   (Na-amu)
Ma Sogolon Condé went and got the *sunsun* staff.   (Na-amu)
She brought it to Simbon.   (Na-amu)
When the *sunsun* staff was thrust firmly into the
    ground,   (Naamu)
2125 When he attempted to stand holding the staff,   (Na-amu)
The *sunsun* staff broke.   (Naamuu)
He said to her, "Ah, mother.   (Naamu)
Go and bring my father's iron staff."   (Naamu)
He said, "They say you have a lame son in the house,   (Na-amu)
2130 But you gave birth to a real son.   (Naaaam')
Nothing happens before its time.   (Naamu)
Go and bring my father's iron staff."   (Na-amu)
She went for the iron staff, but he also broke that.   (Naamu)
He said, "Go and tell my father's blacksmith,   (Naamu)
2135 Let him forge an iron staff so I can walk."   (Na-amu)
(You heard it?)   (Naaaam')
The blacksmith carried one load of iron to the
    bellows,   (Naamu)
Forged it and made it into an iron staff.   (Naamu)
When it was thrust into the ground,   (Naamu)
2140 When he attempted to stand, the staff bent.   (Naamuu)
Where is that iron staff today?   (Na-amu)
It is in Narena,   (Naaaam')
The staff of Sunjata.   (Na-amu)
He broke both of his father's staffs.   (Naamu)
2145 The one that was forged for him is in Narena.   (Naamu)
The one that was bent became a bow.   (Na-amu)

Therefore, when he stood,	(Naamu)
He lifted one foot,	(Na-amu)
Then he lifted the other foot,	(Naamu)
2150 Then the other foot.	(Naamu)
(You heard it?)	(Na-amu)
Then his mother said, "Simbon has walked."	(Na-amu)
The *jeliw* sang this in a song:	(Naamu)
"Has walked,	(Naamu)
2155 Jata has walked.	(Naamu)
Has walked,	(Naamu)
Jata has walked."	(Naamu)
It was rivalry that caused Jata to walk,	(Naamu)
Because of the humiliation to his mother.	(Naamu)
2160 That is why, when I hear people saying they do not	
love their mother,	(Na-amu)
They dismiss their mothers, *oof*!	(Naamuu)
Heh! Jelimori![72]	(Na-amu)
The father is everybody's, the mother is personal.	(Naamu)
When you stand in the crowd,	(Na-amu)
2165 People do not talk about your father,	(Naamu)
It is your mother they will talk about.	(Na-amu)
After that, God gave him feet.	(Naamu)
He went into the house and took his bow.	(Naamu)
Some people say he made the iron staff into his bow,	(Naamu)
2170 But don't repeat that.[73]	(Naamu)
His father's quiver and bow were there.	(Na-amu)
He took the quiver and bow and went out of the	
town.	(Na-amu)
When he got there, he embraced a baobab tree.	(Naamu)
He shook it,	(Naamu)
2175 He shook it,	(Naamu)
He uprooted it,	(Naamu)
And then he put it on his shoulder.	(Naamuu)

[72] During performances, *jeliw* occasionally speak to people in the audience, commenting on something in the narrative (cf. l. 2356, 4169).

[73] The bard himself does not believe that part of the legend.

He brought it into his mother's yard. (Na-amu)

He said, "Now everyone will come here for baobab

    leaves." (Naamu)

2180 (Aah, Sogolon Condé! (Naamu)

When things are hard for you, (Naamu)

Everyone will abuse you. (Naamu)

When things are good for you, (Naamu)

People will say, "We knew this would happen for you." (Na-amu)

2185 May God help us to persevere.) (Aminaaa)

Then when the Mande women came, they said, (Naamu)

"Aah, Sogolon Condé! (Na-amu)

We knew this would happen for you. (Naamuu)

The sacrifice that was made by everybody, (Naamu)

2190 It has been answered through you." (Na-amu)

That was what they said as they picked the baobab

    leaves. (Naamu)

Before the time that So'olon Ma'an[74] could walk, (Naamuu)

His younger brother So'olon Jamori had been born. (Naamuu)

While So'olon Ma'an was still on the ground (Naamu)

2195 Manden Bori was born. (Naamu)

After So'olon Ma'an walked, (Naamu)

So'olon Kolonkan was born. (Naamu)

Sogolon stopped after four births. (Na-amu)

STEP-BROTHER RIVALRY AND NINE SORCERESSES OF MANDEN

[In omitted passages, Sunjata and his brothers assure their half-brother Dankaran Tuman that as long as he lives, his right to their father's legacy will be uncontested. The narrator describes the non-Mande origins

---

[74] Sogolon's Maghan (*maghan* = "king," "lord"), one of several praise-names by which the *jeliw* refer to Sunjata (cf. l. 2408).

*of Sumaworo's father, how he acquired his wives, including Sumaworo's
mother, and how Sumaworo became a hunting apprentice to Sunjata's
father. The four provinces of Soso are introduced, and the boundary be-
tween them and Manden is described. Dankaran Tuman quarrels with
his mother, Sansun Bereté, and they conspire to have Sunjata murdered
by a coven of nine sorceresses, but one of them comes to warn him.]*

	His ally among the nine sorceresses	(Naamu)
2200	Was Jelimusoni Tunku Manyan Diawara.	(Naamu)
	In the middle of the night, she went and told Simbon.	(Naamu)
	She said, "Sunjata, we will kill you the day after	
	tomorrow,	(Naamu)
	If God agrees.	(Na-amu)
	You had better do something.	(Naamu)
2205	The cows from your father's legacy that you declined	
	from your brother,	(Na-amu)
	The big bull that is among them,	(Naamu)
	Dankaran Tuman has called big sister Tasissi	
	Gbandimina,	(Naamu)
	Called Jonmusoni Manyan,	(Na-amu)
	Called me, Jelimusoni Tunku Manyan Diawara,	(Naamu)
2210	Called Nyuma Danba Magasuba,	(Na-amu)
	Called Maramajan Tarawelé,	(Naamu)
	That we should kill you.	(Na-amu)
	If we kill you, he will give us that bull.	(Na-amu)
	Between sorcery and the craving for meat,	(Naamu)
2215	We have agreed to it.	(Na-amu)
	Watch out for yourself.	(Naamu)
	If you don't do something about it,	(Naamu)
	If you don't speak to them about this	(Naamu)
	And make them an attractive offer,	(Naamu)
2220	The day after tomorrow,	(Naamu)
	Hunting in the bush is very important to you,	(Naamu)
	But if you go out we will kill you.	(Naamu)
	You are no match for us."	(Na-amu)
	Sunjata took her hand and said, "You have told me	
	the truth."	(Naamuu)

2225	He said, "Very well, go and tell them	(Naamu)
	That I, the son of a Condé woman,	(Na-amu)
	They must spare me.	(Na-amuu)
	You should tell them that one bull	(Naamu)
	Is not bigger than three male antelope.	(Naamuu)
2230	Tell them that if they spare me,	(Naamu)
	And if God is willing,	(Naamu)
	I will give them three male antelope for the one bull.	(Naamu)
	Tell them to spare me;	
	They should not do what my brother	
	asks."	(Naamu, you are right!)
2235	When she went and told them,	(Na-amu)
	The sorceresses said, "All we want is meat.	(Naamuu)
	Tell him if he does what he has said,	(Naamu)
	He will have no problem."	(Naamuu)
	That night and the next day passed.	(Na-amu)
2240	When the following night had passed,	(Naamu)
	When the *sigbé* bird[75] chirped at dawn,	(Naamu)
	Simbon took his hammock,	(Naamu)
	Put on his crocodile-mouth hat,[76]	(Naamu)
	Hung his hunter's whistle on his chest,	(Na-amu)
2245	Took his quiver and bow,	(Naamu)
	And left the town.	(Naamu)
	When he got one kilometer away from the town,	(Naamu)
	He saw an antelope.	(Naamuu)
	He shot at it and knocked it down.	(Naamu)
2250	He shot another arrow,	(Naamu)
	Hit another antelope and knocked it down.	(Naamuu)
	Again he shot an arrow,	(Naamu)
	The sun did not get white before he had killed	
	all three.	(Naamuu)
	God is with the just.	(Na-amu)

[75] The Fanti rough-winged sparrow, *Psalidoprocne obscursa*.

[76] Maninka *bamada*: a distinctive, cone-shaped hat with flaps at the front and back.

2255 Everybody does what he wants,	(Naamu)
But God makes the final decision.	(Naamuu)
The chick destined to be a rooster will eventually	
crow,	(Naamu)
No matter what is laid in its path.	(Na-amu)
It will overcome.	(Naamu)
2260 After he killed them,	(Na-amu)
He carried the three antelope to the edge of town.	(Na-amu)
Then he went into the town.	(Naamu)
He told Jelimusoni Tunku Manyan Diawara	(Naamu)
That she should go and tell the nine sorceresses	(Naamu)
2265 That their meat was at the edge of town.	(Naaaam')
When they were told this, they set out.	(Naamu)
They went and found the game.	(Naamu)
They butchered them;	(Naamu)
They roasted some of it,	(Naamu)
2270 They boiled some of it,	(Naamu)
They fried some of it,	(Naamu)
And made some of it into meatballs.	(Naamuu)
What did they say then?	(Na-amu)
They said, "Ma'an Sunjata,"	(Naamu)
2275 They said, "Even a female genie will not harm you,	
Much less a human female."	(Na-amuu)
What saved him?	(Naamu)
His hands.	(Na-amu)
When you are popular, you must have an open hand.	(Naamu)
2280 It is a man's generosity that will save him.	(Na-amu)
Nothing saved Sunjata but his hands.	(Naamu)
They blessed him.	(Na-amu)
They said, "We are with you to the death.	(Naamu)
Even a female ant will never sting you.	(Na-amu)
2285 No female genie will ever even chase you.	(Naamu)
No female wild animal will ever harm you,	(Na-amu)
If God agrees,	(Naaaam')
Or we are not producers of kitchen smoke."	(Na-amu)
They spared him.	(Naamu)

MISTAKEN MURDER AND THE QUESTION OF EXILE

[In an omitted passage, Dankaran Tuman and his mother conspire to have Sunjata murdered in his sleep. Meanwhile, Sunjata spends a rainy day playing the hunter's harp while he waits for the weather to change so he can go hunting.]

2290	Because of the rain, Sunjata was impatient to go to	
	the bush.	(Naamu)
	The hunter's harp,	(Na-am)
	The six-stringed harp,	(Naamu)
	He knew how to play it himself.	(Naamu)
	His younger brother Manden Bori was also a player,	(Naamu)
2295	His younger brother So'olon Jamori was also a player.	(Naamu)
	So'olon Ma'an took a hunter's harp;	(Naamu)
	He sat in his hammock,	
	And started singing to himself.	(Na-amu)
	After playing "Kulanjan"[77] for a while,	(Naamu)
2300	He would change and play "Sori."[78]	(Naamu)
	So'olon Ma'an's voice was sweet.	(Naamu)
	As he sang in a low voice, some passing youths	
	heard it.	(Naamu)
	They could not continue on their way,	(Naamu)
	They stood by the door.	(Naamu)
2305	One of them was also an apprentice hunter.	(Naamu)
	He said, "Until the rain stops, I will listen to Sunjata."	(Naamuu)
	As he stood at the door, Sunjata took snuff.	(Naamu)
	He had put some in his mouth.	(Naamu)

[77] One of the oldest melodies in the bards' repertory, often dedicated to hunters. Sumaworo is praised as "Kulanjan" (l. 2899).

[78] A lesser-known melody dedicated to hunters.

When the snuff was wet,	(Naamu)
2310 He stopped playing the harp so he could spit.	(Na-amu)
As he went to spit, he saw the young man by the	
door.	(Naamuu)
He said, "Who is it?"	(Na-amu)
The youth said, "Brother So'olon Ma'an, it is me."	(Naamu)
"Ah," said Sunjata, "What are you doing here?"	(Naamu)
2315 He said, "Your brother sent a message	(Naamu)
That we should bring him some food supplies.	(Naamu)
That's what I did, but it is raining.	(Naamu)
A slave with wet clothes does not enter the house	
of a noble.	(Naamuu)
I am an apprentice hunter at the farm.	(Naamu)
2320 I heard your music, so I am standing here under	
the eaves.	(Naamu)
Let me keep listening to you until the rain stops."	(Na-amuu)
(The musket of conspiracy was being loaded in town.	(Naamu)
You heard it?)	(Na-amu)
So'olon Ma'an said to him, "Come into the house."	(Naamu)
2325 The young man entered the house and sat on the	
edge of the bed.	(Naamu)
Simbon was playing the harp.	(Naamu)
When he played certain parts, the young man would	
tap his feet,	(Naamu)
Because the harp music was so sweet.	(Na-amu)
But he was tired.	(Naamu)
2330 The warm room felt good to him.	(Naamu)
He became sleepy and started to nod.	(Naamu)
Ma'an Sunjata told him, "Lie on the bed."	(Naamu)
When he lay on the bed,	(Na-amu)
Simbon stood up and brought down his blanket and	
covered the young man.	(Naamu)
2335 The young man slept.	(Na-amu)
The young man was still asleep when the rain	
stopped.	(Naamu)
When the rain stopped,	(Naamu)

	Sunjata forgot about the young man there.	(Na-amu)
	Simbon stood up,	(Naamu)
2340	Took his hunter's hammock,	(Naamu)
	Took his quiver and bow,	
	Took his fly whisk,[79]	(Naamu)
	Put on his crocodile-mouth hat.	(Naamuu)
	He shut the front door and went out the back door.	(Naamu)
2345	He took a deep breath and went into the bush.	(Naamu)

	While the young man was still sleeping,	(Na-amuu)
	The musket[80] of conspiracy was loaded in the town.	(Naamu)
	While Simbon was in the bush,	(Naamu)
	Dankaran Tuman came and stood under the eaves and listened.	(Na-amu)
2350	He heard the young man snoring.	(Naamu)
	They did not know that Ma'an Sunjata had left the house.	(Naamuu)
	Dankaran Tuman went and told the seven young men,	(Naamu)
	"Didn't I tell you?	(Na-amu)
	That any time it rains into the evening he sleeps?"	(Naamu)
2355	He said, "Go and get your clubs, he is asleep."	(Naamu)

[79] Ideally made from the tail of a dangerous wild animal and possibly symbolizing the one cut from the slain Buffalo of Dò (l. 1406), although elephant tails were highly prized for this essential hunters' device carrying occult protective qualities.

[80] Maninka *morifa*. The first firearms did not arrive in West Africa until the 16th century, but the *jeliw* frequently speak of muskets in the time of Sunjata. Linear chronology is not a pressing issue in their views of the distant past, but what is of interest is the imagery of a formidable weapon and a hero's power to repel any iron projectile. There may be some bards who actually think firearms existed in Sunjata's day, but most clearly do not. Like many other *jeliw* seeking dramatic effect, Tassey Condé regularly refers to muskets being used (l. 2949, 3602, 4897), but in a later passage not included here, he stresses that "they did not have the *morifa*," specifying that Sunjata and everybody else in his day fought with bow, spear, and sword, according to set rules. Another bard, Demba Kouyaté, remarks that "at that time there were no guns," and that to be able to kill from such a distance is not "real manhood" (Conrad 1999b: 184).

Ah, Nanamoudou!	(Na-amu)
Manden has really suffered.	(Naamu)
(You heard it?)	(Naamu)
Those men got their clubs.	(Naamu)
2360 The seven young men came to the door,	(Naamu)
But they were afraid of Simbon.	(Na-amu)
They said, "Man, don't you know who So'olon Ma'an is?	(Naamu)
One man cannot outdo him,	(Naamu)
Two men cannot outdo him,	(Naamu)
2365 Even the seven of us cannot outdo him."	(Naamuu)
They said, "When we go in,	(Naamu)
Let us listen carefully.	(Naamu)
The place where we hear the sound of his breathing,	(Naamu)
Let us raise the clubs and hit him on the head.	(Naamu)
2370 If we only hit him on the back, he will capture us."	(Na-amu)
They went in and surrounded the young man.	(Naamu)
At the place where they could hear him breathing,	(Naamu)
They raised the clubs and hit him on the head.	(Naamu)
They beat him until he cooled off.	(Naamuu)
2375 When he was cooled off,	(Na-amu)
They went out and told Dankaran Tuman	(Naamu)
That the work he had given them was finished.	(Naamu)
Dankaran Tuman told his mother,	(Naamu)
"Ahah," he said, "Mother.	(Naamu)
2380 The bad thing is now off our necks."	(Na-amu)
(No matter how good one is,	(Naamu)
You always do something bad to your enemy.)	(Naaaam')
He said, "He is dead."	(Na-amu)
"Eh! Dankaran Tuman," she said,	(Naamu)
2385 "Has he died?"	(Naamu)
"Ah!" He said, "The son of the Condé woman has died today!"	(Na-amu)
"Ah, my son!	(Naamu)
I will not be the failure in my husband's home.	(Naamu)
Now my heart is cool.	(Na-amu)

2390 If you have killed Ma'an Sunjata, *aagba*! (Naamu)

Manden Bori cannot stand up to you, (Naamu)

So'olon Jamori cannot stand up to you. (Naamu)

The only one I was worried about is the one who has

been killed." (Na-amuu)

Ma Sansun Bereté did not go back to bed. (Naamu)

2395 Dankaran Tuman did not go back to bed. (Naamu)

Sansun Bereté said, "Heee, (Na-amu)

Just wait until Sogolon Condé knows this." (Naamu)

They spent the night like that. (Na-amu)

When day broke, (Naamu)

2400 As soon as they washed, they went to spy on Sunjata's

mother. (Naamuu)

"Huh!" They whispered, "Don't say anything! (Naamu)

Leave it like that! (Naamu)

When he stays a long time without waking up, (Naamu)

His mother will go and open the door on him." (Na-amuu)

2405 Sansun Bereté said, "You should not say anything, (Naamu)

So it does not appear that you did it." (Naamu)

While they were there, as the soft morning sun was

rising, (Naamu)

They saw Danama Yirindi[81] coming. (Naamuu)

He was carrying three dead animals. (Naamu)

2410 They saw the son of the Condé woman coming with

three dead animals. (Naamuu)

One was hanging over his left shoulder, (Na-amu)

One was hanging over his right shoulder, (Naamu)

One was on his head. (Naamu)

When he got there, (Na-amu)

2415 Sansun Bereté said, "Dankaran Tuman! (Na-amu)

Didn't you say that Sunjata was dead?" (Naamu)

He said, "Mother, we really killed him." (Naamuu)

[81] A praise-name for Sunjata that can be translated as "super hero" (cf. the usage
danama yirindi, l. 4074).

She said, "Then who is this coming?"	(Na-amuu)
She said, "Who is coming?"	(Naamu)
2420 He said, "It is Sunjata who is coming."	(Na-amu)
When they saw that it really was Sunjata,	
Dankaran Tuman peed in his pants.	(Naamuu)
When Sunjata got there,	(Na-amu)
He said to Sansun Bereté, "Big mother,	
2425 Here is some wild game for you."	(Naamu)
He laid another animal before his step-brother and said,	
"Big brother,	
Here is one for you."	(Naamu)
There was no way for them to respond.	(Naamuu)
He carried the last animal to his mother's place.	(Na-amu)
2430 He said, "Mother, here is your animal."	(Naamu)
His mother said, "Ah, my son, thank you."	(Naamuu)
He returned to his own house.	(Na-amu)
When he reached the door and pushed it open,	(Naamu)
Flies were all over the body, *wooooo!*	(Naaaam')
2435 Sunjata shouted, "Mother, Mother!"	(Naamu)
He said, "Come here!"	(Naamuu)
He said, "I will kill today.	(Na-amu)
From the time that I, Sunjata, was born,	(Naamuu)
I have never done anything bad.	(Na-amu)
2440 This is the act of my brother.	(Naaaam', it's true)
I will take revenge."	(Naamu)
(You heard that?)	(Na-amu)
Ma Sogolon Condé came and opened the door.	(Naamu)
Sunjata said, "The one you see lying here,	(Naamu)
2445 I went to the bush and forgot about him.	(Naamu)
My brother's men beat him to death with their clubs."	(Naamuu)
He said, "You see this?	(Na-amu)
I will kill for this young man.	(Naamu)
I know this is Dankaran Tuman's boy,	(Naamu)
2450 But he died my death.	(Naamu)
I will prove to them that I am not the one who died."	(Na-amu)

Ma Sogolon Condé knew that when So'olon Ma'an
    spoke of revenge, (Naamu)
Konfara would be destroyed, (Naamuu)
Because anyone known as a supporter of Dankaran
    Tuman would be killed. (Na-amu)
2455 Sunjata dashed out of the house. (Naamu)
When he reached for his iron staff, (Naamu)
His mother ran and called Jelimusoni Tunku Manyan
    Diawara. (Naamu)
She said, "If you don't go right now,
Your man will kill someone immediately. (Na-amuu)
2460 Jelimusoni Tunku Manyan Diawara went and took hold
    of Simbon. (Naamu)
She said, "Simbon, (Na-amu)
Won't you think about your mother? (Naamu)
Simbon! (Naamu)
Won't you think of me? (Na-amu)
2465 Won't you leave this to God? (Naamu, it's true, naamu)
Don't you realize that the finger has poked
    out its own eye?" (Na-amu)
He tried to break away, but she would not let go. (Naamu)
He struggled to get away, but she would not let go. (Naamu)
Ha! She was able to hold him. (Naamuu)
2470 That was what led to them going into exile. (Naamuu)
Then Ma Sogolon Condé said, (Naamu)
"My son Sunjata, you have no problem except for your
    popularity. (Na-amu)
If they have started murdering people over you, (Naamu)
Should we not go away?" (Na-amu)
2475 (One never sells his father's homeland, (Naamu)
But it can be pawned.) (Na-amu)

DEPARTURE FOR EXILE

*[In an omitted passage, Sunjata repeats his refusal to flee from his step-
brother, but Sogolon argues that neither he nor Dankaran Tuman can
understand the special circumstances of her background in Dò ni Kiri
and how she was brought to their father because of Sunjata's special
destiny. She convinces Sunjata that even if they go away, he will even-
tually take over the leadership of Manden.]*

	Ma Sogolon Condé then set out,	(Na-amu)
	And went to the Somono[82] ancestor, Sansamba	
	Sagado,	(Naamu)
	The Sansamba Sagado you have always heard about	
	in the history of Manden.	(Naamu)
2480	The chief of the Somono was from Manden.	(Naamu)
	Sogolon went secretly to Sansamba Sagado.	(Naamuu)
	She said, "Sansamba Sagado."	(Na-amu)
	She removed her silver bracelet	(Naamu)
	And handed it to the Somono ancestor Sansamba	
	Sagado	(Naamu)
2485	As the price for crossing the river at a future time.	(Na-amu)
	She removed her ankle bracelet	(Naamu)
	And gave it to the Somono ancestor Sansamba	
	Sagado	(Naamu)
	As the price for crossing the river on a future date.	(Naamu)
	Any time that her children might go out in the middle	
	of the night,	(Naamu)
2490	And ask him to take them across the river,	(Naamu)
	He would take them without anybody in Manden	
	knowing about it.	(Naaaam')

---

[82] Maninka- or Bamana-speaking specialists in fishing, canoeing, boating, and the
water-borne transport of people and goods.

During the time of the organization of Manden,	(Naamu)
Sansamba Sagado was involved with that.	(Na-amu)
The Somono villages that you find	(Naamu)
2495 At Jelibakoro,	(Na-amu)
And Sansando,	(Naamu)
And Baladugu,	(Naamu)
Those towns along the bank of the river,	(Naamu)
Those are populated by descendants of Sansamba Sagado.	(Naaaam')
2500 (You heard that?)	(Na-amu)
They are Mande people.	(Naamuu)
If you talk about Manden without talking about Sansamba Sagado,	(Naamu)
You have not covered the subject of Manden.	(Na-amu)

Those days passed, and one day at three o'clock in the morning,	(Na-amu)
2505 Sogolon woke up her children.	(Naamu)
She said, "The time has come for what we talked about."	(Na-amu)
They left together.	(Naamu)
When they came to the riverbank,	(Naamu)
She took the path to go and wake Sansamba Sagado.	(Na-amu)
2510 She told him, "The day we talked about is today."	(Naamu)
He was not a man to break his promise.	(Na-amu)
He took his bamboo pole,	(Naamu)
He took his paddle.	(Naamuu)
They came and met her children in the bushes on the bank of the river.	(Naamu)
2515 The water had risen to the leaves on the bushes.	(Naamuu)
He went and unfastened his canoe that was attached to a *npeku* tree,[83]	(Naamu)
And brought it to them, saying, "Get in!"	(Naamuu)
Ma Sogolon Condé got into the canoe.	(Naamu)

---

[83] *Lannea microcarpa*, a variety of wild grape.

Her daughter Ma Kolonkan got in,	(Naamu)
2520 Manden Bori got in,	(Naamu)
So'olon Jamori got in.	(Naamu)
They told Sunjata to get in, but he refused.	(Na-amu)
Ma Sogolon Condé said, "Ah, Sunjata!	(Naamuu)
Do you want to cause me suffering?"	(Na-amu)
2525 He said, "Mother,	(Naamu)
If I have told you that I will go,	(Naamu)
Take the canoe and I will join you later.	(Naamu)
I will go."	(Na-amuu)
They crossed the river in the canoe.	(Naamu)
2530 Before they could reach the other side, they saw	
Sunjata sitting on the bank.	(Naamuuu)
He had brought his *dalilu* with him.	(Na-amu)

A VISIT TO SOSO

[*In an omitted passage, Sogolon recalls that in Sumaworo's youth, long before he became a problem in Manden, he had been her husband's hunting apprentice, and she decides to stop in Soso. Meanwhile, Sumaworo's personal oracle informs him that the man who will eventually take Soso and Manden away from him has not only been born, but has grown up into a hunter and will be identifiable as the one who violates Sumaworo's taboo.*]

They were now in Soso.	(Naamuu)
Sogolon Condé arrived and said, "Eh, Soso Mansa.	(Naamu)
These are the children of your former master.	(Na-amu)
2535 Their relationship with their brother is strained.	(Naamu)
Because of it, murder has been committed.	(Naamu)
Between two friends,[84]	(Na-amu)

---

[84] Sumaworo and Sunjata's father.

91

When one of them dies, it does not spoil the
    friendship. (Naamu)
The one who survives continues the friendship. (Naamu)
2540 I have brought Ma'an Sunjata and his younger
    siblings, (Na-amu)
To come and put them under your protection. (Naamuu)
You should train them to be hunters,
People who can kill their own game." (Na-amuu)
(Oh! There was still an old message there,[85]
2545 That had been sent by Dankaran Tuman.) (Naamu)
Sumaworo said, "Condé woman, that pleases me. (Naamu)
I agree to take them under my protection,
So long as they do not interfere with my sacred totem. (Naamu)
I agree to care for them." (Naamuu)
2550 (You heard that?) (Na-amu)
She said, "If God agrees, they will never spoil your
    totem." (Naamu)
He said, "Ho, if they do not interfere with my totem," (Naamu)
He said, "I agree to protect them." (Na-amu)
They spent that day there. (Naamu)

2555 That night in the evening, (Naamu)
Ma Sogolon Condé said (Naamu)
That the children of Soso should go and collect a
    pile of dried cow dung, (Na-amu)
That she had brought a small amount of cotton, (Naamu)
That she would like to spin at night, (Na-amu)
2560 So that she could light her lantern of conversation. (Naamu)
(You heard that) (Naamu)
They brought the cow dung to light the lantern of
    conversation.[86] (Na-amu)
Sumaworo had all the musical instruments, (Naamu)
All the musical instruments. (Naamu)

[85] Offering a reward to kill Sunjata.

[86] When villagers gather after dark to socialize and play music, they do it around a
lantern to avoid burning valuable fuel needed for cooking fires.

2565	They were all first brought out by Sumaworo,	(Naamu)
	Except for the *bala*.	(Naamuu)
	He brought out the *kèrèlèngkèngbèng*,[87]	(Naamu)
	He brought out the *kowaro*,[88]	(Naamu)
	He brought out the *donso nkoni*,[89]	(Naamu)
2570	He brought out the three-stringed *bolon*,[90]	(Na-amu)
	He brought out the *soron*,[91]	(Naamu)
	He brought out the *kora*.[92]	(Na . . .)
	That came out after all the other instruments,	
	And that is why they call it *ko la*.[93]	(Naamu)
2575	That is why they call it the last of all musical	
	instruments, *ko la*.	(Naamu)
	Then it came to be called *kora*.	(Na-amu)
	That one is played in Kita,	(Naamu)
	It is played in Senegal.	(Na-amu)
	(You heard that?)	(Naamuu)
2580	Sumaworo took out his *nkoni*,[94]	(Naamu)
	Came, and sat down by people who were conversing.	(Na-amu)
	Ma Sogolon Condé was content.	(Naamu)
	Sunjata and the others came and sat down.	(Na-amu)

[87] Named from the sound it makes (i.e., onomatopoeic), this child's instrument consists of a tin can resonator (or a tiny gourd) and a stick for a neck that supports a single string.

[88] More commonly known as *dan*, an inverted open calabash instrument with a neck for each of its six strings; technically known as a pentatonic pluriac.

[89] The hunters' harp, a large animal-skin–covered calabash with a single neck and six strings, played to praise hunters.

[90] The harp played to praise warriors; larger and deeper-toned than the hunters' harp, an animal-skin–covered calabash with a single neck supporting three or four strings. Tassey also mentioned another type of *bolon*, as yet unidentified.

[91] A large, rarely seen harp of northeastern Guinea, similar to the *kora*, but with twelve strings (for details, see Charry 2000: 121).

[92] With twenty-one strings, largest of the calabash harps.

[93] *Ko la* = "later on," another popular etymology (n. 40).

[94] Bamana *ngoni*; a traditional lute consisting of four to five strings attached to a single neck on a wooden, trough-shaped body covered with animal skin.

Ma Sogolon Condé said, "Wait. (Naamu)

2585 I will sing three songs." (Naamu)

They said, "Very well." (Na-amu)

When anybody sang,

Sumaworo would accompany them on the *nkoni*. (Naamu)

For Ma Sogolon Condé's first song, she sang: (Na-amuu)

2590 "Big ram, (Naamu)

The pen where the rams are kept, (Na-amu)

The leopard must not enter, (Naamu)

Big ram. (Naamu)

The pen where the rams are kept, (Naamu)

2595 The leopard must not enter." (Na-amu)

Sumaworo's *nkoni* was in harmony with her song. (Naamu)

After that, what else did she sing? (Naamu)

She sang: "Pit water, (Na-amu)

Don't compare yourself with clear water flowing

 over rocks, (Naamu)

2600 The pure white rocks. (Naamu)

Pit water, (Naamu)

Don't compare yourself with clear water flowing

 over rocks, (Naamu)

The pure white rocks." (Naamu)

Sumaworo's *nkoni* was in harmony with her song. (Naamuu)

2605 The third song she sang was:

"Big vicious dog, (Naamu)

If you kill your vicious dog, (Naamu)

Somebody else's will bite you, (Naamu)

Vicious dog. (Naamu)

2610 If you kill your vicious dog, (Naamu)

Somebody else's will bite you." (Naamu)

Sumaworo's *nkoni* was in harmony with her song. (Naamuu)

The gathering then broke up. (Naamu)

[In omitted passages, Sumaworo performs a ritual to identify his rival for power, learns that it is Sunjata, and resolves to kill him. Sunjata intentionally violates a taboo by sitting in Sumaworo's sacred hammock, confirming that he is the rival described by the oracle. In an episode

about Sumaworo's youthful rebelliousness and leadership, he invents
different stringed musical instruments at various stages of his youth.]

THE BIRTH OF FAKOLI

[The narrator recites Fakoli's genealogy and claims that his ancestors
in the male line had only one son each.]

Fakoli was himself an only son.	(Naamu)
2615 (You heard that?)	(Na-amu)
What led to Fakoli's birth?	(Naamu)
The first wife of his father, Yerelenko,	(Na-amu)
Was Tenenba Condé.	(Naamu)
He went and married Tenenba Condé	(Na-amu)
2620 At the home of the Condé at Dò ni Kiri.	(Naamu)
She became his first wife.	(Na-amu)
She spent thirty years without bearing a child.	(Na-amu)
(You heard that?)	(Naamu)
It was this Tenenba Condé who told her husband,	(Naamu)
2625 "I will never bear a child."	(Naaaam')
She said, "I now have grey in my hair,	(Naamu)
And your beard is grizzled.	(Naamu)
You should marry another woman,	(Naamu)
So she can bear you a son."	(Naaaam')
2630 Yerelenko said, "Tenenba Condé,	(Naamu)
I am not going to marry another wife.	(Naamu)
People were made for domestic strife,	(Na-amu)
And if I had many wives,	(Naamu)
They would cause problems for you.	(Naamu)
2635 If one marries only one wife,	(Naamu)
If she is understanding,	(Naamu)
If one marries a second wife,	(Naamu)
If she is not understanding,	(Naamu)

It will cause problems for one's manhood.	(Na-amu)
2640 I will not take another wife.	(Naaaam')
If you do not bear a child,	(Naamu)
I will take the place of a child."	(Naamu)
(You heard that?)	(Naamu)
That Ma Tenenba Condé,	(Na-amu)
2645 She wept.	(Naaaam')
As she wept,	(Naamu)
She went to see her husband's friends.	(Naamu)
She said, "Please tell my husband	(Na-amu)
To marry another woman.	(Naamu)
2650 It is important to have a child.	(Na-amu)
Whether it is a son,	(Naamu)
Whether it is a daughter,	(Naamu)
Whether it dies	(Naamu)
Or survives,	(Naamu)
2655 It is important to have a child.	(Na-amu)
If he continues like this,	(Naamu)
Without him siring any child,	(Naamu)
And if death comes to him,	(Naamu)
Without siring any child,	(Naamu)
2660 I will be held responsible."	(Naaaam')
Yerelenko finally agreed.	(Naamuu)
Yerelenko went to Soso.	(Na-amu)
Sumaworo's younger sister was Kosiya Kanté.	(Naamu)
When she was old enough to leave home,	(Naamu)
2665 Yerelenko married Kosiya Kanté.	(Na-amu)
He paid the bride price for her,	(Naamu)
He waited for her,	(Naamu)
And eventually she became pregnant.	(Naamuu)
After she got pregnant,	(Na-amu)
2670 She gave birth to a son.	(Naamu)
That son of Kosiya Kanté was Fakoli.	(Naamu)
The Fakoli that you have been told about,	(Naamu)
Who did well for people to his right,	(Naamu)

	Who did well for people to his left,	(Naamu)
2675	Who did well for Manden,	(Naamu)
	He did not help Manden with the sword.	(Naamu)
	He did not help Manden with the musket.	(Naamu)
	Fakoli helped Manden with his battle axe.	(Na-amu)
	He carried the axe on his shoulder.	(Naamu)
2680	If you hear, "I missed him,"	(Naamu)
	It means you took aim.	(Na-amu)
	A gun might miss you,	(Naamu)
	A sword might miss you,	
	But not a battle-axe.	(Naamu)
2685	That one will not miss you.	(Na-amu)
	The battle-axe was with Fakoli.	(Naamu)
	He was the son of Kosiya Kanté.	(Naamu)

HOW TENENBA ACQUIRED FAKOLI: SUMAWORO'S QUEST FOR THE SOSO BALA

	If you hear people praising Fakoli	(Naamu)
	As Soma Tenenba's son Fakoli,	(Naamu)
2690	How did the Condé woman get Fakoli?	(Naamu)
	When Fakoli was a toddler	(Naamu)
	On the back of Kosiya Kanté,	(Naamu)
	He was beginning to walk,	(Naamu)
	But he was not yet very steady on the ground.	(Na-amu)
2695	Sumaworo was doing his hunting apprenticeship.	(Naamu)
	While Sumaworo was in the bush of Soso,	(Naamuu)
	A genie of Folonengbe came from Kodowari,[95]	(Naamu)

[95] Maninka pronunciation of Côte d'Ivoire, referring to a forested region in the northern part of what foreign traders later called the "Ivory Coast," lying adjacent to today's eastern Guinea.

Jinna Maghan came and stood before Sumaworo	(Naamu)
In the bush of Soso.	(Naamuu)
2700 The genie chief's long hair was down his back.[96]	(Naamu)
Sumaworo followed the genie in the night,	(Naamu)
Traveled through the bush of Soso,	(Naamu)
Traveled through the bush of Manden,	(Naamu)
Went all the way to Folonengbe.	(Na-amu)
2705 When they came to the edge of Folonengbe,	(Naamu)
Jinna Maghan entered a cave.	(Naamu)
Sumaworo stood at the opening of the cave.	(Na-amu)
How was Sumaworo's manhood completed?	(Naamu)
If you hear,	(Na-amu)
2710 "Kukuba and Bantamba,	(Naamu)
Nyèmi-Nyèmi and Kambasiga,	(Naamu)
Sègè and Babi,	(Naamu)
Manden Pi-Pa-Pi,	(Naamu)
And big wind that blows in Manden,"	(Naamu)
2715 Sumaworo could transform himself into anything that flies through the air.	(Naamu)
Sumaworo could transform himself into anything on the ground.	(Naamu)
He could become air,	(Naamu)
He could rise into the sky,	(Naamu)
He could do anything on the ground.	(Naamuu)
2720 Here is how he developed to maturity:	(Na-amu)
When they came to the cave entrance,	(Naaaam')
The genie entered the cave.	(Naamu)
Sumaworo stood at the opening of the cave.	(Na-amu)
He was in unfamiliar bush.	(Naamu)
2725 He was not in the bush of Manden,	(Na-amu)
He was not in the bush of Soso.	(Naamu)

---

[96] As supernatural beings, genies are perceived by Manding peoples in a variety of physical manifestations. Jinna Maghan (*jinna* = genie; *maghan* = king/chief) is ubiquitous, conjured by the bards wherever they wish to place him in their narratives (cf. l. 3135 ff.).

He was not in the bush of Dò ni Kiri,	(Naamu)
He was not at Folonengbe.[97]	(Na-amu)
As he stood at the entrance of the cave,	(Naaaam')
2730 He raised his eyes and saw a big *siri* tree[98] standing	
there.	(Naamuu)
It had some ripe fruit on it.	(Naamu)
He climbed into the tree, saying, "Mba,	(Naamu)
Let me hang my hunter's hammock here until	
daybreak.	(Naamu)
If the animals come to eat the ripe *siri* seeds,	(Naamu)
2735 I'll have a shot at them."	(Naaaam')
(It is animals that bring trouble to hunters.)	(Na-amu)

While he was lying up there,	(Naamu)
A defining moment had arrived.	(Na-amu)
No animal came while he was lying up there.	(Naamu)
2740 The genie that brought him there saw to it that,	(Naamu)
In that time of the night,	(Naamu)
The cave entrance was all lit up as if there were a	
fire there.	(Na-amu)
Sumaworo was in the tree.	(Naamu)
He was not afraid.	(Naamu)
2745 God had removed all fear from him.	(Na-amu)
When the cave entrance was all lit up,	(Naamu)
Jinna Maghan came out and stood, and looked	
around.	(Naamu)
Sumaworo was up in the tree.	(Naamuu)
(You heard it?)	(Na-amu)
2750 The genie chief brought out two young male genies.	(Naamu)
They were both carrying knives.	(Naamu)
They circled the area and took their seats.	(Naamuu)
Sumaworo was watching them.	(Na-amu)

---

[97] An apparent contradiction (cf. l. 2704), but possibly meant to indicate that Sumaworo had stepped into the spirit world.

[98] *Burkea africana*, also known as *guéléba*.

Then the genie brought out two others.	(Naamu)
2755 They circled the area and took their seats.	(Naamu)
Sumaworo was watching from up in the tree.	(Naamuu)
After that, the genie brought out two more.	(Naamu)
They circled and sat down.	(Naamu)
The number of young male genies was now complete	
at six.	(Naamuu)

2760 After those six were arranged, the genie reentered	
the cave,	(Naamu)
Went and got the *bala*,[99] and brought it out.	(Naamu)
When the *bala* was set down,	(Na-amu)
He went back into the cave.	(Naamu)
He went and took the mallets and the wrist bells;[100]	(Naamu)
2765 He came and laid them on the *bala*.	(Naamu)
If you hear that the *bala* came from the genies,	(Naamu)
That is the *bala* that is in Manden.	(Naamu)
This is how it was acquired.	(Na-amu)
When the sticks and bells were laid on it,	(Naamu)
2770 Then he went back inside and got the small drum,	
dunun mutukuru.[101]	(Naamu)
He came and set it on the *bala*.	(Naamu)
After that, he went in,	(Naamu)
Took three arrows and laid them on the *bala*.	(Naamu)
When the three arrows were laid on the *bala*,	
2775 Sumaworo jumped down.	(Naamu)
That is what he was after.	(Na-amuu)
(You heard it?)	(Naaaam')

[99] Also known as *balafon*, the traditional xylophone. This legendary one is still revered as a sacred object known as the Soso Bala.

[100] A mallet is held in each hand to strike the melodious, resonating slats of the *bala*, while small brass bells attached to the player's wrist add accompanying rhythm.

[101] Dunun: A double-headed, cylinder-shaped drum with a name that corresponds to the sound it makes (i.e., onomatopoeic). In Maninka legend, the names of certain instruments become proper nouns, as in the case of Dunun Mutukuru, which, like the sacred *bala* called Soso Bala, is a musical and spiritual icon.

When Sumaworo jumped from the tree,	(Naamu)
He went and crouched over them.	(Naamu)
2780 Jinna Maghan took a seat facing the *bala*.	(Naamu)
Sumaworo said, "Aah, genie!	(Naamu)
It was you who brought me here.	(Naamuu)
If it is true that a promise should be kept,	(Na-amu)
Won't you sell me this *bala*?	(Naaaam')
2785 Please sell me your *bala*.	(Na-amu)
I am the one who made the musical instruments.	(Naamu)
I made the *kèrèlèngkèngbèng*,	(Naamu)
I made the *koworo*,	(Naamu)
I made the *donso nkoni*,	(Naamu)
2790 I made the three-stringed *bolon*,	(Naamu)
I made the *soron*,	(Na-amu)
After that I made the *kòra*,	(Naamu)
But I have never seen this kind of instrument.	(Na-amu)
Please agree.	(Naamu)
2795 Mba, sell this to me.	(Naamu)
Let me add this to the others so I can have them all."	(Naamuu)
But what he really wanted were the arrows.	(Na-amu)
It was for the arrows that his father moved him away	
from Folonengbe.	(Naaaam')
The diviners had said, "These can only be acquired in a	
foreign land.	(Naamu)
2800 You cannot acquire them while you are in	
Folonengbe."	(Na-amu)
(If you see the Mande people struggling with the issue	
of Sumaworo,	(Naamu)
That is the reason.)	(Na-amu)
He said, "Sell me the *bala*."	(Naamu)
Jinna Maghan said, "Aha."	
2805 He said, "Sumaworo,	(Naamu)
You do not have the price of the *bala*."	(Na-amu)
"Ah," said Sumaworo, "Please agree to sell it to me."	(Naamu)
"Ah!" he said, "If you say you want to buy this *bala*,	(Naamu)

What do you people have that would equal the price
 of this *bala*?"   (Na-amu)

2810 Sumaworo said, "Sell it to me in *gbensen*."   (Naamu)

People of early times used *gbensen*.   (Naamuu)

The money we used was *gbensen*.   (Naamu)

They would forge a piece of black iron,   (Naamu)

Cross it the way a Catholic thing[102] looks,   (Naamu)

2815 And make a *gbensen* like that.   (Naamu)

This is what we made into our money.   (Na-amu)

Sumaworo said, "Sell it to me for *gbensen*."   (Naamu)

Jinna Maghan said, "We do not want *gbensen*.   (Na-amu)

Genies have no use for *gbensen*."   (Naamu)

2820 Sumaworo said, "Mba, sell it to me for gold."   (Naamu)

Jinna Maghan said, "Human beings don't have that
 much gold."   (Na-amuu)

He said, "God gave gold to the genies."   (Naaaam')

*[In an omitted passage, Jinna Maghan tells a story of Adam asking God
for wealth with which to try to return to paradise, and being told that
the gold had already been given to the genies and that humans could
only reach paradise by avoiding sin, respecting one another, and being
faithful.]*

Jinna Maghan said, "What do you have to offer us,   (Naamu)

Other than gold, cowries, and *gbensen,* which we genies
 already have?"   (Naamu)

2825 Disappointed, Sumaworo said, "Jinna Maghan,

I have not met any other genies.   (Na-amu)

You are the only one I have met.   (Naaaam')

If you should decide to sell the *bala*,   (Naamu)

If you should decide to sell the things that go with it,   (Na-amu)

2830 What would you wish to sell it for?"   (Naamu)

---

[102] Indicating that the *gbensen*, a unit of trade currency made of thick strands of
iron wire, was bent into the shape of a rough cross.

Jinna Maghan said, "I am not the only owner of the
bala. (Naamu)

It belongs to all the genies. (Na-amu)

But the genies say that if they should decide to sell
the bala, (Naamu)

They will only sell it for a human being." (Naamu)

2835 (You heard it?) (Naamu)

He said, "The only thing they will sell it for is a
human being. (Na-amu)

If they say they want to sell it for a human being, (Naamu)

The price for which they would sell it is four people. (Naamuu)

The bala, one person! (Naamu)

2840 The mallets and wrist bells, one person! (Naamu)

The small drum, one person! (Naamu)

The three arrows that are on it, one person! (Naamu)

Anybody who brings four people, (Na-amu)

We will give those things to him." (Naamu)

2845 If the genies had demanded just anybody, (Naamu)

Sumaworo would have gotten ordinary people. (Na-amu)

Sumaworo was hopeful, (Naaaam')

But then Jinna Maghan said, "Sumaworo, (Naamu)

We are not talking about just any people, (Na-amu)

2850 They must all be related to you. (Naamu)

The four people we are talking about, (Naamu)

Anybody who brings his mother, (Naamu)

Brings his father, (Naamu)

Brings his first wife, (Naamu)

2855 Brings his sister, (Naamu)

We will give the things to that person." (Naamu)

Uh! Sumaworo was again disappointed. (Na-amu)

Because if the people were not his real relatives, (Naamu)

They would not be acceptable. (Naamu)

2860 The genies would never agree to that. (Naamu)

*[In an omitted passage, the narrator informs his listeners that the young
hunter Sumaworo had been missing from his homeland for three months,*

and that he was being searched for by the people of Soso, Manden, Dò ni
Kiri, Negeboriya, Tabon, and Kirina, because they did not know that he
was in Folonengbe, which was not part of the "seven lands" of Manden.]

Then Sumaworo said to Jinna Maghan,

"Tell me to bring ordinary people. (Naamu)

I, Sumaworo, am the son of three Touré women, [103] (Naamu)

But they are all dead. (Naamu)

2865 If they were alive and were told about this, (Na-amu)

And my father was included with them, (Naamu)

They would make up the four people. (Naamu)

But my mothers are dead, (Na-amu)

My father is dead, (Naamu)

2870 I have not yet married, (Naamu)

And I have only one sister. (Naamu)

My father gave her in marriage to the Koroma family

in Negeboriya. (Naamu)

I would not have agreed to give her up for anything, (Naamu)

Especially since she is married. (Na-amu)

2875 In fact, she has given birth to a boy child. (Naamu)

You should agree, and tell me that it can be ordinary

people." (Naamu)

"Ahuh!" The genie said, (Na-amu)

"Humans do that, but we do not do that. (Naamu, it's true)

Forget about these things and go on home. (Naamu)

2880 Anybody who brings those four people, (Naamu)

We will give the things to that person. (Naamu)

Anybody who does not bring those four people, (Naamu)

He will not get these things." (Naamuu)

Sumaworo appealed to them, (Na-amu)

2885 But he realized that the genies would not accept his

proposal. (Naamu)

Sumaworo said, "Jinna Maghan, (Naamu)

Then let me take my leave to return to Soso." (Na-amu)

---

[103] According to the tradition, Sumaworo's father was married to three sisters of
the Touré family, all of whom are said to be mothers of the Soso *mansa*.

Jinna Maghan said, "Go with my blessing."   (Naamu)
Sumaworo took his leave and went back to Soso.   (Naamu)
2890   When he got there, Soso, Manden, Dò ni Kiri,   (Naam . . .)
No one had doubted that Sumaworo was dead.   (Naamuu)
Before Sumaworo could return,   (Na-amu)
His hair had grown from his head down to below
      his neck,   (Naamu)
He had grown long hair.   (Naamu)
2895   For three months he had been in the bush.   (Naamuu)
When he arrived, the news spread.   (Naamu)
"Oooh," they said,
"The son of the three Touré women has been found.   (Naaaam')
Ooh, Kulanjan[104] has been found.   (Naamu)
2900   The Kulan of the riverbank has been found."   (Na-amu)

After he returned,   (Na-amu)
A message was sent to his sister in Negeboriya,   (Naamu)
His sister who was married to Yerelenko,   (Na-amu)
Who had given birth to Fakoli.   (Naamu)
2905   Fakoli had just started to talk, but was still being
      carried on her back.   (Naaaam')
Kosiya Kanté was told that her brother had returned.   (Naamu)
She took Fakoli, put him on her back,   (Naamu)
And went to tell her husband.   (Naamuu)
She said, "Sumaworo has been found and I am going
      to Soso."   (Naamu)
2910   Her husband said, "Go and see him,   (Naaaam')
Find out if he is all right."   (Naamu)
She went and told Ma Tenenba Condé,   (Naamu)
"Big sister, my brother has been found,   (Naamu)
And I am going to lay my eyes on him."   (Naamuu)
2915   Ma Tenenba Condé said,   (Naamu)
"If it were not for cooking for your husband,   (Naamu)
I would go with you,   (Naamu)

---

[104] "Tall Kulan." Hunters (in this case Sumaworo) are praised as the pelican (*kulan*),
because it is a hunting bird (cf. song title, l. 2299).

	Because my brothers are in Dò ni Kiri.	(Naamu)
	You and I, our brother is Sumaworo.	(Naamuu)
2920	Go and lay your eyes on him.	(Na-amu)
	When you come back, I myself will go."	(Naamuu)
	(You heard it?)	(Naamu)
	Kosiya Kanté set out for Soso.	(Na-amu)
	She went there and found that people were still welcoming Sumaworo.	(Naaaam')
2925	Kosiya Kanté said, "Eh, Sumaworo,	(Naamu)
	Where were you?"	(Naamu)
	He replied, "Only God knows."	(Na-amu)
	"Eh, Sumaworo,	(Naamu)
	A hunting apprentice can get lost for fifteen days;	(Naamu)
2930	That is not bad.	(Naamu)
	But for a hunting apprentice to get lost for three months,	(Naamu)
	Where were you?	(Naamu)
	Were you never told that when you get lost,	(Naamu)
	You are going to hurt someone?	(Na-amu)
2935	It is me that you hurt.	(Naaaam')
	Sisters need brothers.	(Naamu)
	Did you fall out of your hammock?	(Na-amu)
	Did your gun barrel blow up?	(Naamu)
	Were you attacked by a leopard?"	(Naamu)
2940	He said, "I was not attacked by a leopard."	(Naamu)
	"Ah," she said, "Then what happened?"	(Naamu)
	He said, "M'ma, Allah!"	(Naamu)
	They shook hands.	(Naamuu)
	After she saw that he was all right,	(Naamu)
2945	She said, "I did not tell my husband that I would spend the night here.	(Naamu)
	I want you to agree	(Na-amu)
	To let me go back and tell them that you are well so they will not worry."	(Naamu)
	Sumaworo said, "Go with my blessing."	(Na-amu)
	He took his musket,	(Naamu)

2950	Put it on his shoulder,	(Naamu)
	And escorted his sister.	(Naamuu)
	When they were one kilometer out of the town,	(Na-amu)
	He explained the situation to her.	(Naamu)

[In an omitted passage, Sumaworo confides in his sister, cautioning secrecy because of his rival step-brothers. He details his experience with the genies in Folonengbe, describing the wonderful bala *and other objects, including the three magic arrows that he knows he must possess in order to achieve his political ambitions. He tells Kosiya that the genies are demanding a family member in exchange for the* bala, *and says he will return to renew his pleas that they accept some other human instead.]*

THE SACRIFICE OF KOSIYA KANTE

	Kosiya Kanté set off on her way back to Negeboriya.	(Naamu)
2955	When she got to the town,	(Naamu)
	She went and reported to her husband Yerelenko;	(Naamu)
	She reported to Ma Tenenba Condé.	(Naamu)
	She sat and reflected for a long time.	(Naamu)
	In the afternoon, she spoke to Ma Tenenba Condé.	(Naamu)
2960	She said, "Big sister Tenenba Condé,	(Naamu)
	If Fakoli is orphaned now, what will happen to him?"	(Na-amu)
	Ma Tenenba Condé said, "Eh!	(Naamu)
	Little sister Kosiya Kanté,	(Naamu)
	Why are you talking like that?"	(Naamu)
2965	"Ah," said Kosiya,	(Naamu)
	"When I go to search for firewood,	(Naamu)
	Does he usually cry while I am gone?"	(Naamu)
	The Condé woman was slow to understand.	(Naamu)
	Ma Tenenba Condé said, "When you go to gather firewood,	(Naamu)
2970	Once he is full of porridge	(Naamu)

And you have gone searching for wood,	(Naamu)
He will last a long time, *wrrrrr*.	(Naamu)
During the time until you return,	(Naamu)
He will not cry, but he is mischievous.	(Na-amu)
2975 If he does start to cry, he will never quiet down."	(Naaaam')

Oh, once Kosiya knew about Fakoli being filled with porridge,	(Naamu)
She felt it was possible to leave.	(Naamuuu)
Kosiya Kanté went into the house.	(Naamu)
She took soft white rice and pounded it,	(Naamu)
2980 And filled a container with clean rice.	(Naamuu)
That night passed.	(Naamu)
She took one ladle of pounded rice,	(Naamu)
Cooked it, and cooled it.	(Naamu)
She took Fakoli and put him on her lap.	(Naamu)
2985 She fed Fakoli the porridge.	(Naamu)
When he was full of porridge,	(Naamu)
She gave him her breast.	(Naamu)
After he suckled it, she gave him the other one.	(Naamu)
After he suckled that one, he was full.	(Naamuu)
2990 (You heard it?)	(Naamuu)
She took Fakoli and said, "Big sister Tenenba Condé,	(Naamu)
Take care of Fakoli."	(Naamu)
She said, "I am going to look for firewood."	(Naaaam')
Ma Tenenba Condé said, "Eh,	(Naamu)
2995 Little sister Kosiya Kanté!	(Na-amu)
The thing you told me yesterday,	(Naamu)
I am worried about it.	(Naamu)
You have given Fakoli to me so you can go to fetch wood,	(Naamu)
But do not stay long."	
3000 "Uh uh," she said, "I will not stay long."	(Naaaam')
(You heard it?)	(Naamu)

Ma Tenenba Condé took Fakoli and stood him at her side.	(Naamuu)
Kosiya Kanté went inside.	(Naamu)
She took the wood-chopping axe,	(Naamu)

3005	She took the wood-carrying head pad,[105]	(Naamu)
	She took the wood-carrying frame,	(Naamu)
	She went out to the other side of the yard.	(Naamu)
	She looked back at Fakoli.	(Naamu)
	She gazed at him for a long time.	(Naamu)
3010	Then she passed out of the yard.	(Naamu)
	She looked back at Fakoli,	(Naamu)
	Watched him for a long time.	(Naamu)
	When she arrived at her husband's door,	(Naamu)
	She looked back at Fakoli,	(Naamu)
3015	Looked back at him,	(Naamu)
	Looked at him,	(Naamu)
	And then she entered the house.	(Naamu)
	From there she left the town.	(Naamuu)
	She went into the bush.	(Naamu)
3020	When she was one kilometer away from the town,	(Naamuu)
	She heard that Sumaworo had again disappeared.	(Naamu)
	(You heard it?)	(Na-amu)
	You know, she knew where he had gone.	(Naamu)
	When she was one kilometer away from the town,	(Na-amu)
3025	The beads she wore on her ankles,	(Naamu)
	She cut them off.	(Naamu)
	Those that were around her neck,	(Naamu)
	She cut them off.	(Naamu)
	The wood-carrying pad on her head,	(Naamu)
3030	She put it with the carrying frame,	(Naamu)
	Added the axe to them,	(Naamu)
	Put the ropes on them,	(Naamu)
	And set them down.	(Naamuu)
	She ran toward Folonengbe.	(Na-amu)

[In an omitted passage, Sumaworo continues his negotiations for the bala and other objects, begging Jinna Maghan to accept any form of payment other than members of his own family.]

[105] A doughnut-shaped pad of cloth or twisted grass used to cushion and help balance loads carried on the head.

3035	Sumaworo was pleading with Jinna Maghan when	
	Kosiya Kanté arrived.	(Naamu)
	Jinna Maghan was watching her as she drew near,	(Naamu)
	But Sumaworo had not yet seen her.	(Naamu)
	Kosiya Kanté arrived just as he was saying,	(Na-amu)
	"The only sister I have I would not give away,	(Naamu)
3040	Especially since she has been married."	(Naamu)
	Kosiya Kanté appeared at his side and said,	
	"Sumaworo?"	(Naamu)
	She said, "Whether you send me	(Naamu)
	Or you do not send me,	(Naamu)
	I have come myself.	(Naamu)
3045	I prefer your success to my life."	(Naamu)
	Then she entered the cave.	(Naamuu)
	From the time of Sumaworo's birth	(Naamu)
	To the time of his death,	(Naamu)
	For any man to see him shed a tear,	(Naamu)
3050	That was the only day.	(Na-amu)
	The tears came down, *tur, tur, tur.*	(Naaamu)
	(You heard it?)	(Naamu)
	Jinna Maghan then said, "Sumaworo,"	(Naamu)
	He said, "Take heart.	(Naamuu)
3055	The reason you are weeping,	(Na-amu)
	That you will never see your sister again,	(Naamu)
	The genies will never let her out.	(Naamu)
	But we had said that the price of the *bala*	(Naamu)
	And everything with it is four persons.	(Naamu)
3060	But since your sister has done this,	(Na-amu)
	Go on back home.	(Naamu)
	We are giving you the *bala* and everything with it,	(Na-amu)
	In exchange for your sister,	(Naamu)
	Because we know that this has touched you deeply.	(Naamu)
3065	Go on back home and we will send you the *bala*.	(Naamuu)
	Deeply troubled, Sumaworo went back home.	(Na-amu)
	He did not say anything to anyone.	(Naamuu)
	They were the only two offspring of the three Touré	
	women.	(Naamu)

	This was his only sister who had gone.	(Na-amu)
3070	His nephew had been left an orphan.	(Naamu)
	He could not say anything to anyone.	(Na-amu)
	He was ashamed to face his in-laws at Negeboriya.	(Naamu)
	He kept silent.	(Naaaam')
	On the day that the *bala* arrived,	(Na-amu)
3075	On the occasion when he received it,	(Naamu)
	Kosiya Kanté was spoken of.	(Na-amu)
	The people of Negeboriya wept.	(Naamu)
	Ma Tenenba Condé wept,	(Naamu)
	"Ah! Little sister Kosiya Kanté,	(Na-amu)
3080	Is this how you treat me?	(Naaaam')
	When a child-bearing mother leaves her child with a barren woman,	(Naamu)
	Fakoli is not yet grown.	(Na-amu)
	Eh! Kosiya Kanté!	(Naamu)
	Eh! This Kanté woman has real courage!"	(Na-amu)
3085	Ma Tenenba Condé was saying this as she went home.	(Naamu)
	She went and reported to her husband.	(Naamu)
	Yerelenko said, "Tenenba Condé,	(Naamu)
	The way you feel about this,	
	It does not make me feel that bad."	(Na-amu)
3090	He said, "God does as He pleases.	(Naamu)
	I was not thinking of marrying another woman.	(Naamu)
	It was you who said that I should marry,	(Naamu)
	So I could sire my only son.	(Naamu)
	Since that child has been born,	(Naaaam')
3095	If Kosiya Kanté has done this,	(Naamuu)
	What you requested from God,	(Naamu)
	Heh! That boy with you is now your son.	(Naaaam')
	You do not need to weep."	(Naamuu)
	That is how God brought the end to Kosiya Kanté.	(Na-amu)

[In an omitted passage, the narrator advises his listeners on domestic relationships, and how men should comfort their wives when they are in distress.]

TENENBA AND FAKOLI VISIT THE SACRED SITES

3100	Yerelenko calmed Tenenba with sweet talk.	(Na-amu)
	Ma Tenenba Condé dried her tears.	(Naamu)
	From then on, Ma Tenenba Condé took care of Fakoli.	(Naamu)
	If you see that Fakoli grew to become a man,	(Naamu)
	The source of that was the Condé's place.	(Naamu)
3105	It was a Condé woman who gave him his *dalilu*.	(Na-amu)
	After she heard this from her husband,	(Naamu)
	Ma Tenenba Condé took him away	(Naamu)
	To the Kulubali ancestor, Kani Simbon.	(Naamu)
	She said, "Simbon,	(Naamu)
3110	I have given birth to a child without getting pregnant[106]	(Naamu)
	If relations between Kulubali and Condé are	
	meaningful,	(Na-amu)

	If something goes wrong with this child,	(Na-amu)
	It will be said that Kosiya Kanté meant for it to happen.	(Naamu)
	It will be said that since her own birth,	
3115	This woman[107] has never borne a child.	(Naamu)
	They will say,	
	'How can you bear a child and give it to that person?	(Naamu)
	She meant to kill Fakoli.'[108]	(Na-amu)
	If relations between Kulubali and Condé are meaningful,	(Naamu)
3120	Heh! I have brought Fakoli.	(Naamu)
	Make him into a hunter who will kill game for	
	himself."	(Naamu, it is true)

[106] She has become Fakoli's foster mother.

[107] Ma Tenenba Condé.

[108] Teneba is saying that if Fakoli dies for any reason (l. 3112) she will be blamed for it; this is why she is taking him on *dalimasigi*, a journey to the sacred sites of Manden to acquire protective medicines and amulets (*basiw*).

(You heard it?) (Naamu)

They bathed Fakoli with protective medicine. (Na-amu)

They prepared Fakoli,

3125 Providing him with protective medicines (Naamu)

So Fakoli would never die in fire, (Naamu)

No man would ever get the better of him, (Naamu)

So God would make him a hunter,

A killer of animals for himself. (Na-amu)

3130 Tenenba took Fakoli from there, (Naamu)

And carried him to Tabon Wana Faran Kamara at

Sibi mountain, (Naamu)

And said the same thing to him. (Naamu, great Kamara)

When she went to Kamanjan, (Na-amu)

She explained everything to him, saying, (Naamu)

3135 "I have brought him for you to set on the lap of

Jinna Maghan; (Naamu)

You must address him as 'Nya Maghan and

Jinna Maghan.'" (Naamu)

Kamanjan passed through the entrance of Sibi

Mountain,[109] (Naamu)

And came out through the exit of Tabon Mountain. (Naamu)

He carried Fakoli in his arms, (Na-amu)

3140 Brought him back, (Naamu)

And handed him to Tenenba Condé. (Naamu)

Kamanjan said,

"He has become a hunter who will kill wild game for

himself." (Naamu)

He said, "Nothing can harm this one now." (Naamuu)

3145 She took Fakoli from there on the road to Kirina. (Naamu)

When she arrived at Kirina, (Naamuu)

She gave him to Tenen Mansa Konkon.

When Fakoli was given to that veteran warrior, (Naamuu)

---

[109] This and the reference to an exit (l. 3138) refer to a large, natural stone arch on Tabon Mountain above the village of Sibi, visible from the road running north to Bamako, Mali's capital.

	Tenen Mansa Konkon carried him into the cave.	(Naamu)
3150	He went and rolled him in the pit of Kirina.	(Naamu)
	He rolled him in the dust of the cave,	(Naamu)
	And than came back out with Fakoli.	(Naamu)
	Tenen Mansa Konkon returned him to Tenenba Condé.	(Na-amu)
	When she took Fakoli away from there,	(Naamu)
3155	She carried him to Nema.	(Naamu)
	She gave him to Nema Faran Tunkara in Kuntunya.	(Naamuu)
	The important places that Ma'an Sunjata visited in his travels,	(Naamu)
	Ma Tenenba Condé took Fakoli to all of them.	(Naamu)
	Now, when she came back from there,	(Naamu)
3160	She took Fakoli to her brothers in Dò ni Kiri.	(Naamu)
	Ancestor Donsamogo Diarra said, "Tenenba Condé,	(Naamu)
	You are the sister who always obeyed me.	(Naamu)
	You were not like Dò Kamissa.	(Na-amu)
	Ha! You see the old place of Dò Kamissa,	(Naaaam')
3165	Where she settled after she started changing into a buffalo?"	(Naamu)
	He said, "But since the time you were given for marriage	(Naamu)
	To the people of Negeboriya,	(Naamu)
	Up to the present,	(Naamu)
	You have never come back here for a visit.	(Naamu)
3170	You have never violated our taboo.[110]	(Naamu)
	We never heard about anything bad between you and your husband.	(Naamu)
	Now that you have brought your son here,	(Naamu)
	Send a message to your husband saying	(Naamu)
	That if you had given birth to a child,	(Naamu)
3175	You would have taken three months here,	(Naamu)
	To care for your baby.	(Naamu)
	Therefore, let him allow you to spend three months here,	(Naamu)

[110] See n. 38.

So we can prepare Fakoli."	(Na-amu)
(You heard it?)	(Naaaam')

3180 The Koroma[111] *kamalenw* call us Condé "uncle," (Naamu)

Although that Condé woman did not actually give birth
    to any Koroma. (Naamu)

Ma Tenenba Condé sent her husband a message at
    Negeboriya. (Naamu)

Yerelenko replied that the Condé should be told (Naamu)

That even if they should request seven months, (Naamu)

3185 It was all right as long as Fakoli would become a
    hunter. (Naaaam')

Our ancestor said, "Ahhh, three months is enough." (Naamuu)

Our ancestor prepared Fakoli. (Naamuu)

Three hundred and thirteen heads of the *kolon* bird,[112] (Naamu)

Our Condé ancestor attached them to a hat. (Naamu)

3190 The heads of three hundred and thirteen cats, (Naamu)

He attached them to a hat. (Naamu)

The heads of three hundred and thirteen *gwara*
    snakes,[113] (Naamu)

He attached them to a hat. (Naamu)

He said, "This hat is for Fakoli." (Naamu)

3195 When Fakoli used to put this on his head, (Naamu)

He would be called "Jamujan Koli." (Naamu)

People were sometimes taller than him, (Naamu)

But even when he sat down, (Naamu)

He could be taller than them.[114] (Naamu)

---

[111] One of the patronymics or lineage identities (*jamuw*) identified with Fakoli (for details, see Conrad 1992: 174–80).

[112] Not definitively identified, but the skull of the hornbill is favored for sorcerer's bonnets. The numbers of such amulets are purposely exaggerated for emphasis.

[113] Very deadly according to Maninka informants; probably a species of viper, but not positively identified.

[114] Reference to the later episode where Fakoli demonstrates his sorcery by increasing his size (l. 4300–13). "Jamujan" in the praise-name (l. 3196) translates as "lengthy *jamu*," possibly referring to Fakoli's many praise-names, or the fact that many blacksmith families claim him as an ancestor.

3200 This hat came from Dò ni Kiri. (Na-amu)

It was the Condé who gave that to him. (Naamu)

My ancestor said, "This is not all that I will give." (Naamu)

He took him into a little room (Naamu)

And bathed him with water from seven pots. (Naamu)

3205 My ancestor said, "I will not stop with that." (Naamu)

The buffalo wraith of Dò Kamissa that was killed, (Naamu)

He took a horn of that buffalo, (Naamu)

He took its skull and prepared it. (Naamuu)

If you hear about our war totem, (Naamu)

3210 That was our war totem. (Naamu)

It was the skull of Dò Kamissa's buffalo wraith. (Naamu)

After that, (Naamu)

He circled Fakoli with the buffalo skull. (Na-amu)

He sat him on the buffalo skull, (Naamu)

3215 And said, "This one will not die in fire, (Naamu)

He will not die in water, (Naamu)

This one has become the nephew of the Condé." (Naamu)

After that, (Na-amu)

He gathered together the unmarried girls, (Naamu)

3220 Those who had not had sex. (Naamuu)

He put them in a house, (Naamu)

In the darkness of the twenty-eighth day of the moon, (Naamu)

And put out the lamp. (Naamuu)

He sent in some cotton and spindles, (Na-amu)

3225 And told them to spin it and give it to him in the
morning. (Naamu)

The girls entered the house. (Naamu)

They spun the cotton. (Naamu)

In the morning, (Naamu)

That amounted to nine spindles full of thread. (Naamuu)

3230 They gave it to our ancestor. (Na-amu)

He then took the spindles into his little room, (Naamu)

Came back out, and gave them to Tenenba Condé. (Naamu)

He said, "Go and give this to the weavers. (Naamu)

Let them weave it; (Na-amu)

3235 Let them dip it into the dye." (Naamu)

He said, "This will be for Fakoli." (Naamuu)

The weavers wove it; (Naamu)

They dipped it into the dye, (Naamu)

Gave it to Ma Tenenba Condé. (Naamu)

3240 They said, "Tenenba Condé, this is for Fakoli." (Naamu)

Then it was given to Fakoli. (Naamu)

He looked at it. (Naamu)

It was not enough to make a hat, (Naamu)

It could not make a shirt, (Naamu)

3245 It could not make trousers. (Naamuu)

"Uh, this is supposed to be worn," said Fakoli. (Na-amu)

"Ah, this thing, (Naamu)

Since my uncles have given me this, (Naamu)

If God agrees, (Naamu)

3250 Men do not wear head-ties, (Naamu)

But I will tie this on my head (Naamu)

And make it my warrior headband (Naamu)

For when I go in pursuit of enemies." (Naamu)

This Fakoli headband is in Norasoba.[115] (Naamuu)

3255 (You heard it?) (Na-amu)

Fakoli's battle headband that came from Dò ni Kiri, (Naamu)

That is in Norasoba. (Naamu)

That Fakoli, (Naamu)

Ma Tenenba Condé took him back home. (Naamuu)

3260 He grew up being thankful to her. (Naamu)

The days of this Fakoli (Naamu)

And the days of Ma'an Sunjata (Naamu)

Were at the same time. (Naamu)

It was this Fakoli who joined the government of
    Ma'an Sunjata. (Naamu)

3265 He also took part in the war with Soso. (Naamuu)

[115] A town in Guinea, located on the north bank of the Niger River between Siguiri and Kouroussa.

*[In an omitted passage, the scene shifts back to Soso at the time of So-
golon's visit with her children, when Sumaworo is in power. Sumaworo
interprets the meaning of the songs sung earlier by Sogolon. Sunjata vi-
olates Sumaworo's sacred taboo, the two men engage in the deadly
snuff-taking ritual, and Sunjata is banished from Soso. Continuing the
journey into exile, Sunjata violates sacred taboos in each of the places
they stop, including Nema, where they remain.]*

SUMAWORO'S TYRANNY
OVER MANDEN

When Sogolon and her children were in Nema,	(Naamu)
When they were with ancestor Faran Tunkara at Kuntunya,	(Naamuu)
He would send Sunjata between himself and where the sun sets.	(Naamu)
Whenever war broke out, they would send for him.	(Naamu)
3270 Then Sunjata would come and join the army of Kuntunya.	(Naamu)
They would march.	(Naamu)
Whenever he captured three prisoners,	(Naamu)
One captive would be for him.	(Naamu)
Whenever he captured five prisoners,	(Naamu)
3275 Two captives would be for him.	(Naamu)
Whenever he captured ten prisoners,	(Naamu)
His share would be four captives.	(Naamu)
The Kuntunya *mansa* would take six of the captives.	(Naamu)
This is how Sunjata collected his own band of men.	(Naamu)
3280 He stayed there for twenty-seven years.	(Naamuu)
Mhmm, before the end of the twenty-seventh year,	(Naamu)
Heh! Things were very bad in Manden.	(Naaaam')
Things were terrible in Manden!	(Naamu)
Sumaworo had sent his warriors.	(Naamu)

3285	He was looking for Sunjata.	(Na-amu)
	He did not know where he was.	(Naamu)
	Whenever he consulted Nènèba, his oracle,	(Naamu)
	It would say, "Your successor has grown."	(Naamuu)
	Whenever he consulted Nènèba,	(Na-amu)
3290	Three age sets of young men used to fetch wood,	(Naamu)
	And pile it under the cauldron of Nènèba,	(Naaaam')
	Morning and evening.	(Naamu)
	That same oracle said, "Fire, fire, fire, fire, fire, fire."	(Naaaam')
	Whenever he went to it,	(Na-amu)
3295	He would bathe in the cauldron's medicines.	(Naamu)
	Whenever they would set out for war,	(Naamu)
	It was that Nènèba that would tell them what to sacrifice for the war.	(Naamuu)
	Each time he woke up in the morning,	(Naamu)
	It would tell him, "Sumaworo,	(Naamuu)
3300	Only God knows the day.	(Na-amu)
	Your successor has grown up."	(Naamu)
	Sumaworo would question some Mande people,	(Naamu)
	Saying, "Has Ma'an Sunjata returned to Manden?"	(Naamu)
	Meanwhile, he laid waste to Manden nine times.	(Naamu)
3305	As he searched for Sunjata,	(Naamu)
	The Mande people struggled	(Naamu)
	And rebuilt it nine times.	(Naamuu)
	He failed to find Sunjata.	(Na-amu)
	When Sumaworo would kill,	(Naamu)
3310	He would tell his people to search among the bodies,	(Naamu)
	To find out if the Condé woman's son was among them.	(Na-amu)
	When Sumaworo's people would go and look,	(Naamu)
	They would say, "The Mande people do not know The whereabouts of the Condé woman's son."	(Naamuu)
3315	What he did then, was send a message to Manden,	(Naamu)
	That he wanted to see all of them at Kukuba.	(Naamu)
	He summoned all of them.	(Naamu)
	The leaders at that meeting were	(Naamu)

	Turama'an,	(Naamu)
3320	Kankejan,	(Naamu)
	And Fakoli.	(Naamuu)
	Ma'an Sunjata and his brothers were not there.	(Na-amu)
	When those men came,	(Naamu)
	All the men who came at that time,	(Naamu)
3325	Sumaworo killed them all.	(Naaaam')

The people of Manden mourned. (Naamu)
He killed all the men, (Na-amu)
Except for Turama'an and Kankejan, who could
    disappear in broad daylight, (Naamuu)
And Fakoli, who could stand and vanish instantly. (Naamuu)
3330 The people who had that kind of *dalilu* (Na-amu)
Were the only ones he did not kill. (Naamu)
He killed all the other men who went. (Naamu)
The people of Manden wept. (Naaaam')
(You heard it?) (Naamu)
3335 After another month had passed, (Naamu)
He summoned them to Bantamba, (Naamuu)
Saying, "I have to finish them off. (Naamuu)
If I continue doing that, (Naamu)
I will get my successor. (Na-amu)
3340 If I continue killing human beings,
My successor will be among them." (Naamu)
He called them to Bantamba. (Naamu)
When they arrived at Bantamba, (Na-amu)
After the meeting he looked at the Mande people, *rrrr*,
3345 And said, "Kill them all." (Naamu)
Only those who had the power to disappear in broad
    daylight escaped. (Na-amu)
Again Manden wept. (Naamuu)

He summoned them to Nyèmi-Nyèmi. (Naamu)
Manden also wept for that. (Na-amu)
3350 Every time Mande people were summoned, (Naamu)
Manden would be in mourning. (Naamu)

Sumaworo was killing the people of Manden.   (Naamuu)

He would search among the bodies, hoping to identify
    his successor.   (Naamu)

Every time he killed like that,   (Naamu)

3355 He would go to his Nènèba.   (Naamu)

That Nènèba is with the Kantés at Balandugu.   (Naamu)

Since the days of Sumaworo,   (Na-amu)

From that time until now,   (Naamu)

The Kantés have only one town;   (Naamu)

3360 The Kanté town of Balandugu.   (Naamu)

Aside from that,

Sumaworo's descendants did not establish any other
    towns,   (Naamu)

Because he was so ruthless.   (Na-amu)

(You heard it?)   (Naamu)

3365 He summoned them again,   (Naamu)

To Kambasiga.   (Naamu)

After doing that,   (Naamu)

He would go and consult his Nènèba.   (Naamu)

The Nènèba would say, "Sumaworo, uh heh."   (Naamu)

3370 It would say,

"Up to now you have still not found him."   (Naamuu)

It would say,

"Of all those who have been killed, he is not among
    them."   (Na-amuu)

Sumaworo asked, "What should I do?"   (Naamu)

3375 It said, "Search for him."   (Naamu)

It said, "He has reached maturity."   (Naamuu)

When the Mande people were summoned to
    Kambasiga,   (Naamu)

Fakoli went to see the Kulubali ancestor, Kani
    Simbon.   (Naamuu)

He said, "Simbon.   (Naamu)

3380 Manden is about to be wiped out.   (Naamu)

We must sit down together;   (Naamu)

Let us find a solution to this problem in Manden.   (Naamu)

Manden will be reduced to being Soso's peanut farm,	(Naamu)
Because Sumaworo has said two things.	(Na-amu)
3385 He has said, 'Manden's reputation is better than	
Manden itself.'	(Naamu)
He has said, 'When one goes to Manden,	(Naamu)
The Mande women are better than the Mande men.'	(Naamu)
He said Manden has only women;	
He did not see any men there.	(Na-amu)
3390 Since it was said that his successor had been born,	(Naamu)
He has tried to provoke Sunjata into responding."	(Naaaam')
(You heard it?)	(Naamu)
After saying that,	(Na-amuu)
Fakoli then returned to Manden and said, "Let us	
build a council hall.	(Naamu)
3395 Let the surviving men of Manden have a meeting,	(Naamu)
Let us hold meetings at the edge of town.	(Naamu)
Otherwise, Manden is doomed."	(Na-amu)
(You heard it?)	(Naaaam')
When it was said that they should meet outside the	
town,	(Naamu)
3400 They worked hard and built the council hall.	(Naamu)
After that they sat in front of the council hall,	(Naamu)
And Fakoli addressed the men of Manden.	(Naamuu)
He said, "We have finished building this council hall.	(Naamu)
We all share the ownership of this council hall,	(Naaaam')
3405 Except for the one who wants to destroy Manden.	(Naamu)
If you are a man of courage,	(Naamu)
You share the ownership of this council hall.	(Naamu)
If you are a man of truth,	(Naamu)
You share the ownership of this council hall.	(Naamu)
3410 If you are a master of sorcery,	(Naamu)
You share the ownership of this council hall.	(Naamu)
If you have the love of Manden at heart,	(Naamu)
You share the ownership of this council hall.	(Naamu)

THE EXPEDITION TO FIND SUNJATA AND RETURN HIM TO MANDEN

*[In an omitted passage, the assembled elders decide to summon diviners to
learn who will be the liberator of Manden, and where he can be found.
After an extended period of divination it is determined that Ma'an Sun-
jata is the one who was foreseen, and that a special delegation must be
sent to find Sogolon and her children. Volunteering are the Muslim divin-
ers Manjan Bereté and Siriman Kanda Touré, as well as the female bard
Tunku Manyan Diawara and the female slave Jonmusoni Manyan. They
plan to visit distant markets with special sauce ingredients that can only
be found in Manden, as a way of finding the people they seek.]*

After they left the town,	(Naamu)
3415 Manjan Bereté laid down his prayer skin.[116]	(Naamu)
He stood and made two invocations to God.	(Naamu)
Those travelers did not meet anybody;	(Naamu)
Nobody saw them going.	(Naamu)
Whatever town they slept in,	(Na-amu)
3420 Manjan Bereté would say,	(Naamu)
"Siriman Kanda Touré,	(Naamu)
I want to tell to you	(Naamu)
That where we are now,	(Naamu)
There is no problem whether you are a man,	(Naamu)
3425 There is no problem whether you are a woman.	(Naamu)
Everybody must exercise their *dalilu*.	(Naaaam')
We must not be seen on the road."	(Na-amu)
When he finished making the two invocations,	(Naamu)
As he shook hands with his companions,	(Naamu)
3430 They asked where they would sleep that night.	(Naamu)
"Ahhh," he said, "Let us try to reach Soso today."	(Naamu)

[116] His Muslim prayer rug, the hide of a goat or sheep.

123

He said, "Because tomorrow is Soso's market day." (Naamuu)

When he had finished with the two invocations, (Na-amu)

When he shook hands with a companion, (Naamu)

3435 The companion became invisible. (Naamuu)

When he gave his hand to another companion and
 withdrew it, (Naamu)

The person became invisible. (Naamu)

When he gave his hand to the third companion and
 withdrew it, (Naamu)

That person became invisible. (Naamu)

3440 Then he circled his prayer skin, (Naamu)

And he himself became invisible. (Naamu)

They went on and met at the outskirts of Soso. (Naamuu)

When they met there, they spent the night; (Naamu)

They slept outside the town. (Naaaam')

3445 When the market opened at daybreak, (Mmmm)

Manjan Bereté said, "Take the things to the market." (Naamu)

They set them out in the Soso market, (Naamu)

But nobody asked for them. (Naamu)

They went on to the market of Tabon; (Naamu)

3450 The things were not asked for. (Naamu)

They went to the market of Kirina; (Naamu)

The things were not asked for. (Naamu)

They took the road to Kuntunya. (Naamuu)

When they arrived at Kuntunya, (Naamu)

3455 The Kuntunya market was held on Friday. (Naamu)

They arrived there on Thursday evening. (Naamuu)

They slept outside the town. (Naamu)

At a house in that same town,

Ma Sogolon Condé said to her daughter Ma Kolonkan, (Naamu)

3460 She said, "Ma Kolonkan, *aaaoy!* (Naamu)

My stomach is hurting me. (Na-amu)

Since I came from Manden, (Naamu)

This is the twenty-seventh year that I have not had *dado*.[117] (Na-amu)

---

[117] Dried hibiscus blossoms and/or leaves, used as a condiment in sauces. A related product, *datu*, is a pungent condiment made by fermenting the seeds of the *dado*.

Tomorrow morning,	(Naamu)
3465 Do not wash the dishes,	(Naamu)
Do not scrub the pots,	(Naamu)
Be the first one into the market, my child,	(Naamu)
So I can have some *dado* to eat."	(Naamuu)
When an eater of *dado* goes a long time without any,	
the stomach hurts.	(Na-amu)
3470 All night she was complaining of that to her daughter.	(Naamu)
The Mande people had brought *dado*,	
But they spent the night outside of town.	(Naamu)
As soon as the sun started to show its face,	(Naamu)
Manjan Bereté said, "Take the things into the market."	(Naamu)
3475 The two women went and sat outside the covered part	
of the market.	(Naamu)
The two women had the *dado* there,	(Naamu)
With the *namugu* and the *nèrè* seeds.[118]	(Naamu)
They set them out on display.	(Naamu)
Ma So'olon Wulen Condé said to Ma Kolonkan,	(Naamu)
3480 "Go early to the market so you can get what you want."	(Naamu)

When Kolonkan arrived at one place,	(Naamu)
She saw two women standing there with *dado*.	(Naamu)
She clapped her hands.	(Na-amu)
She said, "My mother has *dalilu*.	(Naamu)
3485 From the time we came from Manden,	(Naamu)
She has not said anything about *dado*,	(Naamu)
Nothing at all.	(Naamu)
It was only yesterday that she suddenly spoke of *dado*,	(Naamu)
And here it is.	(Naamu)
3490 Heh! My mother has *dalilu*."	(Naamu)
When she reached the *dado*,	(Naamu)
She did not even stop to greet the *dado* seller.	(Naamu)

---

[118] *Namugu* is powdered leaves of the baobab tree, used as an ingredient in sauces. *Nèrè: Parkia biglobosa*. The seeds are pounded into a paste that is fermented and rolled into balls to make a pungent condiment called *sumbala*.

She immediately reached for the *dado* and put some in	
her mouth.	(Naamu)
Jelimusoni Tunku Manyan Diawara said,	(Naamu)

3495 "Eh! You, girl, are impolite!   (Na-amu)

If you don't greet us first,

Don't touch our merchandise without asking us."   (Na-amu)

"Eeeh," said the girl, "I was so surprised!   (Naamu)

My mother told me to come to the market today to

see if I could find *dado*.   (Na-amu)

3500 She said she has gone so long without eating the old

things of Manden,

That her stomach hurts.   (Naamu)

Since we arrived here, we have not seen *dado*;

We have not seen anyone who sells it.   (Naamu)

I have just seen it and tasted it,   (Naamu)

3505 Because it is something we always used to have."   (Naamu)

Tunku Manyan Diawara said, "Who are you?"   (Naamu)

She asked, "Where do you come from?"   (Naamu)

"Ah, mother," replied Kolonkan,

"We come from Manden."   (Na-amu)

3510 "Who is with you here?"   (Naamu)

Kolonkan said, "I am here with my mother Sogolon

Wulen Condé,   (Na-amu)

With my elder brother Ma'an Sunjata,   (Naamu)

With my elder brother So'olon Jamori."   (Naamu)

"Aaah! You are the people we have come for!   (Na-amu)

3515 Our road has been good.   (Na-amu)

Let us go to your house."   (Na-amu)

[In an omitted passage, Kolonkan conducts the Mande delegation to her house for a joyful reunion with Sogolon. Manjan Bereté announces that they have been sent to ask Sogolon to return to Manden because her children are needed there. Sogolon explains that her sons are hunting in the bush and concerns herself with providing the customary hospitality to the guests.]

KOLONKAN FINDS MEAT FOR GUESTS FROM MANDEN

When they had given lodgings to the visitors from
    Manden, (Naamu)
Sogolon called Ma Kolonkan. (Naamu)
She said, "Ma Kolonkan, come here." (Naamu)
3520 When Ma Kolonkan came, (Naamu)
She said, "Go and look on the meat-drying rack. (Naamu)
See if there is any meat, (Naamu)
Because these people who came from Manden are
    hungry." (Naamu)
Ma Kolonkan went and looked. (Naamu)
3525 She came back and said, "Mother!" (Naamu)
She said, "There is no fresh meat." (Naamu)
"Eh," said Sogolon, "It will take a long time for the
    dried meat to cook." (Naamu)
Ma Kolonkan was very happy. (Naamu)
She had long since reached the age of marriage, (Naamu)
3530 And she knew that (Naamu)
These people would not leave her behind. (Naamu)
When she arrived in Manden, (Naamu)
She would be married. (Naamu)
She was feeling happy. (Naamu)
3535 She told her mother, "Just let things be for now." (Naamu)
Ma Kolonkan went out of the town. (Naamu)
She sniffed over here, (Naamu)
But she did not smell her brothers in that direction. (Naamu)
She sniffed over there, (Naamu)
3540 She did not smell her brothers in that direction either. (Naamu)
When she sniffed in the direction of the sunset, (Naamu)
She smelled her brothers there. (Naamu)
She went into her *dalilu, shuwe*! (Naamu)

	She went after her brothers.	(Naamu)
3545	When she went after them, she found	(Naamu)
	That they had killed a bushbuck[119] that day.	(Naamu)
	They had also killed a roan antelope.[120]	(Naamu)
	She opened the animals,	(Naamu)
	She removed some internal pieces.	(Naamu)
3550	She took them out of there,	(Naamu)
	And went home with them,	(Naamu)
	Without making any exterior cuts on the animal carcasses.	(Naamu)
	Ma Kolonkan brought home the meat.	(Naamu)
	She said, "Mother!"	(Naamu)
3555	She said, "I went after my brothers,	
	And I have brought back some fresh meat."	(Naamu)
	Her mother said, "Did you see them?"	(Naamu)
	"Oh," she said, "I saw the work they did."	(Naamu)
	Her mother said, "Did you not tell them that they should meet you in town?"	(Naamu)
3560	Kolonkan replied, "I thought you only wanted fresh meat."	(Naamu)
	Sogolon said, "Go and cut the meat into pieces,	(Naamu)
	Cook some and put it over rice,	(Naamu)
	And serve it to our guests."	(Naamu)
	Ma Kolonkan did that.	(Naamu)
3565	After saying that,	(Naaam)
	Ma So'olon Wulen Condé herself went out of the town.	(Naamu)
	She had agreed on a way of signaling Ma'an Sunjata,	(Naamu)
	And she went to do that.	(Naamu)
	Ma'an Sunjata heard her and said to his younger siblings,	(Naamu)
3570	"Let us butcher the game."	(Naamu)
	He said, "My mother has called me."	(Naamu)
	(You heard it?)	(Naamu)

[119] *Adenota Kob*, Maninka *sòn*.

[120] *Kobus defassa unctuosus*, Maninka *sensen*.

He said, "Mother has called me."	(Naamu)
He said, "Let us go home."	(Naaaa')
3575 The game they had killed,	(Naamu)
They went to butcher the roan antelope.	(Naamu)
They found that its internal organs were missing.	(Naamu)
They went to butcher the bushbuck.	(Naamu)
They found that its internal organs were missing.	(Naamu)
3580 Ma'an Sunjata said, "Manden Bori,	(Naamu)
Can God create an animal without internal organs?"	(Naaaa')
Manden Bori said, "Brother, that is not possible."	(Naamu)
He said, "Any animal created by God,	(Naamu)
They all have internal organs.	(Naamu)
3585 Let us butcher what remains of the animals."	(Naamu)
He said, "This was done by our little sister, Ma Kolonkan."	(Naamu)
He said, "I will not spare her;	
She will soon know that I am wearing trousers.	(Naamu)
Eh! Ma Kolonkan came from town,	(Naamu)
3590 Came and took the internal organs of the animals we killed,	(Naamu)
Without making any external cuts.	(Naamu)
Does she have to prove her female powers to us?	(Naamu)
We will not fail to see her in town."	(Naamu)
Everyone has his own *dalilu*.	(Naamu)
3595 That is why it is good for children of the same mother to be in harmony.	(Naaaa')

MANDEN BORI'S ANGER AND KOLONKAN'S CURSE

When the hunters returned,	(Naamu)
When Ma Kolonkan and Manden Bori made eye contact,	(Naamu)

	Eyes that often watch one another do not forget.	(Naamu)
	Ma Kolonkan ducked behind her mother.	(Naamu)
3600	Manden Bori paid no attention to the strangers,	(Naamu)
	He was ready to pounce.	(Naamu)
	Manden Bori stood his musket against the wall.	(Naamu)
	He passed through the gathering of people.	(Naamu)
	He started to run after Ma Kolonkan,	(Naamu)
3605	Chased her into the main house.	
	They did not stop there,	(Naamu)
	They ran into a cooking hut.	(Naamu)
	They did not stop there.	(Naamu)
	On their way back,	(Naamu)
3610	He tripped her and threw her down.	(Naamu)
	Her wrapper came loose.	(Naamuu)
	(You heard it?)	(Na-amu)
	Ma Sogolon Condé said, "Eh!	
	Manden Bori, you are envious."	(Naamu)
3615	Ma Kolonkan stood up.	(Naamu)
	She said, "You have shamed me in front of the Mande people.	(Naamu)
	I am the one who has been shamed.	(Na-amu)
	Could you not overlook this when I was acting in your own interest?"	(Naamu)
	Because of the power of Manden Bori's sorcery,	(Na-amu)
3620	The meat that had been fried and saved for them,	(Naamu)
	When he touched it, fresh blood began to flow from it.	(Naamuu)
	Ma Kolonkan said, "Are you still trying to embarrass me?	(Naamu)
	I was protecting your reputation.	(Na-amu)
	The Mande people came to you on the question of kingship.	(Naamu)
3625	Because you have done this to me,	(Naamu)
	The kingship will eventually be passed to your descendants,	(Naamu)
	But they will never agree on one ruler until the trumpet is blown."	(Naamu)

[In omitted passages, Tassey Condé digresses to explain how Kolonkan's curse still affects the descendants of Manden Bori in today's Hamana

region of Guinea, and what sacrifices would be required to remove the
curse. Tassey mentions a childhood experience with his famous father
Babu Condé toward the end of the colonial era, and describes how he,
Tassey, became the spokesman for the bards of Fadama. Reverting to his
story, Tassey describes Sogolon's great happiness at the prospect of her
sons returning to Manden. The next episode describes a momentous
family meeting of Sogolon and her children, in which the rarely men-
tioned brother Jamori plays a conspicuous part.]

SOGOLON BESTOWS THE LEGACY OF MAGHAN KONFARA

	Sogolon said to her children, "Let us go outside the town.	(Naamu)
	Let me give you my last words."	(Na-amuu)
3630	When she took them out of the town,	(Naaaam')
	They left the Mande delegation behind them in town.	(Naamuu)
	When they arrived outside the town,	(Naamu)
	Ma So'olon Condé said to Manden Bori,	(Naamu)
	"Break off that termite mound."[121]	(Naamu)
3635	When Manden Bori broke off the termite mound,	(Naamu)
	She said, "Pick some leaves."	(Naamu)
	He picked some leaves.	(Naamu)
	She said, "Lay them on the termite mound."	(Naamu)
	When they were laid on it,	(Naamu)
3640	She said, "Ma'an Sunjata, you sit on that."[122]	(Na-amu)
	She said, "Go and break off another termite mound."	(Naamu)

---

[121] As the youngest of the three sons, Manden Bori is ordered to perform the menial tasks.

[122] Of the many kinds of termite mounds (some well over 6 ft. tall), the type referred to here is c. 1–2 ft. high, shaped like a hard clay mushroom, and the larger ones could be used as stools.

He went and broke another one and put leaves[123] on it. (Naamu)

She said, "So'olon Jamori, you sit on that." (Naamu)

She said, "Go and break off another one." (Na-amu)

3645 Manden Bori broke off another termite mound and
      brought it. (Naamu)

She said, "You sit on that one yourself." (Na-amu)

The three men sat. (Naamu)

Ma So'olon Condé stood up. (Na-amu)

Ma Kolonkan stood behind her. (Naamu)

3650 Women would have sat during a hunter's ceremony,[124] (Na-amu)

But here they did not sit down. (Na-amu)

While they were standing, (Na-amu)

Ma So'olon Wulen Condé said, "Manden Bori!" (Na-amu)

She said, "What I say to you (Naamu)

3655 Is also for So'olon Jamori and for Ma'an Sunjata.[125] (Naamu)

The people of Manden have come for you. (Na-amu)

They are calling you to war." (Naamu)

(You heard it?) (Naamu)

"The reason for the bad relations between you and
      Dankaran Tuman, (Naamu)

3660 Dankaran Tuman plotted against you (Naamu)

Because he claimed you had usurped your father's
      legacy. (Na-amu)

When your father died, (Na-amu)

Dankaran Tuman saw the gold; (Naamu)

He saw the silver. (Naamu)

---

[123] For a soft and clean seat.

[124] If present at a hunters' meeting, women would be seated in the background. In this and the following line, the bard explains that mother and daughter remain standing because Sogolon is in charge of this solemn occasion.

[125] On occasions where oral communication must be precise, it is customary for an important speaker's words to be repeated several times by various people in the presence of the person addressed. When a *jeli* is available, the speaker addresses the bard, who repeats and validates what was just heard. At Sogolon's secret meeting, the youngest son serves to repeat and affirm her words (cf. Fakoli's remarks to Sunjata via Turama'an, l. 4273 ff., and to Sumaworo via Bala Fasali, l. 4423 ff.).

3665	He said your father also had *dalilu*.	(Naamu)
	But he did not know where to find the *dalilu*.	(Naamu)
	That is why he was plotting against you,	(Naamu)
	Thinking that when he killed you,	(Naamu)
	He would get the *dalilu*.	(Na-amu)
3670	My son,	(Naamu)
	You do not have the *dalilu*.	(Naamu)
	He does not have it either.	(Naamu)
	I have your father's *dalilu* here.	(Naamu)
	If you see that a man's *dalilu* went to the last wife,	(Na-amu)
3675	It is because I obeyed my husband."	(Naaaam')
	(You heard it?)	(Naamu)
	"When my husband was dying,	(Na-amu)
	He gave it to me,	(Naamu)
	That I should keep it safe for you,	(Naamu)
3680	That when you reached maturity,	(Naamu)
	I should give it to you.	(Naamu)
	Now that the Mande people have come for you,	(Na-amu)
	And you are going to war,	(Naamu)
	That is why I have brought you here,	(Naamu)
3685	To give you your father's *dalilu*.	(Naamuu)
	But what worries me	(Na-amu)
	Is that there are three things,	(Naamu)
	And they cannot be separated.	(Na-amu)
	They can only go to one person.	(Naaaam')
3690	Ah! There are three things,	(Naamu)
	There are three people.	(Na-amu)
	If the things should be divided up,	(Naamu)
	They would not benefit any of you.	(Na-amu)
	Since the Mande messengers have come,	
3695	They brought the name of your brother Ma'an Sunjata.	(Naamu)
	You must allow him to be given the three things.	(Naamuu)
	Because the three things,	(Na-amu)
	The sorcery horse,	(Naamu)
	The sorcery bow,	(Naamu)
3700	And the sorcery mask,	(Na-amu)

When you sit on the sorcery horse,	(Naamu)
You put on the sorcery mask,	(Naamu)
You take up the sorcery bow.	(Naamu)
Then you are ready for combat against all comers.	(Naamuu)
3705 If you mount the sorcery horse	(Na-amu)
Without carrying the sorcery bow,	(Naamu)
Without wearing the sorcery mask,	(Naamu)
While the horse is galloping,	(Naamu)
Somebody will strike you down.	(Na-amu)
3710 If you put on the sorcery mask	(Naamu)
Without carrying the sorcery bow,	(Naamu)
And you are not on the horse,	(Naamu)
You will see enemies,	(Naamu)
But you will not be able to kill them.	(Naamuu)
3715 If you take up the sorcery bow	(Naamu)
Without wearing the mask,	(Naamu)
And without being on the horse,	(Naamu)
What good is that?	(Naamu)
The three must go to one person.	(Na-amu)
3720 Allow them to be given to Ma'an Sunjata."	(Na-amu)

So'olon Jamori spoke.	(Naamu)
He said, "Manden Bori,	(Naamu)
Tell our mother that I do not agree to what she is saying.	(Naamu)
Ah! She herself says there are three things.	(Naamu)
3725 There are three of us.	(Naamu)
They are easily divided.	(Naamu)
Have you not heard the Mande people say	(Na-amu)
That if you cannot take your father's legacy on your head,	(Naamu)
You must at least drag part of it behind you?	(Naamu)
3730 If I cannot carry it, I will drag it behind me.	(Na-amu)
There are three of us,	(Naamu)
There are three things.	(Naamu)
Let her bring them out and divide them among us."	(Naamu)
Ma So'olon Condé said,	(Naamu)

3735	"Eh, So'olon Jamori my son!	(Na-amu)
	Eh, So'olon Jamori!	(Naamu)
	If you see that I brought you out of the town,	(Naamu)
	It is because of the fear of you alone.	(Na-amu)
	Did you not hear me say,	(Naamu)
3740	There are three things but they can only solve one	
	problem?	(Naamu)
	Will you not be agreeable?"	(Naamu)
	Manden Bori spoke.	(Na-amu)
	He said, "Big brother So'olon Jamori,[126]	(Naamu)
	Will you not have pity on our mother?	(Na-amu)
3745	What is worrying our mother,	(Naamu)
	This is it.	(Naamu)
	Let us agree to give it to brother So'olon Maghan."	(Naamu)

Ah!

Jamori said if Manden Bori did not take his mouth away
    from him,

3750	He would slap his ears.	(Na-amu)
	Manden Bori said, "You cannot slap my ears.	(Naamu)
	Why should you slap my ears for this?	(Naamuu)
	Aside from our father's legacy,	(Na-amu)
	Don't you know our brother can battle Soso without	
	our father's legacy?	(Na-amuu)
3755	And this mother of ours,	(Naamu)
	Who was it that used up her legacy?	(Naamu)
	You and I did.	(Naamu)
	My brother did not take part in that.	(Naamu)
	Our mother took her gold earring	(Na-amu)
3760	And gave it to the Somono ancestor Sansamba Sagado,	(Naamu)
	For a future day's river-crossing fee.[127]	(Naamu)
	She took her silver bracelet	(Naamu)
	And gave it to the Somono ancestor Sansamba Sagado,	(Naamu)

---

[126] In many variants of the epic, Sogolon's son Jamori is not mentioned at all, and the claim here that Manden Bori was the youngest of the three brothers is an especially rare detail.

[127] See l. 2481–88.

For a future day's river-crossing fee. (Naamu)

3765 The day that we left Manden, (Naamu)

When we arrived at the river, (Na-amu)

How many of us got into the canoe? (Naamu)

The price for crossing in the canoe was our mother's
    legacy. (Naamu)

Our mother went in the canoe, (Naamu)

3770 Our little sister got into the canoe, (Naamu)

You got into the canoe, (Naamu)

I got into the canoe. (Naamu)

Did my brother get in? (Naamu, he did not get in)

Hah! (Na-amu)

3775 Didn't my brother say he was not getting in? (Naamu)

Didn't my mother weep? (Naamu)

Didn't he say for us to go ahead and that he would
    follow? (Naamu)

By the time we got to the other side of the river, (Naamu)

Didn't we see my brother sitting down there? (Naamu)

3780 Wasn't that our father's legacy? (Na-amu)

The *dalilu* with which he crossed the river, (Naamu)

He can battle Sumaworo with that. (Naamuu)

But you say you will slap my ears? (Na-amu)

Why didn't you slap my ears on the riverbank?" (Naaaam')

3785 Ma'an Sunjata spoke. (Naamu)

He said, "Manden Bori, be quiet. (Na-amu)

Tell my mother that we will not quarrel. (Na-amu)

If you see somebody taking your friend's share of
    the sauce, (Naamu)

Your own sauce cannot satisfy you. (Na-amu)

3790 Does she think I will quarrel with this foolish person?" (Naamu)

He said, "I will never quarrel with So'olon Jamori over
    our father's legacy. (Na-amu)

Even if he says I should give it all to him, I will give
    him all. (Naamu)

Tell my mother to bring out the legacy. (Naamu)

But mother, (Na-amu)

3795	You have done two things for us.	(Naamu)
	We will never forget them.	(Na-amu)
	We were born in legitimacy.	(Naamu)
	It is because of our legitimacy that people have come to get us.	(Naamu)
	The second thing,	(Naamu)
3800	My father married fifty women and two women.	(Naamuu)
	Fifty wives!	(Na-amu)
	None of them gave birth to a child.	(Naamu)
	The other two wives,	(Naamu)
	Sansun Tuman Bereté,	(Naamu)
3805	She was the one who gave birth to Dankaran Tuman and Nana Triban.	(Na-amu)
	You!	(Naamu)
	You were the fifty-second wife.	(Naamu)
	Eh! Why did you acquire the legacy?	(Naamu)
	Because of your devotion.	(Naamu)
3810	If was for us that you did that.	(Naamu)
	I have trusted in God.	(Naamu)
	Even if you do not give me the legacy,	(Naamu)
	Because of your devotion,	(Naamu)
	I will vanquish Sumaworo.	(Na-amuu)
3815	Bring out the legacy."	(Naaaam')
	Ma So'olon Wulen Condé said, "I am pleased with that."	(Na-amu)
	She said, "Excuse me."	(Naamu)
	She pushed her hand into her abdomen.	(Naamu)
	When she did that, *ho*!	(Naamu)
3820	The *dalilu* fell out.	(Na-amu)
	When the three *dalilu* were piled together,	(Naamu)
	Ma'an Sunjata laughed.	(Naamu)
	Ma'an Sunjata spoke.	(Na-amu)
	He said, "So'olon Jamori. . . ."	(Naamu)
3825	Suddenly the mother began to shake.	(Naamu)
	So'olon Ma'an held his mother until the dizziness stopped.	(Na-amu)

When the dizziness left her eyes,   (Naamu)

Sunjata said, "Manden Bori,   (Naamu)

Tell our mother   (Naamu)

3830 That she should tell my younger brother   (Naamu)

That he should choose one of the things."   (Naamu)

He said, "Let So'olon Jamori choose one of the things. (Na-amu)

Aheh!" he said,

"My little brother and I will not quarrel over my

    father's legacy."   (Naamu)

3835 (You heard it?)   (Naamu)

So'olon Jamori said   (Na-amu)

That he chose the sorcerer's mask.   (Naamu)

They said, "Have you chosen that?"   (Naam . . .)

He said, "Ahuh, that is mine."   (Naamu)

3840 They said, "Very well, take it."   (Na-amu)

Sunjata said, "Manden Bori."   (Naamu)

He said, "Choose one."   (Naamu)

Manden Bori said, "I will not take a share in this

    legacy,   (Naamu)

I am holding your shirt-tail.   (Na-amu)

3845 So long as I hold your shirt-tail,   (Naamu)

Nothing will happen to me in the war with Soso. (Naamu)

If I take a share of the legacy,   (Naamu)

When you die, Sunjata,   (Naamu)

Your legacy will be mine anyway.   (Na-amu)

3850 It is my father's legacy,   (Naamu)

You are my father,   (Naamu)

And that belongs to you.   (Na-amu)

My share and your share, take them both."   (Naamu)

Ma'an Sunjata said, "Is that your word?"   (Naamu)

3855 Manden Bori said, "Ahuh.

The bow and the *mansaya*[128] that we are quarreling

    about,"   (Na-amu)

He said, "Neither I nor So'olon Jamori,   (Naamu)

---

[128] The bow and quiver were symbolic of Mande kingship (*mansaya*).

It is not our names that will be attached to this bow,
    but yours." (Na-amu)
(That is why, when people go outside town for a
    private meeting, they say:
3860 "Let us speak with the truth of Manden Bori.") (Naamu)

Manden Bori was the youngest of the brothers. (Naamuu)
The blessing of his brother remained with him. (Na-amu)
Ma So'olon Wulen Condé spoke. (Naamu)
She said, "Manden Bori, is that your word?" (Na-amu)
3865 She said, "Come here." (Naamu)
She took Manden Bori behind a bush. (Naamu)
She said, "Manden Bori, (Naamu)
You have honored me. (Naamu)
God will honor you. (Naamu)
3870 Manden Bori, (Na-amu)
You have honored me. (Naamu)
Nobody will ever dishonor you. (Na-amu)
The way So'olon Jamori acted,
If you act like that the Mande people will know your
    secret. (Naamu)
3875 If your rival knows your secret, he will vanquish you. (Na-amu)
You prefer the secret to be kept so I will not be
    shamed. (Naamu)
Come and let me give you my legacy. (Naamu)
My legacy is something that did not come from here at
    Nema. (Naamu)
This legacy of mine, (Naamu)
3880 It did not come from Manden. (Na-amu)
It came from Dò ni Kiri, the home of my brothers. (Naamu)
I will give that to you. (Naamu)
As long as the world exists, (Naamu)
Whenever things become difficult for you in the bush, (Naamu)
3885 When the genies trouble you, (Naamu)
When enemies threaten you, (Naamu)
If you look at this, (Naamu)
Saying, 'Ah, mother!' (Naamu)

God will spare you from that.	(Naamu)
3890 If you say 'Ah, genie!'	(Naamu)
God will spare you from that.	(Naamu)
If you say, 'Genie and man!'	(Naamu)
God will spare you from that."	(Naamu)
That is the brass ring the hunters wear on their fingers.	(Naamu)
3895 Some people call it "Genie and man."	(Naamu)
That is what So'olon Wulen Condé gave to Manden Bori.	(Na-amu)
She said, "This is your keepsake."	(Naaaam')
Manden Bori took the road and came back;	(Naamu)
They all came back to town.	(Naamu)

[In the next scene, Sogolon suddenly dies, and Sunjata tells Manden Bori to request a plot of land for her burial.]

THE BURIAL OF SOGOLON AND DEPARTURE FROM NEMA

3900 Manden Bori took the path to town.	(Na-amu)
He met with Faran Tunkara, the *mansa* of Nema.	(Naamu)
He said "Mansa,"	(Na-amu)
He said, "My brother says that I should come and tell you	(Naamu)
That my mother is dead.	(Naaaam')
3905 If you agree,	(Naamu)
You should give him land,	(Naamu)
So he can bury his mother."	(Na-amu)
Faran Tunkara had been unhappy to see the messengers come from Manden	(Na-amu)
Because from the time Sunjata arrived, up to that day,	(Naamu)

140

3910   He did not engage in any battle that was lost by the
      people of Kuntunya.   (Na-amu)
  Every campaign he went on, he returned with slaves.   (Naamu)
  But he could not detain Sunjata, because they came by
      their own choice.   (Na-amu)
  He wanted to start a quarrel so he could detain
      Sunjata.   (Naamu)
  Nema Faran Tunkara said, "Manden Bori,   (Na-amu)
3915   Go and tell your brother   (Naamu)
  That I, Nema Faran Tunkara, say   (Na-amu)
  That you did not bring a piece of land with you from
      Manden,   (Naamuu)
  That I am the owner of this place,   (Na-amu)
  That you should take your corpse,
3920   Load it on your head, and go to Manden.   (Naamu)
  Carry her back the same way you brought her.   (Naamu)
  Tell him that if you bury her in my land,   (Naamu)
  I will force her removal with gunpowder."   (Naamu)
  (You heard it?)   (Na-amu)

3925   He said, "Go and tell your brother that."   (Naamu)
  When Manden Bori was told this,   (Na-amu)
  He took the path back to report to Sunjata.   (Naamu)
  Manjan Bereté said, "What kind of man is this?"   (Naamu)
  He said, "Simbon, let me go and give him the
      message."   (Na-amu)
3930   "Eee," said Sunjata, "Leave it like that.   (Naamu)
  Huh, he will provide the land.   (Na-amu)
  Ah! I have spent twenty-seven years here.   (Naamu)
  I am in his army.   (Na-amu)
  And he says I should carry my mother's body back to
      Manden?   (Naamu)
3935   He will soon provide the land."   (Na-amu)
  He said to Manden Bori, "Go back and tell him,   (Naamu)
  That I, the son of the Condé woman, say,   (Naamu)
  That he should give me land,   (Naamu)
  So my mother can be buried there.   (Naamuu)

3940 Tell him it is I who say so."	(Na-amu)
When Tunkara was told this,	(Naaaam')
He said to Manden Bori,	(Naamu)
"I do not want ever to see you here again."	(Na-amu)
He said, "I have known from the time you first came here,	
3945 That you are a hotheaded man.	(Naamu)
Go and tell your brother	(Na-amu)
That I do not go back on what I said twice.	(Naamu)
Tell him I have no land for him here."	(Naamu)
Manden Bori went and told this to Ma'an Sunjata.	(Naamu)
3950 Manjan Bereté and Siriman Kanda Touré became angry.	(Na-amu)
They were all brave men.	(Naaaam')
They all had *dalilu*, and they all knew how to fight.	(Naamuu)
As they started to leave the house,	(Na-amu)
Ma'an Sunjata said, "You be patient and take your seats.	(Naamuu)
3955 He will soon provide the land."	(Naamu)
He took the path that went behind the house.	(Naamu)
He picked up a fragment of old clay pot,	(Naamu)
He picked up a piece of old calabash,	(Na-amu)
He picked up the feather of a guinea fowl,	(Naamu)
3960 He picked up a partridge feather.	(Na-amu)
He added a stick of bamboo to these.	(Naamu)
He put the things together, gave them to Manden Bori, and said,	
"Tell him that I say he should give me land to bury my mother in.	(Naamu, his land price)
If he needs a price for his land, this is his land price.	(Naamu)
3965 Let him agree for me to lay my mother in the ground."	(Na-amu)
When Faran Tunkara was given these things,	(Naamu)
Manden Bori said, "My brother says this is your land price,	
That you should agree to give him land."	(Naamu)
Faran Tunkara said, "Is this what you pay for land in your country?	(Na-amu)

142

3970	Huh, Manden Bori?	(Naamuu)
	I do not ever want to see you here again.	(Na-amu)
	Take these things and go away."	(Naamu)
	His *jeli* man was sitting there beside him.	(Naamu)
	He said, "He should not take those things away	
	from here.	(Na-amu)
3975	Heh! This is an important message that has been sent	
	to you."	(Naaaam')
	The *jeli* said, "Mba, when these people came,	(Naamu)
	Did I not tell you that you should kill Sunjata?	(Naamuu)
	Did you not say he had come to place himself in	
	your care,	(Na-amu)
	And that you must not do anything to him?	(Naamu)
3980	Ahuh! He has said something to you.	(Naamu)
	There is a message in these things that were sent.	(Naamu)
	If you do not understand it, I will tell you the	
	meaning."	(N . . .)
	Faran Tunkara said, "All right, tell me the meaning."	(Na-amu)
	The *jeli* said, "This piece of bamboo means	(Naamu)
3985	That you should give him land so he can bury his	
	mother in it.	(Naamu)
	If you do not give him land,	(Naamu)
	The Mande people will come and take it.	(Naamu)
	If they came and called him for the kingship,	(Na-amu)
	After he finishes fighting that war for Manden,	(Naamu)
3990	He will take the army of Manden,	(Naamu)
	He will bring it here to Nema.	(Naamu)
	He will break Nema like an old clay pot.	(Naamu)
	He will break Nema like a calabash.	(Naamu)
	This is the old calabash.	(Naamu)
3995	The guinea fowls and the partridges will take dust	
	baths in the ruins of Nema.	(Naamu)
	These are the feathers of those guinea fowls and	
	partridges.	(Naamu)
	You will not see anything growing here but weeds.	(Naamu)
	This piece of bamboo stick is from the ruins."	(Naamuu)
	(You heard it?)	(Na-amu)

143

4000 Mansa Tunkara was a good debater.	(Naamu)
All arguments went in his favor.	(Na-amu)
Faran Tunkara said, "I am right."	(Naamu)
The *jeli* said, "How can you be right in this?"	(Na-amu)
Faran Tunkara said, "The reason I am right,"	(Naamu)
4005 He said, "Since these people arrived here,	(Naamu)
This is their twenty-seventh year.	(Naamu)
Those three men are in my army.	(Naamu)
During that time, I lost no battles.	(Naamu)
They never cheated me,	(Naamu)
4010 They were never disobedient to me,	(Naamu)
I never had to discipline them for women trouble.	(Naamu)
But since their mother has died,	(Naamu)
Are they going to say the corpse is mine,	
Or will they just demand that I give them land?"	(Naamu)
4015 Everyone agreed that they should have observed the custom of saying,	
"This is your corpse."	(Naamu)
Faran Tunkara said, "Ah! This is why I refused."	(Naamu)
(You heard it?)	(Na-amu)
Faran Tunkara said, "Eh! If they are children,	(Naamu)
4020 A child that is well-mannered,	(Naamu)
They should have said that God has made this my opportunity,	(Naamu)
That this is my corpse.	(Naamuu)
Should they look for land to lay their mother in?	(Na-amu)
Did they show me any respect?"	(Naamu)
4025 Everybody said, "You are right!"	(Naamu)
Manjan Bereté himself came and said, "You are right."	(Naamu)
"Very well," he said, "If I am right,	(Naamu)
Give her to me and I will do the funeral."	(Na-amu)
The woman's funeral was conducted as if she were a man.	(Naamu)
4030 Cows were killed,	(Naamu)
Guns were fired,	(Naamu)
The special drum was beaten.	(Naamu)
This all started with Ma So'olon Wulen Condé.	(Na-amu)

	Then they took the body to the town of Kuntunya.	(Naamu)
4035	On Thursday,	(Naamu)
	They did the burial.	(Naamu)
	When they were finished with the burial,	(Naamu)
	Simbon asked permission to take his leave.	(Na-amu)
	He said, "I will leave tomorrow."	(Naamu)
4040	When it was said, "I will go tomorrow,"	(Na-amu)
	There was no problem of debt between them.	(Naamu)
	Faran Tunkara said, "Go with my blessing."	(Naamuu)
	He said, "I give you the road."	(Naamu)
	When Sunjata and his brothers had gone back to	
	their lodging,	(Na-amu)
4045	Faran Tunkara gathered his warriors.	(Naamu)
	He said, "I cannot accept this,	(Naamu)
	Because when he arrived here, he had no men of	
	his own.	(Na-amu)
	Prepare yourselves and go ahead of them.	(Naaaam')
	Go as far as the second village and wait for them	
	there.	(Na-amu)
4050	When they get there, you attack them.	(Naamu)
	Try to capture them.	(Naamu)
	When you bring them back, they will never leave	
	again."	(Na-amuu)
	When the warriors went,	(Na-amu)
	They passed one village and prepared their attack at	
	the second.	(Na-amu)
4055	When Sunjata and the others got there,	(Naamu)
	They were attacked.	(Naamu)
	So'olon Jamori remained there.	(Naamu)
	So'olon Jamori did not survive that!	(Na-amu)
	He did not live to reach Manden.	(Naamu)
4060	(You heard it?)	(Naamu)
	The three parts of the legacy were combined and given	
	to Simbon.	(Naamu)
	That is why if a *kamalen* of the Mansaré lineage becomes	
	selfish,	(Na-amu)

Do not bother to curse him.	(Naamu)
He will not have a long life.	(Naamuu)
4065 (You heard it?)	(Na-amu)
They got past that ambush,	
And the captives they took from among those	
warriors,	(Naamu)
Sunjata added them to his own troops.	(Naamu)

[The narrator explains that despite the ambush that killed So'olon Jamori, Faran Tunkara sent troops to support Manden's campaign against Soso, and Sunjata never attacked Nema. Claiming that he wants to notify Sumaworo of his return so he will not be accused of sneaking back into Manden, Sunjata stops in Soso. Sumaworo issues a series of warnings to Sunjata that he must not attack Soso. They engage in a traditional boasting contest, concluding with Sunjata's promise to return and Sumaworo's reply that he will be waiting.]

THE RETURN OF SUNJATA

Sunjata took the road toward home.	(Naamu)
4070 When they arrived at the edge of town,	(Na-amu)
The townspeople could hear *nege* music[129]	(Naamu)
Played by Jelimusoni Tunku Manyan Diawara.	(Naamu)
She sang to Manden:	(Na-amu)
"The *danama yirindi*[130] that we have been looking for,	
4075 He is at the edge of town.	
Come, let us go.	(Naamu)
For the sake of the Condé woman's son,	
Come, let us go.	(Naamu)

---

[129] *Nege* = iron; syn. *nkarinyan*: a rhythm instrument consisting of a notched iron tube, 7–8 inches long, held in one hand and scraped with a thin metal rod.

[130] Roughly translated as "super hero" (cf. l. 2408 for alternate usage).

The person that Manden was busy searching for,

4080   Known as So'olon Ma'an,   (Na . . .)

Come, let us go."   (Na-amu)

Sansamba Sagado crossed the river with his canoe
that day.   (Naamu)

He took the canoe onto the river without his pole or
paddle.   (Naamu)

As soon as he untied the canoe, it went *prrrr*, as if it
had a motor.   (Na-amu)

4085   It went straight to them.   (Naamu)

He said, "You will soon see the power of my *dalilu*."   (Na-amu)

He loaded them into the canoe,   (Naamu)

He struck the water.   (Naamu)

The canoe went *prrrr*, and landed on the riverbank in
Manden.   (Na-amu)

4090   Simbon stepped out.   (Naamu)

His fathers and brothers,   (Naamu)

The men of Manden, greeted him and embraced him.   (Naamu)

(You heard it?)   (Na-amu)

The shade tree under which he was welcomed,   (Naamu)

4095   Even up to tomorrow, that tree is still living.   (Na-amu)

Even up to tomorrow,   (Naamu)

That is the shade tree under which Sunjata was
welcomed.   (Na-amu)

When he was welcomed,   (Naamu)

Manden was jubilant,   (Naamu)

4100   Manden celebrated.   (Na-amu)

They named that place for being the town of
happiness,   (Naamu)

As being the town of rejoicing, *ko anyè nyani so*.[131]   (Naamu)

They named it Niani.   (Naamuu)

That is in Manden.   (Na-amu)

4105   (You heard it?)   (Naamu)

---

[131] This and the following line comprise a popular etymology (see n. 40).

When Manden welcomed them back,	(Na-amu)
They said, "Manjan Bereté, you are welcome;	(Naamu)
Siriman Kanda Touré, you are welcome;	(Na-amu)
Tunku Manyan Diawara, you are welcome;	(Naamu)

4110 Jonmusoni Manyan, you are welcome.[132]   (Na-amu)

You have brought a gift for Manden.	(Naamu)
You have found Simbon.	(Naaaam')
This one's father,	(Naamu)
We knew this would happen for the son of
Farako Manko Farakonken.	(Naamu, it's true)

4115 We knew this would happen for the son of the

Condé woman,	(Na-amu)
But Manden suffered while he was away.	(Na-amuu)
We have suffered.	(Naamuu)
Let him see for himself	(Na-amuu)
That so many of those he knew here have been killed.	(Naaaam')

4120 It was Sumaworo who did it.   (Naamu)

The only people left here are those with *dalilu*.	(Na-amu)
Those who had *dalilu*,	(Na-amu)
Sumaworo has caused even them to suffer."	(Naamu)
They said, "Since Sunjata has come,	(Naaaam')

4125 We carried out divination and swore oaths.   (Na-amu)

It was seen that only he could receive the legacy of
ancestor Mamadi Kani.[133]	(Naamu)
Therefore, since he has come,	(Naamu)
Heh! The Kulubali say,	(Naamu)
The Konaté say,	(Naamu)

4130 The Douno say,   (Naamu)

That you should take the legacy,	(Na-amuu)
So that Manden can be helped.	(Naamuu)
You have been called to take the legacy."	(Naamu)
"Take your legacy," *ko ila kè ta*, came to be spoken
as "Keita."	(Na-amu)

4135 (You heard it?)   (Naamu)

---

[132] The four people listed here are famous for their journey to find Sunjata and bring him back from exile (see p. 123).

[133] See l. 126.

CONDE PRIDE AND DESCENT FROM ADAMA

If you should hear Tontajontaniwooro,[134]

We are among them. (Naamu)

Fadama is part of that. (Na-amu)

Between me and God,

4140 Anybody who wants to take our *jeliya* from us,[135]

They will not succeed. (Naamu)

(You heard it?) (Na-amu)

We will not surrender *jeliya*. (Naamu)

(I say this to you.) (Na-amu)

4145 Tontajontaniwooro! (Naamu)

No one is older than us. (Na-amu)

No one ever defeated us. (Naamu)

We used to lend everyone support in the wars. (Na-amu)

Nobody could defeat us, (Naamu)

4150 Because we possess all the *dalilu* of war. (Na-amu)

A Condé *kamalen* might claim he has nothing, (Naamu)

That his mother did not give him anything. (Naamu)

I swear to God, a Condé *kamalen* did get something. (Na-amu)

(I say this to you.) (Naamu)

4155 There is no Maninka in the seven *jamanaw* (Naamu)

Who can boast of his patronage to us;[136] (Naamu)

---

[134] Lit. "sixteen slaves who carried the quiver," a mnemonic term referring to the oldest lineages of Manden who are recalled, not as "slaves," but as staunch supporters of Sunjata in unifying the ancient *jamanaw* into the basis of empire (for details, see Conrad 1992: 175–77).

[135] The following lines are related to the fact that, among the great numbers of Maninka people named Condé, only a few are bards, while the primary occupational identity of people named Kouyaté and Diabaté is *jeliya*, and the latter are generally recognized as the earliest *jeli* lineages, although Tassey denies this (l. 4146).

[136] *Jeliw* are customarily regarded as dependent on patrons whom they serve as orators and musicians (see Conrad and Frank 1995). Tassey boasts that the Condé

	There is nobody!	(Na-amuu)
	We fought against everyone,	
	Nobody defeated us.	(Na-amu, true, naamu)
4160	When you go to a certain place,	(Naamu)
	Tell the white people,	(Na-amu)
	Just as the Americans are among the white people,	(Naamu)
	So are the Condé among the blacks.	(Naamu)
	Let me tell you about that.	(Na-amu)
4165	We all descended from the same ancestor.	(Naaaam')
	Us?	(Naamu)
	The Americans?	(Naamu)
	We all descended from Isiaaka.	(Naamuu)
	Have you not heard, Mamady Kouyaté?	(Na-amu)
4170	It was ancestor Adama who sired us all.	(Naamu)
	Adama's first child was Sita![137]	(Naamu)
	Sita's child was Yunusi!	(Naamu)
	Yunusi's child was Hayayulu!	(Naamu)
	Hayayulu's child was Fariku!	(Naamu)
4175	Fariku's child was Iyada!	(Naamu)
	Iyada's child was Kanuga!	(Naamu)
	Kanuga's child was Lamaki.	(Naamu)
	Lamaki's child was Nuha.	(Naamu)
	He was brought by the flood;	(Na-amu)
4180	The whole world was destroyed.	(Naamu)
	When the water receded,	(Na-amu)
	Nuha sired three sons:	(Naamu)
	Sama,	(Naamu)
	Hama,	(Naamu)
4185	Yafisu.[138]	(Na-amu)

bards were never beholden to anyone, thus implying that their historical discourse is less influenced by such obligations.

[137] See notes 10 and 11. In addition to Adam, a few other names identified as Prophets in the Koran are recognizable in the following lines, including Seth (Ar. Shīth, Tassey's "Sita"), who was the third son of Adam and Eve, Luqman (Lamaki), and Noah (Nuha).

[138] In the Koran: Sām, Hām, and Yāfith; Bible: Shem, Ham, and Japheth.

Sama sired Shalihu,	(Naamu)
Shalihu sired Hamidu,	(Naamu)
Hamidu sired Salimaya,	(Naamu)
Salimaya sired Hajara.	(Naamu)
4190 It was Hajara who sired our ancestor Ibrahima.[139]	(Na-amu)
We are now *jelilu*.	(Naamuuu)
It was he who built the Kaaba.[140]	(Na-amu)
Nobody can surpass us.	(Naamu)
(I say this to you.)	(Na-amu)
4195 Ibrahima sired two sons:	(Naamu)
Ishmaila,	(Naamu)
And Isiaaka.	(Na-amu)
Ishmaila!	(Naamu)
The Nyiminyeme[141] descended from him.	(Naamu)
4200 Isiaaka!	(Naamu)
We the Condé descended from him.	(Naamu)
What have we to fear?	(Na-amuu)
(I say this to you.)	(Naamu)
If you say "scientist,"	(Naamu)
4205 Make the airplane fly!	(Naamu)
Make watches!	(Naamu)
Make radios!	(Naamu)
All scientists!	(Naamu)
They all came from the descendants of Isiaaka.	(Naamu)

[139] According to the *Shorter Encyclopaedia of Islam* (1965: 154), the names of Abraham's ancestors extend back through six ancestors to Shālikh (Tassey's "Shalihu"), and through two more generations to Sām (Shem) and Nūh (Noah).

[140] Ar. Ka'ba (lit. "cube"). A large, nearly cubic stone structure covered by a black cloth that stands in the center of the Grand Mosque of Mecca. This and a black stone inside its southeast corner represent a sanctuary consecrated to God. According to Islamic tradition, God ordered Adam to build the Ka'ba, and Gabriel taught him the pilgrimage ceremonies; it was rebuilt by Adam's son Seth, later rebuilt by Ibrāhīm (Abraham) and his son Ismā'īl (Ishmael), and then rebuilt many times thereafter (see Glassé 2001: 245).

[141] One of many names for the Prophet in Mande tradition. In Islamic belief, Abraham is the ancestor of Muhammed through Abraham's son Ishmael.

4210	Us!	(Na-amu)
	Us!	(Na-amu)
	You know that!	(Naamu)
	That is why	(Na-amu)
	The Frenchmen asked my father	(Naamu)
4215	If he could say anything about how Paris was built.	(Naamu)
	My father said, "Yes, I can say something.	(Na-amu)
	The history of Paris."	(Naamu)
	My father said,	(Naamu)
	"The Paris you ask about,	(Naamu)
4220	It was not built by Frenchmen!	(Naamu)
	It was not built by Americans!	(Na-amu)
	It was not built by the English!	(Naamuu)
	It was not built by the Russians!	(Naamu)
	None of them built it.	(Naamu)
4225	They only saw it appear.	(Naamuu)
	Because they only saw it appear, they called it Paris."	(Naamu)
	(You heard it?)	(Na-amu)
	If Paris was ever built by anyone, it was	
	God.	(Naamu, true, naamu)
	(I say this to you.)	(Na-amu)
4230	Do not be too concerned with blackness,	(Naamu)
	Do not be too concerned with whiteness,	(Naamu)
	Be more concerned with humanity.	(Naamuu)
	We are all equal.	(Na-amu)
	We all have life.	(Naaaam')
4235	We all go to sleep.	(Naamu)
	We all eat food.	(Na-amu)
	We all suckle breasts.	(Naamu)
	If you have come, you have come to your father's home.	(Naamu)

[In an omitted passage, Sunjata accepts the leadership of Manden, and an elaborate series of sacrifices is performed in preparation for war against Soso.]

FAKOLI REVEALS HIS POWER

While they were in a meeting,	(Naamu)
4240 A message from Sumaworo arrived,	(Naamu)
Saying that the Mande people must be told	(Na-amu)
That he has been expecting them for a long time.	(Mmmm)
He said it had been a long time since their *mansa*	
arrived.	(Na-amu)
He said he had not seen any messenger.	(Naamu)
4245 He said that since So'olon Ma'an was now there,	(Naamu)
He wanted to see those people	(Naamu)
On the fourteenth of the new month at Dakajalan.	(Na-amu)
The battle had now been set.	(Naamu)
(You heard it?)	(Mmmm)
4250 After that, So'olon Ma'an responded.	(Na-amuu)
As soon as he heard that message,	
He had them beat the signal drum.	(Naamu)
Everybody went to the council hall.	(Na-amu)
On their way to the council hall,	(Naamu)
4255 Fakoli was thinking, *frrrru!*	(Na-amuu)
They were going to march against Soso.	(Naamu)
But his mother and Sumaworo had suckled at the	
same breast.	(Na-amu)
He was wondering if he and the Mande people should	
attack Sumaworo.	(Naamu)
Fakoli's mind was on that.	(Na-amu)
4260 Fakoli thought, "As soon as I get to the council hall,	(Naamu)
I will ask the Mande people	(Na-amu)
If they will give me leave so I can go to Soso.	(Na-amu)
Let Manden come and fight both me and my uncle."	(Na-amu)
(You heard it?)	(Naaaam')

4265	When he got to the council hall,	(Naamu)
	That is what he told them.	(Naamu)
	But before he entered,	(Naamu)
	Manden Bori ridiculed him.	(Na-amu)
	When he was laughed at by Manden Bori,	(Naamu)
4270	Fakoli became angry.	(Na-amu)
	Whenever he entered the council hall,	(Naamu)
	Manden Bori would laugh at him.	(Naamu)
	That is why Fakoli said, "Turama'an,	(Na-amu)
	Let me say this to you.	(Naamu)
4275	Tell this to Simbon:	(Na-amu)
	Let him ask his younger brother why he laughs at me.	(Naaaam')
	Everyone enters the council hall,	(Naamu)
	But whenever I enter, Manden Bori laughs at me.	(Na-amu)
	Why does he laugh at me?	(Naamu)
4280	What have I done to him?"	(Naamuu)
	When Ma'an Sunjata was told this,	(Na-amu)
	Ma'an Sunjata said, "Stop laughing at him.	
	Did you not hear Fakoli saying that you are ridiculing him?"	(Naamu)
	He said, "Why are you laughing at him?"	(Naamu)
4285	"Ah," Manden Bori said, "Big brother,	(Naamu)
	Whenever the tall men enter the council hall,	(Na-amu)
	They duck their heads.	(Naamu)
	Fakoli is only one and a half arm-spans tall,	(Naamu)
	But when he enters, he also ducks his head.	
4290	That is what makes me laugh.	(Na-amu)
	Aaah, Fakoli, heh, heh."	(Naamu)
	Fakoli said, "Turama'an, tell Simbon	(Naamu)
	That he should tell his younger brother	(Naamu)
	That short Mande people can do things that tall Mande people cannot do."	(Na-amu)
4295	He said, "Let him believe that."	(Naamuu)
	When Manden Bori was told this,	(Na-amu)
	He said, "I will not believe that until I see it.	(Naamu)

	Do you believe that?	
	I do not believe that."	(Naamu)
4300	Fakoli picked up his goatskin rug.	(Naamu)
	He laid it in the center of the council hall.	(Na-amu)
	He sat down on the rug.	(Naamu)
	He waved his hand,	(Naamu)
	He grunted,	(Naamu)
4305	He grunted.	(Naamu)
	He raised the roof from the house.	
	The sun shone in on everybody.	(Na-amuu)
	He said, "Manden Bori, what about that?"	(Naamu)
	Manden Bori said, "You spoke the truth."	(Naamu)
4310	They were fair about crediting one another with	
	the truth;	(Na-amu)
	They were always in search of more *dalilu*.	(Naamuu)
	They asked Fakoli to replace the roof where it	
	belonged.	(Naamu)
	They said, "No tall man of Manden has done such	
	a thing."	(Na-amu)
	Then Fakoli placed his hand in the middle of the	
	council hall floor.	(Naamu)
4315	He crouched there and wrinkled his face,	(Naamu)
	Wrinkled his face!	(Naamu)
	Wrinkled his face!	(Naamu)
	He squeezed everyone against the wall.	(Na-amu)
	That was the beginning of the song "Nyari Gbasa."	(Naamu)
4320	They sang: "Fakoli, our arms will break,	(Na-amu)
	Fakoli, our heads will burst,	(Naamu)
	Fakoli, our stomachs will rupture."	(Na-amu)
	That song belongs to the Koroma family.	(Naamu)
	They said, "Stop that!"	(Na-amu)
4325	They said, "No tall man of Manden has done such	
	a thing."	(Naamu)

FAKOLI EXPLAINS HIS DILEMMA AND TAKES HIS LEAVE FROM MANDEN

After Fakoli did that, he spoke to the assembled elders.		(Naamu)
He said, "Turama'an, I say to you,		
I say to Simbon,		(Naamu)
I say to everyone in the council hall,		(Na-amu)
4330	Sumaworo has sent a message	(Naamu)
That we should meet at Dakajalan.		(Naamu)
My mother and Sumaworo,		(Naamu)
They are children of three Touré women.		(Na-amu)
For me to participate in Manden's attack on my uncle,		(Naamu)
4335	I would be shamed by that.	(Na-amu)
If you will permit me,		(Naamu)
Give me leave and let me go to Soso.		(Naamu)
Let them come and attack me and my uncle.		(Naamu)
Let them fight me and my uncle."		(Na-amuuu)
4340	Manden Bori refused to repeat this to Ma'an Sunjata,	
But Ma'an Sunjata heard about it anyway.		
He said, "Manden Bori, have I not told you?		(Na-amu)
Fakoli is right.		(Naamu)
You and I have uncles whose home is Dò ni Kiri.		(Naamu)
4345	What if it were said that Dò ni Kiri would be attacked?	(Na-amu)
Would you and I stay here?"		(Naamu)
Manden Bori said, "Would anyone dare to do that?"		(Naamu)
"Oh," said Sunjata, "There you are.		
If Fakoli says he is going to help his mother's kinsman,		(Na-amu)
4350	Leave him alone and let him go."	(Naamu)
"But," said Sunjata, "Fakoli,		(Na-amu)
You have done well for Manden.		(Naaaam')

The nine invasions of Manden that are talked about, (Na-amu)

And the nine efforts to rebuild it, (Naamu)

4355 You did well in all of that. (Na-amu)

Therefore, if you should say that (Naamu)

You are going to help your uncle, (Naamu)

Very well. (Na-amu)

But if we meet during the battle, (Naamu)

4360 There is no brotherhood, (Naamu, true, naamu)

There is no friendship. (Na-amu)

It must not be said that so-and-so is ungrateful. (Naamu)

When the shooting starts, that is not in the
gunsmoke. (Naaaam')

That is all I have to say." (Na-amu)

4365 Fakoli said, "Bisimillahi." (Naamu)

(You heard it?) (Na-amu)

Fakoli returned to his house for the night. (Naamu)

In the morning, he bathed in the water of his seven
medicine pots. (Naamu)

He took his battle-axe and hung it on his shoulder. (Naamu)

4370 He brought out his horse and mounted it. (Na-amu)

His groom, Nyana Jukuduma,[142] was with him. (Naamu)

His wife, Keleya Konkon, (Naamu)

He lifted her up and sat her behind him. (Na-amu)

He took the ends of his scarf and tied them together. (Naamu)

4375 He said, "Because I know the kind of man my uncle is, (Naamu)

He might wait for me on the road."[143] (Naamuu)

While Fakoli was getting ready to leave, (Naamu)

Another message came from Sumaworo, (Na-amu)

That Fakoli should be told (Naamu)

4380 That Sumaworo had been informed of Fakoli's plan to
go and help him, (Naamu)

And that he must not go to Soso. (Na-amu)

[142] Fakoli's groom, a slave that cared for his horse.
[143] To ambush him.

(You heard it?) (Naaaam')

Sumaworo said he had been informed that if Fakoli
  went to Soso,

And if the Mande people should succeed in conquering
  him, (Naamu)

4385 That they would replace Sumaworo with Fakoli. (Na-amu)

He said that if Fakoli went to Soso, (Naamu)

His feet would bring his head. (Naaaam')

The Mande people said if Fakoli went, (Naamu)

They would cut off his head. (Na-amu)

4390 The Soso people said if he went, (Naamu)

His feet would bring his head. (Na-amu)

Fakoli laughed, (Naamu)

"I will not die for Sunjata,

I will not die for Sumaworo." (Na-amu)

4395 Even up to tomorrow, that expression is often quoted. (Naamu)

He said, "Go and tell my uncle that I will soon be
  there. (Na-amu)

If I really plan to do what he said, (Naamu)

Then he will succeed with what he threatens to do
  to me. (Na-amu)

But if that is not my intention, (Naamu)

4400 I will go to Soso today. (Naamu)

Tell him to get ready." (Na-amuu)

[In an omitted passage, Sumaworo deploys soldiers to intercept Fakoli
and kill him, but Fakoli makes himself and his companions invisible
and arrives unscathed at the gates of Soso.]

FAKOLI FINDS TROUBLE IN SOSO

When Sumaworo was told that Fakoli came alone, (Naamu)

With only him, his wife, and his slave, (Naamu)

Sumaworo told Bala Fasali,[144] "Take the *bala* and welcome

    my nephew." (Naamu)

4405 He took the *bala*, (Naamu)

And that was the beginning of the song "Janjon":[145] (Na-amu)

"Eh, Fakoli! (Naamu)

You became a son. (Na-amu)

If death is inevitable, (Naamu)

4410 A formidable child should be born. (Na-amu)

The Mande people said (Naamu)

That if you come, they will wait for you on the road. (Naamu)

The people of Soso said (Naamu)

That if you come, your feet will bring your head. (Na-amu)

4415 Knowing that, you still had no fear. (Naamu)

If death is inevitable, (Naamu)

A formidable child should be born." (Na-amu)

"Janjon" belonged to the Koroma family. (Naamu, it's true)

Sumaworo stood up and raised his elephant tail

    in salute. (Naamu)

4420 He was welcoming Fakoli. (Na-amu)

Fakoli came and sat down. (Naamu)

He explained why he had come. (Naamu)

He said, "Bala Fasali, you take part in this.[146] (Na-amu)

Let Sumaworo be a part of this. (Naamu)

4425 If you see that I have come, (Naamu)

Sumaworo has done many things. (Na-amu)

If you see that I was invisible, (Naamu)

I came in good faith. (Na-amu)

[144] An unusual pronunciation of this famous bard's name, which is usually given as Bala Fasaké, or a variant thereof. He is related to Nyankuman Duga, ancestor to the Kouyaté lineage of bards.

[145] One of the oldest and most famous songs of Manden, said to have been originally composed for Fakoli, but in later times played to honor any distinguished personage.

[146] Custom dictated that the dignitary, in this case Fakoli, would speak to the *jeli*, who would then add weight to the message by repeating it to the person addressed (see n. 125).

The three Touré women gave birth to two of you,

4430 My mother and Sumaworo. (Naamu)

Since a war has been declared, (Na-amu)

I have thought about my mother. (Naamu)

If my mother had been a man, (Naamu)

The war would have come to her as well as to

Sumaworo. (Naamu)

4435 That is why I decided to be here in place of my

mother. (Na-amu)

That is the reason I came. (Naaaam')

I have come to him through the will of God. (Naamu)

Let us unite. (Naamu)

The war that is coming, (Naamu)

4440 Let us fight it together." (Na-amu)

Sumaworo was pleased. (Naaaam')

Sumaworo said, "Bala Fasali, I say this to you,

I say this to Fakoli. (Naamu)

Tell him that I appreciate his words. (Na-amu)

4445 I am well pleased, (Naamu)

I am glad." (Naamu)

Fakoli came and met Sumaworo's wives. (Naamu)

Three hundred wives, thirty wives, and three wives. (Naamuu)

Fakoli's only wife was Keleya Konkon. (Na-amu)

4450 What did Sumaworo say then? (Naamu)

He said, "Fakoli has come at the time when (Naamu)

The oracle Nènèba says that I am going to fight a war, (Na-amu)

That the sacrifice for that is (Naamu)

Three hundred dishes, thirty dishes, and three dishes. (Na-amu)

4455 That is what I want to be prepared the day after

tomorrow, on Friday. (Naaaam')

If we are allies, let Fakoli be told about that." (Na-amu)

Then Fakoli said, "That is a good thing. (Naamu)

Since I have come to take the place of my mother, (Na-amu)

The one bowl that my mother would have provided, (Naamu)

4460 My wife will cook that." (Naamu)

When they heard that, the Soso women said, "*Paki!*" (Na-amu)

They said, "The Soso women and the Mande woman,

We will soon see how they cook." (Naamu)

That was insulting to Keleya Konkon. (Na-amu)

4465 Keleya Konkon said, "I have said that I would build my

fire near theirs. (Naamu)

Go and look for a pot and bring it to me. (Na-amu)

Since they have said that, (Naamu)

They will learn that Manden also has kitchens." (Naamu)

(You heard it?) (Na-amu)

4470 "They will realize that Manden has kitchens." (Naamu)

She told her husband to find a cooking pot. (Na-amu)

Her husband found a cooking pot and gave it to her. (Naamu)

Sumaworo's three hundred dishes and thirty dishes and

three dishes, (Naamu)

Among them were beans, (Naamu)

4475 Among them was rice, (Naamu)

Among them was fonio, (Na-amu)

Among them was cereal paste, (Naamu)

Among them was millet wafers, (Naamu)

Among them was wheat meal, (Na-amu)

4480 Among them was cassava, (Naamu)

Among them was porridge, (Naamu)

All of those were among the three hundred dishes. (Na-amu)

Fakoli's wife said, "Look for a cooking pot. (Naamu)

Bring rice, (Na-amu)

4485 Bring pounded cassava, (Naamu)

Bring fonio. (Naamu)

If God agrees, (Naamu)

Whatever the consequences, (Naamu)

The *jelilu* will bear witness to this." (Na-amu)

4490 She set her one pot on the fire. (Naamu)

Those who were cooking rice, (Naamu)

When they were putting rice in their pots, (Naamu)

She would put rice in her one pot, (Naamu)

Then she would sit down. (Na-amu)

4495 Those who were cooking the fonio, (Naamu)

When they were putting fonio in their pots, (Naamu)

She would put the fonio in her one pot, (Naamu)

Then she would sit down. (Naamu)

Those who were cooking *monie*,[147] (Naamu)

4500 As they were rolling the *monie* balls, (Naamu)

Keleya Konkon was also rolling *monie* balls. (Naamu)

When they were putting *monie* balls in their pots, (Naamu)

She would put the *monie* balls in her one pot, (Na-amu)

Then she would take her seat. (Naamu)

4505 Those who were baking *takura*,[148] (Naamu)

When they had finished rolling the *takura* balls, (Naamu)

As they were putting the *takura* balls in their pots, (Na-amu)

She would make *takura* (Naamu)

And put it in her one pot, (Naamu)

4510 Then she would sit down. (Na-amu)

Everything the Soso women put in their individual

pots, (Naamu)

She put all the same things in her one pot. (Naamu)

When the women started dishing out rice, (Naamu)

She would take her rice bowl, (Naamu)

4515 She would dish out her rice. (Naamu)

When the women started dishing out the fonio, (Naamu)

She would take her fonio bowl, (Naamu)

She would dish out her fonio from the same pot, (Naamu)

And put it into the fonio bowl. (Naamu)

4520 Three hundred things, (Naamu)

And thirty things, (Naamu)

Were produced by Sumaworo's wives. (Naamu)

Three hundred things, (Naamu)

Thirty things, (Naamu)

4525 And three things, (Naamu)

---

[147] A millet porridge made with small balls of millet flour flavored with tamarind or lemon.

[148] A millet cake made with five balls of soaked millet flour and baked or steamed in a clay pot buried in the ground; one of the preferred foods for sacrifice or alms-giving.

Were produced by Fakoli's wife in one pot, (Naamuu)
So the scandalmongers would not get the best of her. (Na-amuu)
(You heard it?) (Naamu)

The scandalmongers went and told Sumaworo, (Na-amu)
4530 "Did we not tell you (Naaaam')
That Fakoli came to take your place? (Na-amu)
You have three hundred wives and thirty wives and
    three wives. (Naamu)
You have produced three hundred dishes, thirty dishes,
    and three dishes. (Naamu)
Your nephew has only one wife, (Naamu)
4535 But he has also prepared three hundred dishes, thirty
    dishes, and three dishes. (Naamu)
In fact, his dishes are bigger than yours. (Na-amu)
Everything that you produced, he also produced. (Naamu)
He came to take your place. (Naamuu)
If you think this Fakoli business is not serious, (Na-amu)
4540 He will take Soso away from you even before you go
    to war." (Naamu)
Sumaworo said "Huh?" (Na-amu)
He said "Oho." (Naamu)
He assembled his people. (Naamu)
The scandalmonger who brought the gossip to him, (Na-amu)
4545 Sumaworo told him (Naamu)
That he should go and call Fakoli. (Naamu)

The scandalmonger went and stood on the road. (Na-amu)
He did not go to where Fakoli was, (Naamu)
Then he went back to Sumaworo. (Naamu)
4550 He came and said, "I have called him,"
But he had not gone to Fakoli. (Na-amu)
Much time passed without Fakoli coming to see
    Sumaworo. (Naamu)
When Sumaworo called someone, (Naamu)
He expected the person to arrive one minute after the
    messenger returned. (Na-amu)

4555	"Ah!" He said,	
	"Did you not see my nephew?"	(Naamu)
	The scandalmonger said, "I saw him."	(Na-amu)
	"Ah, did you not call him?"	(Naamu)
	"I called him."	(Naamu)
4560	"All right, go and tell him I am waiting for him."	(Naamu)
	The scandalmonger went again and stood on the road.	(Naamu)
	He came back and told Sumaworo,	(Naamu)
	He said, "I have called him."	(Naamu)
	Much time passed and Fakoli did not appear.	(Naamu)
4565	Sumaworo sent another person.	(Naamu)
	He said, "You go and tell Fakoli	(Naamu)
	That I am waiting for him."	(Naamu)
	Sumaworo was very angry.	(Naamu)
	The messenger went	(Naamu)
4570	And told Fakoli.	(Naamuu)
	He said, "Fakoli,	(Naamu)
	This is the third time you have been called,	(Naamu)
	But you did not come.	
	Who do you think you are?"	(Naamu)
4575	Fakoli said "Me?"	(Naamuu)
	Was I called three times?"	(Na-amu)
	"Yes, the message came and came again."	
	Fakoli said "Me?"	(Naamu)
	He said, "Mba, I refuse."	(Naamu)
4580	That messenger ran back to tell Sumaworo,	(Naamu)
	"Your nephew refuses to come."	(Na-amu)
	Sumaworo said, "*Paki!*"	(Naamu)
	He said, "I have heard it.	(Naamu)
	You tell me, Sumaworo, 'I refuse'?"	(Na-amu)
4585	When the last messenger had returned from Fakoli's place,	(Naamu)
	Fakoli put on his hat with three hundred bird's heads.	(Naamu)
	He put his axe on his shoulder,	(Naamu)
	He tied his headband around his head,	(Naamu)
	Because he knew there was going to be a falling-out.	(Na-amu)
4590	When Fakoli was on his way,	(Naamu)

When they saw Fakoli coming,	(Na-amu)
Sumaworo stood up from his royal seat.	(Naamu)
He said, "Fakoli, am I the one to whom you said,	
'I refuse'?"	(Naamu)
Fakoli said, "I refuse."	(Naamu)

4595   Fakoli believed that to explain himself to Sumaworo
      would be cowardly.   (Na-amu)

Sumaworo said, "Am I the one to whom you said,	
'I refuse'?"	(Naamu)
Fakoli said, "I refuse."	(Na-amu)
He said, "Why?"	(Naamuu)
He said, "I refuse."	(Na-amu)

4600   "Ah, very well."   (Naamu)

Sumaworo said, "What they told me is the truth."	(Na-amu)
He said, "You claim that you came to help me.	
You have not come to help me."	(Naamu)
He said, "You know what you came for.	(Na-amu)

4605   I have three hundred wives, thirty wives, and three
      wives.   (Naamu)

I have prepared three hundred dishes, thirty dishes, and	
three dishes.	(Na-amu)
You have only one wife.	(Naamu)
You also produced three hundred dishes, thirty dishes,	
and three dishes.	(Naamu)
Did you come to help me?	(Na-amu)

4610   Were you told that your head and my head are
      equal?   (Naamu, true, naamu)

But your wife, with whom you are boasting,	(Na-amu)
I was the one who gave you your mother's	
namesake.[149]	(Naamu)
I am taking her back.	(Naamu)
If you boast about anything,	(Na-amu)

4615   It means you have what you are boasting about.   (Naamu)
    The namesake of Kosiya Kanté that you have,   (Na-amu)

---

[149] Fakoli's mother was Kosiya, so his wife Keleya was not exactly her namesake.

She is my daughter.[150]	(Naamu)
I am now taking her back."	(Na-amu)

	Fakoli said, "Ah!	(Naamu)
4620	Uncle, have things come down to that level?	(Naamu)
	Has the dispute between us come to the point of taking	
	back a wife?	(Na-amu)
	Oooh, in fact I do not even want her now,	(Naamu)
	Until after the battle smoke has settled.	(Na-amu)
	Since you have sent a message to the Mande people	(Naamu)
4625	That we must meet at Dakajalan,	(Naamu)
	I do not want to keep Keleya Konkon now."	(Na-amu)
	He brought out his blanket and tore off a strip, *prrrr!*	(Naamu)
	He threw it to Keleya Konkon and told her to use it for	
	a mourning veil.	(Na-amu)
	He said, "If I defeat your brother,[151]	(Naamu)
4630	I will not marry you again until I marry you in	
	gunsmoke.	(Na . . . naamu)
	I am returning to Manden."	(Na-amu)
	He turned his back on Keleya Konkon.	(Naamu)
	He gave the tail of his horse to Nyana Jukuduma.[152]	(Naamu)
	They took the road to Manden.	(Naamuu)
4635	The diviners were still praying to God.	(Na-amu)

When Fakoli got back to Manden,	(Naamu)
He went and stood at the door of the council hall.	(Naamu)

[150] Family relationships among Manding peoples are perceived on several levels, or "paths." Keeping in mind that this is the storyteller's viewpoint, this is probably meant in the sense that the wife Sumaworo provided for Fakoli was a classificatory "daughter" of Sumaworo. In Manding societies, the children of one's cousins are considered to be one's own children.

[151] In the same way that Keleya Konkon could be a classificatory "daughter" of Sumaworo (n. 150), she could also be a classificatory "sister." Indeed, on one path a person can be classified as one's sibling, while on another path the same person can be referred to as one's father, uncle, mother, or aunt. This reflects the polygynous practice of men marrying wives of the same age as some of their children (Kassim Koné, pers. com. 2004).

[152] The slave would run behind the horse, hanging onto its tail.

He said, "Simbon, my uncle and I have quarreled.

He has taken my wife from me. (Na-amu)

4640 I will not take back Keleya Konkon until I do it in

gunsmoke." (Naamu)

"Huh," Ma'an Sunjata laughed, (Na-amu)

Manjan Bereté laughed, (Naamu)

Siriman Kanda Touré laughed. (Naamu)

They said, "Manden is now complete." (Na-amu)

4645 They said they put their trust in Turama'an. (Naamu)

If you hear that they put their trust in Turama'an

instead of Fakoli,[153] (Naamu)

It is because, at that time, Fakoli had gone to help

his uncle. (Na-amu)

The trust was placed during the time he was gone. (Naamu)

When Fakoli came back, (Na-amu)

4650 He did not settle in Manden. (Naamu)

He went and stepped on the threshold of the council

hall. (Naamu)

He said, "Simbon, (Naamu)

My uncle and I have quarreled. (Naamu)

He has taken my wife from me, (Naamu)

4655 But I do not want a wife from Soso. (Naamu)

I do not want a wife from Manden. (Naamu)

I do not want a wife from Negeboriya. (Na-amu)

Since he has taken my wife from me, (Naamu)

Send a message to your uncles in Dò ni Kiri, (Na-amu)

4660 Let them give you your nephew wife.[154] (Naamu)

You give her to me. (Naamu)

Before we go to the battle at Dakajalan, (Naamu)

---

[153] Turama'an had acquired a leadership position or military command that was formerly held by Fakoli.

[154] In Maninka and Bamana society, it is claimed, both jokingly and seriously, that it is the uncle's duty to give his nephew a wife, the so-called "nephew wife." The obligation of this uncle–nephew bond is implied in the Bamana proverb: "When your uncle fails to give you a wife, he is no longer your uncle but your mother's brother" (Kassim Koné, pers. com. 2003).

Let me have that woman. (Naamu)

Then any work that I do, (Naamu)

4665 It will not be said that it was because of the loss

    of my wife. (Na-amu)

If I do not get a wife, (Naamu)

Whatever work I do on the battleground,

They will say it is because if I did not do it,

I would remain a bachelor. (Na-amu)

4670 Let me have a wife. (Naamu)

Let your nephew wife be with me before we leave

    for the war." (Naamu)

Ma'an Sunjata sent a message to Dò ni Kiri. (Na-amu)

When the message reached our ancestor, (Naamu)

He took Ma Sira Condé (Na-amu)

4675 And gave her to a messenger (Naamu)

Who brought her to Ma'an Sunjata, (Naamu)

As his nephew wife. (Naamu)

Ma'an Sunjata in his turn took her (Naamu)

And gave her to Fakoli. (Naamu)

4680 At that time, Fakoli was feeling bitter. (Naamu)

He had refused to live at Negeboriya, (Naamu)

He had refused Manden, (Naamu)

He had refused Soso. (Naamuu)

He had gone and built his own hamlet, (Na-amu)

4685 Where he remained until time for the battle at

    Dakajalan. (Naamu)

It was there that Sira Condé was brought to him. (Na-amu)

Everyone said, "Eeeh, Fakoli is bitter! (Naamu)

He has refused. (Naamu)

He has built his own hamlet." (Naamu)

4690 That hamlet became Bambugu. (Naamuu)

That Bambugu is in Manden. (Na-amu)

There he remained. (Naamuu)

A VISIT TO KAMANJAN IN SIBI

Sunjata dressed in his ritual attire.	(Na-amu)
He said, "My mother told me	(Naamu)
4695 That when I come to Manden,	(Na-amu)
That her first blessing	(Naamu)
Was that God should help me be on good terms	(Naamu)
With any elder whose *dalilu* is greater than mine.	(Naamu)
Fakoli, since you have settled,	(Na-amu)
4700 I say to you,	
I say to Turama'an,	(Naamu)
I say to Kankejan,	(Na-amu)
I say to Tombonon Sitafa Diawara,	(Naamu)
I say this to all the Simbons,	(Na-amu)
4705 Give me sixty men;	(Naamu)
Let me go to greet Kamanjan.	(Na-amu)
I must not go to war without doing that.	(Naamu)
Let me go and greet Kamanjan,	(Na-amu)
Because I esteem him above all other elders."	(Naamu)
4710 There was a distance of age between him and Kamanjan,	
Because Kamanjan and his father Maghan Konfara had lived at the same time.	(Naaaam')
Kamanjan never committed a shameful deed in his entire life.	(Naaaam')
Anybody who commanded an army would seek the advice of Kamanjan.	(Naamu)
Sunjata said, "Let us go and greet Kamanjan."	(Naaaam')
4715 He took sixty men and went to salute Kamanjan.	(Naamu)
The place where he went to greet Kamanjan	(Naamu)
Is the battle site near Sibi mountain, called Kalasa.	(Naaaam')
They used to light torches for meetings at night,	(Naamu)

	Night meetings.	(Naaaam')
4720	Kamanjan used to light torches,	(Naamu)
	And hold a torchlit meeting.	(Naaaam')
	When the meeting was crowded with people,	(Naamu)
	The special ones he had selected,	
	Those *kamalenw* of whom he had been told,	
4725	"This one is outstanding in such-and-such a town,	(Naaaam')
	That one is outstanding in such-and-such a town."	(Naamu)
	After choosing those people, they would extinguish	
	the torches.	(Naaaam')
	Sunjata came at such a time.	(Naamu)
	Sunjata arrived when Kamanjan was having a meeting,	
4730	And the torches were aflame.	(Naaaam')
	Sunjata took his hand and extinguished all the torches.	(Naamu)
	After they were all extinguished,	(Naaaam')
	He had a thing that he used, *kan!*	(Naaaam')
	Everything was illuminated.	(Naamu)
4735	It was there that they said he lit his own torch.	(Naaaam')
	They said, "As soon as Sunjata put out the torches,	
	He lit his own torch."	
	Its light was as powerful as the light from a pressure	
	lamp.	(Naamuu)
	That little town became known as	(Naamu)
4740	The town where Sunjata extinguished the torches.	
	It is near Tabon and is called Kalasa.	(Naamu)
	It is on the Bamako road.	(Na-amu)
	It is populated by the Konaté.	(Naaaam')
	That Kalasa is where they held that meeting.	(Naamu)
4745	(You heard it?)	
	After that, Sunjata approached Kamanjan and saluted	
	him.	(Naamu)
	He explained the purpose of his visit.	(Naamu)
	He said, "I left from your place with my mother."	(Naaaam')
	He said, "Now I have returned."	(Naamu)
4750	Kamanjan said, "Simbon!"	(Naaaam')

Have you come?"

He said, "I have come." (Naamu)

"Ah, are you the one that Manden sent for against

Sumaworo?" (Naaaam')

Sunjata said, "Ahuh, father Kamanjan." (Naamu)

4755 He said, "That is why I have come to greet you." (Naaaam')

He said, "When you inform a person that you are

leaving on a trip,

The person you informed must be greeted upon

your return." (Naamu)

Kamanjan said, "Sunjata, what *dalilu* did you bring

with you? (Naaaam')

Hm! Sumaworo is a bad one. (Naamu)

4760 Have you not heard his praises?:

'Transforms in the air,

Sumaworo, (Naaaam')

Transforms on the ground,

Sumaworo. (Naamu)

4765 Manden *pi-pa-pi*,

Whirlwind of Manden, (Naaaam')

Kukuba and Bantamba,

Nyemi-Nyemi and Kambasiga,

Sege and Babi'?" (Naamu)

4770 Sunjata said, "Father Kamanjan, I know that." (Naaaam')

Kamanjan said, "What kind of *dalilu* did you bring?" (Naamu)

He said, "Ah, father Kamanjan,

That is why I have come to greet you, (Haaaa)

To come and tell you my thoughts." (Naamu)

4775 Kamanjan said, "We whom you first met here,

I have become old. (Naaaam')

I cannot go to war again." (Naamu)

He said, "No one else can do it either. (Naaaam')

All those who have attacked Sumaworo have been

defeated. (Naamu)

4780 It was Manden that made it possible for him to become

what he is. (Naaaam')

It was a mistake to give him the four *jamanaw*.[155] (Naaaam')

Not satisfied with that, he wants to add Manden to
    Soso. (Naamu)

That is what we must fight to avoid." (Naaaam')

When Kamanjan said, "Ah!" (Naamu)

4785 They were under the *balansan* tree,[156] (Naaaam')

The tree that in Manden is called *balansan*. (Naamu)

As they were there under the *balansan* tree, (Naaaam')

When Kamanjan said, "Ah!" (Naamu)

The *balansan* flipped upside down onto its top
    branches. (Aaaaa)

4790 Sunjata also said, "Ah!" (Naamu)

The *balansan* flipped back over onto its
    roots. (It's true, *binani tinima*)

(You heard it?) (Naamu)

Kamanjan said, "Ah!" (Naaaam')

The *balansan* flipped over onto its top branches. (Naamu)

4795 Before Sunjata could say, "Ah,"

His sister said, "Big brother, (Naaaam')

This is not what my mother told you to do. (Aaaaa)

Leave it to him. (Naamu)

Our mother prayed that you would be blessed (Naamu)

4800 By an elder with *dalilu* stronger than yours. (Aaaaa)

He is trying to demonstrate his *dalilu* for you.

If you show him your own,

He will not give you anything. (Naamu)

Leave it to him,

4805 And when he is satisfied, he will flip the tree back. (Aaaaa)

If you get this one's *dalilu* and add it to what you
    already have, (Naamu)

---

[155] The four main provinces of Soso that commonly appear in praise-lines to Suma-
woro (though rarely identified in the same way): Kukuba, Bantamba, Nyemi-Nyemi,
and Kambasiga. This comment, which the bard attributes to a contemporary of Sun-
jata's father, appears to imply a failed policy of appeasement toward Sumaworo.

[156] *Acacia albida*; in Mande lore, one of many trees, including the baobab and the
dubalen, that carry strong associations with the spirit world.

Maybe you will succeed."   (Aaaa)

She said, "You should act like you do not know
    anything,

So he will give you what he has."   (Naaaam')

A STRATEGIC ALLIANCE: KOLONKAN'S MARRIAGE

4810 After Sunjata had that meeting with Kamanjan,

The battle that would follow did not go well for
    Manden.   (Naaaam')

The lamenting over that would go to Manden.   (Naamu)

But Kamanjan did give something to Simbon.   (Naaaam')

He told him, "Since you have returned,

4815 I see that your sister has matured.   (Naamu)

Your sister has matured,

And you should give her to me.   (Naaaam')

I will marry her.   (Naamu)

Your mother is of the best stock.   (Naaaam')

4820 This girl has spent twenty-seven years at Nema.

Your mother said she would never be given to a man
    there,

And you agreed that she would not be given to a man
    there.

Only here in Manden would she be married.   (Naaaam')

Give her to me."   (Naamu)

4825 Ma'an Sunjata said, "Eh!

Father Kamanjan, that will not be possible.   (Naaaam')

If I give you my younger sister,

I would be embarrassed to discuss certain subjects
    with you.   (Naaaam')

If there is no marriage between us,

4830	I can discuss them with you.	(Naamu)
	With both my father and mother having died,	(Naaaam')
	You are the one I am depending on for counsel.	
	So, a marriage between us would make it embarrassing	
	for me."[157]	(Naamu)
	He said, "Besides that, you are a battle commander.	(Naaaam')
4835	If we do something to displease you,	
	If you become offended, we might quarrel."	(Naamu)
	Kamanjan said, "Ah, give her to me."	(Naaaam')
	Ma'an Sunjata said, "But if I give her to you,	(Naamu)
	Then you should advise the Kamara people	(Naamu)
4840	That they must show respect for the Mansaré people.	(Aaaaa)
	Let them show respect for us,	(Naaaam')
	Let them show respect for me."	(Naamu)
	He said, "The Kamara should respect us,	
	Kamaralu yé dan a na."	
4845	That became those people's family name, the	
	Dannalu.	(Naaaam')
	Those are the Danna who live between Balia and	
	Wulada.	(Naamu)
	Whenever the Kamara are spoken of,	
	The Danna must also be mentioned.	(Naamu)
	That was because of Ma Kolonkan's marriage.	(Naaaam')
4850	Once the promise was made,	
	Ma Kolonkan was taken and given to Kamanjan	
	Kamara.	(Naamu)
	He went into her and she gave birth to his son	
	Fadibali.	(Naaaam')

---

[157] In this case of *buranya* ("having an older in-law), Sunjata would have to practice great restraint and lack of familiarity toward his sister's husband, and would no longer be able to appeal to him for help or advice.

THE BATTLE OF NEGEBORIYA

	Kamanjan said, "Simbon, I respect you."	(Naamu)
	He said, "You will succeed,	(Na-amu)
4855	But what I have to tell you is,	(Naamu)
	Do not go to Dakajalan yet.	(Na-amu)
	Before you go to Dakajalan,	(Naamu)
	Go to Negeboriya.	(Na-amu)
	Go there and salute the relatives of Fakoli.	(Naamu)
4860	Fakoli has accomplished much here in Manden,	(Naamu)
	But he is not a man of Manden.	(Na-amuu)
	He is from Negeboriya.	(Naaaam')
	Have you not heard,	
	'Negeboriya Maghan,	
4865	Kayafaya Maghan'?[158]	(Naamu)
	They are our in-laws.	(Na-amu)
	Fakoli has eliminated doubt from us all.	(Naamu)
	He says, 'If the Mande people think	(Naamu)
	That my reason for helping them is to win the *mansaya* for myself,'	(Naamu)
4870	He says he does not want that.	(Naamu)
	That is why none of the Koroma in our Mansaré towns here aspire to *mansaya*.	(Na-amu)
	Fakoli says, 'I am only helping Manden because of Ma Tenenba Condé.	(Naaamu)
	It was Tenenba Condé who raised me.	(Na-amuu)
	She blessed me.	(Naamu, its true)
4875	Tenenba Condé's sister is So'olon Wulen Condé,	
	So'olon Wulen Condé's son is Ma'an Sunjata.	(Naamu)
	I am not helping you because of personal ambition.	(Naamu)

[158] Kayafaya is said to have been a *jamana*, or province attached to Negeboriya under the Koroma ruling lineage.

If you listen to the Mande people's gossip about me
    now,   (Na-amu)
You will be ashamed to face me later.'   (Naaaam')
4880 Turama'an has said similar things.   (Na-amu)
Kankejan has also said similar things."   (Naamu)
Kamanjan said, "Go and salute the people of
    Negeboriya."   (Na-amu)

Ma'an Sunjata and his companions took their leave
    from Tabon.   (Naamu)
They mounted their horses   (Naamu)
4885 And went straight to Negeboriya.   (Na-amu)
By the time they arrived there,   (Naamu)
Sumaworo had built a wall around it.   (Naamuu)
He had built walls around all the towns of Manden,   (Na-amu)
Sumaworo's walls.   (Naamu)
4890 As many towns as Manden has,   (Naamu)
Aside from Soso,   (Na-amu)
As many towns as Manden has,   (Naamu)
Sumaworo had built walls around all of them;
His troops occupied all of them.   (Naamu)
4895 When it was said that So'olon Ma'an and his troops
    were going there   (Naamu)
To salute the people of Negeboriya,   (Na-amu)
They laid the musket barrels along the top of the
    wall.   (Na-amu)
They waited for them.   (Naaaam')
When they arrived,   (Naamu)
4900 The musket battle errupted.   (Na-amu)
They opened fire!   (Naamu)
They opened fire!   (Naamu)
They opened fire!   (Naamuu)
Manden mourned,   (Na-amu)
4905 But Sumaworo lost his sacred drum Dunun Mutukuru
    there.   (Na-amu)
Up to tomorrow it has never been found.   (Naamu)
Only the *bala* remained.   (Naamu)

The Dunun Mutukuru was lost,	(Na-amu)
During the Battle of Negeboriya.	(Naamu)
4910 Sunjata returned to lamenting in Manden,	(Naamu)
But his powerful army was not destroyed.	(Naamu)

[In omitted passages, back in Manden two rams that are named for Sunjata and Sumaworo, respectively, fight one another in a symbolic preview of the battle to come. Preparing for the Battle of Dakajalan, Sunjata calls for volunteers. The army of Manden is divided into companies of men who possess occult powers, companies of those who have no magic, and one unit made up of famous ancestral figures with the power to become invisible. In a secret meeting with Manjan Bereté, Sunjata learns the elaborate strategy he must adopt to defeat Sumaworo. He exchanges his sorcery horse for the sorcery mare of the jelimuso *Tunku Manyan Diawara. He also sends a messenger to his sister, Nana Triban, who is in Soso, to retrieve from her the* dibilan *medicine that she steals from the tail of Sumaworo's horse.]*

TRADING INSULTS AND SWEARING OATHS

Manden had mourned after every battle against	
Sumaworo.	(Naamu, it's true)
He made all the women widows.	(Na-amuu)
He sewed shirts of human skin,	(Naamu)
4915 With the skins of Mande and Soso people.	(Naamu)
He sewed trousers of human skin,	(Naamu)
With the skins of Mande and Soso people.	(Na-amu)
He sewed a hat of human skin.	(Naamu)
After that, he sewed shoes of human skin.	(Naamu)
4920 He summoned the Mande people	(Naamu)
To come and give his shoes a name.	(Naamuu)
Anyone who came,	(Na-amu)

If the person said, "Finfirinya Shoes,"	(Naamu)
He would say, "That is not the name."	(Naamu)
4925 If somebody said, "Dulubiri,"	(Naamu)
He would say, "That is not the name."	(Naamu)
They asked him,	(Naamu)
"All right, Sumaworo,	(Naamu)
What are your shoes called?"	(Na-amu)
4930 He said, "My shoes are called,	(Naamuu)
'Take the Air,	(Naamu)
Take the Ground from the Chief.'	(Naamu)
People must always be around me, Sumaworo.	(Naamuu)
I will always keep Manden in my power.	(Na-amu)
4935 That is the name of my human-skin shoes."	(Naamu)
After they had made their preparations, the war	
began.	(Na-amu)
To shorten this narrative,	(Naaaam')
When the war began,	(Naamu)
The three Mande divisions arrived.	(Na-amu)
4940 Those who could become invisible in the daytime,	(Naamu)
The five *mori* diviners,	(Na-amu)
Simbon was over here,	(Naamu)
Simbon was placed like this.	(Na-amu)
They placed Manjan Bereté in front of him.	(Naamu)
4945 The head of his horse was touching the tail of the	
horse in front.	(Na-amu)
Sanbari Mara Cissé and Siriman Kanda Touré were	
there,	(Naamu)
Kòn Mara and Djané were there,	(Na-amu)
Manden Bori,	(Naamu)
And Tombonon Sitafa Diawara,	(Na-amu)
4950 And Turama'an,	(Naamu)
And Kankejan,	(Naamu)
And Fakoli.	(Naamu)
They were placed out here,	(Naamu)
Like when ants are marching,	(Na-amu)
4955 Back and forth,	(Naamu)

Back and forth. (Na-amu)

Sunjata said they should maintain those positions on
    the battlefield. (Naamu)

(You heard it?) (Na-amuu)

Simbon was in the middle! (Naamu, true, naamu)

4960 When they marched and arrived at the
    battlefield, (Naaaam')

Ma'an Sunjata said, "You Mande people, wait here." (Na-amu)

He left the Mande troops there. (Naamu)

He and the masked flag bearers, (Naamu)

He crossed the field with those men. (Na-amuu)

4965 As they crossed the field, (Naaaam')

They approached Sumaworo's position. (Naamu)

Sumaworo's troops were also there. (Naamu)

They were waiting in position. (Na-amu)

Sumaworo was astride his horse; (Naamu)

4970 He was surrounded by his corps of guards. (Naamu)

Sunjata drew nearer to Sumaworo. (Na-amu)

As Sunjata drew near, (Naamu)

He said, "Father Sumaworo, good morning." (Naamu)

(True manhood is revealed by the mouth.) (Na-amu)

4975 Sumaworo said, "Marahaba, good morning." (Naamu)

He said, "Where are the Mande troops?" (Na-amu)

"Ah, Father Sumaworo, they are over on the
    Mande side." (Naamu)

"Ah, is that your usual way of doing it?" (Na-amuu)

Sunjata said, "Ah, I have been away." (Naaaam')

4980 He said, "This is our first encounter in battle. (Naamu)

If I bring them, (Naamu)

I cannot allow them to mingle with your troops.

We would not be able to tell them apart.[159] (Na-amu)

You can see them standing over there on the Mande
    side." (Naamu)

---

[159] The problem of distinguishing between ally and enemy in the heat of battle was
a serious concern. In an episode not included in this book, the narrator describes
how Kamanjan Kamara introduced facial scarification for that purpose.

4985   "Ah, So'olon Ma'an, this is not the usual procedure."   (Na-amu)

Sunjata said, "Well, there was nobody else available to
    do this."   (Naaaam')

He was very bold in his speech.   (Na-amuu)

Sumaworo said, "I say to you, Bala Fasali,

I say to Simbon,   (Naamu)

4990   It was I who issued the challenge.   (Na-amu)

I have been told   (Naamu)

That the Mande people sent for their battle
    commander.   (Na-amuu)

They did not inform him of anything that happened
    in his absence.   (Naamu)

That is why I have challenged him   (Na-amu)

4995   To come and meet in the field.   (Naamu)

I will tell him what I have to say,   (Naamu)

And let him tell me what is on his mind.   (Naamu)

Then I will do to him what I planned to do.   (Naamu)

Or, he can try to do to me what he wants to do.   (Na-amuu)

5000   That is why I challenged him to come here."   (Naamu)

Simbon said, "I appreciate that.   (Na-amu)

Ah! You are my respected elder."   (Naamu)

(You heard it?)   (Na-amu)

He said, "The person who assisted one's father,   (Naamu)

5005   Is also one's father."   (Naamu)

(You heard it?)   (Na-amu)

He said, "But, father Sumaworo,   (Naamu)

People may refuse peanuts,   (Naamu)

But not ones that have been placed right in front of
    them.   (Na-amu)

5010   Let me say this to you."   (Naamu)

Sumaworo said, "Mba, give me some snuff from
    Manden."[160]   (Naamuu)

---

[160] This request commences a standard ritual called *sigifili*, conducted between opposing commanders before a battle; it involved boasting about one's powers and swearing oaths while taking poisonous snuff that would kill a liar.

Simbon said,	(Na-amu)
"Ah! Father Sumaworo,"	(Naamu)
He said, "It is appropriate for the master to give snuff to his apprentice,	
5015 Rather than for the apprentice to give snuff to his master."	(Na-amu)
He said, "Give me some snuff from Soso,	(Naamu)
So that I will know I have seen my father."	(Naamu)
Sumaworo took out his snuffbox	(Naamu)
And handed it to him.	(Na-amu)
5020 Simbon put some in his palm,	(Naamu)
Took a pinch and snorted it,	(Naamu)
Took another pinch and snorted it,	(Naamu)
And put some in his mouth.	(Naamu)
He closed the snuffbox and gave it back to Sumaworo.	(Naamu)
5025 It did not even make his tongue quiver.	(Naamu)
Sumaworo was surprised.	(Na-amu)
Anybody who took that snuff would immediately fall over.	(Naamu)
It was poison!	
(You heard it?)	(Na-amu)
5030 So'olon Ma'an sucked on the snuff.	(Naamu)
He did not even cough.	(Naamu)
He spit the snuff on the ground.	(Naamu)
Sumaworo said, "Give me some Mande snuff."	(Na-amu)
Simbon reached in his pocket,	(Naamu)
5035 And took out his snuffbox and handed it to him.	(Naamu)
Sumaworo put some in his palm.	(Naamu)
He took a pinch and snorted it,	(Naamu)
Took some more and snorted it,	(Naamu)
And put the rest in his mouth.	(Naamu)
5040 That was specially prepared snuff,	(Naamu)
But it did not do anything to him.	(Naamuu)
Sumaworo said to him,	(Na-amu)
He said, "I summoned you,	
Since the Mande people brought back their *mansa*.	(Naamu)

5045	You would not be here without *dalilu*.	(Naamu)
	The *dalilu* you brought,	(Naamu)
	I told you when you passed through Soso	(Naamu)
	That if they sent you against me,	(Naamu)
	That you should refuse.	(Naamu)
5050	I said that because,	(Naamu)
	As you have now learned,	(Naamu)
	I have become hot ashes surrounding Manden and Soso,	(Naamu)
	And if a toddler walks in it,	(Naamu)
	I will burn him	(Naamu)
5055	Up to his thighs.	(Naamu)
	But here you are."	(Naamuu)
	"Ah, father Sumaworo, I also told you,	(Naamu)
	This is my father's home that you came to.	(Na-amu)
	You are not a son of this place.	(Naaaam')
5060	Your grandfather came from Folonengbe,	(Naamuu)
	He came to us.	(Na-amu)
	It was not your grandfather, it was your father who came.	(Naamu)
	You are the second generation since your people arrived.	(Na-amu)
	Since we have been here,	(Naamu)
5065	It was our ancestor Mamadi Kani who came from Hejaji.[161]	(Naamu)
	It was that Mamadi Kani who came,	(Naamu)
	Mamadi Kani's son,	(Naamu)
	Kani Simbon,	(Naamu)
	Kani Nyogo Simbon,	(Naamu)
5070	Kabala Simbon,	(Naamu)
	Big Simbon Mamadi Tanyagati,	(Naamu)
	Balinene,	(Naamu)
	Bele,	(Naamu)
	And Belebakòn,	(Naamu)

[161] Hejaji: see n. 34.

5075 And Farako Manko Farakonken.	(Naamu)
I am his son,	(Naamu)
The eighth generation.	(Naamu)
I have been here.	(Na-amu)
You only came yesterday,	(Naamu)
5080 Dawn has broken today.	(Naamu)
Huh!" continued Sunjata,	(Na-amu)
"And you say that I have just arrived?	(Naaaam')
Mba, huh!	(Na-amu)
You are my respected elder.	
5085 I will not be the first to make a move.	
You who summoned me,	(Naamu)
Saying that your child is growing disrespectful,	(Naamu)
You go ahead and show what you have."	(Naamuu)
Sumaworo said, "Bisimillahi."	(Na-amu)
5090 (You heard it?)	(Naamu)

THE BATTLE OF DAKAJALAN
AND FAKOLI'S REVENGE

When something is filled to the brim,	(Naamu)
It will overflow.	(Naaaam')
Sumaworo took his sword and struck at Sunjata.	(Naamu)
The sword blade flexed like a whip.	(Naamu)
5095 Sunjata also struck with his sword.	(Naamu)
The blade of his sword also bent.	(Naamu)
Sumaworo raised his musket and fired at him.	(Naamu)
Nothing touched So'olon Ma'an.	(Na-amu)
So'olon Ma'an then fired his musket at Sumaworo.	(Naamu)
5100 It did not pierce Sumaworo.	(Na-amu)
The *dalilu* was finished.	(Naamu)
They were just standing there.	(Na-amu)
Sumaworo reached into his saddlebag,	(Naamu)

And took his whip.	(Naamu)
5105 As he raised his hand like this,	(Naamu)
So'olon Ma'an seized his reins like this,	(Naamu)
Clap! He dashed away.	(Na-amu)
(You heard it?)	(Na-amu)
The two armies were waiting.	(Naamu)
5110 Soso waited on one side,	(Naamu)
Manden waited on the other side.	(Naamu)
Everybody was watching the commanders on the battlefield.	(Na-amu)
Fakoli was off to one side of Sunjata.	(Naamu)
Turama'an was on his other side.	(Naamu)
5115 Sumaworo's men were flanking him.	(Na-amu)
Blu, blu!	(Naamuu)
They dashed across the field;	(Naamu)
They started up the hill.	(Na-amu)
As they began to climb,	(Naamu)
5120 They disappeared from sight.	(Na-amu)
Even their dust faded from sight.	(Naamu)
They reached the edge of a ravine.	(Naamu)
It was a very deep ravine!	(Naamu)
When they got there,	(Naamu)
5125 Sunjata's sorcery mare,	(Naamu)
Tunku Manyan Diawara's mare,	(Naamu)
Approached the deep ravine.	(Naamu)
The horse gathered itself to spring.	(Naamu)
It jumped and landed on the other side.	(Naamu)
5130 (You heard it?)	(Na-amu)
Sumaworo approached the ravine.	(Naamu)
When his horse tried to jump,	(Naamu)
It tumbled into the ravine.[162]	(Naamu)

[162] Though not usually seen in versions of the Sunjata epic, the incident of the horse tumbling into a ravine is a popular motif in *jeli* storytelling, a favorite way of disposing of the hero's enemy (cf. a Bamana version in Conrad 1990: 313–14).

	Fakoli's horse jumped and landed on the other side	
	of the ravine.	(Naamu)
5135	Turama'an's horse also jumped to the other side.	(Naamu)
	They turned their horses and went to the edge of	
	the ravine.	(N . . .)
	Sumaworo was wearing the human-skin trousers.	(Naamuu)
	(You heard it?)	(Na-amu)

	Sunjata said, "Sumaworo, what is the matter?"	(Naamu)
5140	He replied, "So'olon Ma'an, kill me here;	
	Do not carry me to the town.	(Na-amu)
	Do not bring such shame to me."	(Naamu)
	Sumaworo said, "God controls all time.	(Na-amu)
	Do not take me back."	(Naamu)
5145	Sumaworo removed his *dalilu*;	(Na-amu)
	He released his horse-whip.	(Naamu)
	He dropped everything and took off his human-skin	
	shirt.	(Naamu)
	He stripped his body.	(Na-amu)
	Sunjata said, "I am not going to finish you off.	(Naamu)
5150	From where you are, nobody can climb out."	(Na-amuu)
	He said, "I do not want your shirt of human skin,	(Naamu)
	Because it is the skin of my father's relatives.	(Na-amu)
	I do not want it."	(Naamu)
	Ma'an Sunjata would not take it.	(Naamu)
5155	When they said, "Come, let us go home,"	(Na-amu)
	They had gone some distance	(Naamu)
	When Fakoli made a decision, turned, and went back.	(Naamu)
	When he got back to Sumaworo,	(Na-amu)
	He said "Sumaworo, what did I say to you?	(Naamu)
5160	When you took back your sister,[163] what did I say?"	(Na-amu)
	He took his axe from his shoulder,	(Naamu)
	And struck Sumaworo on the head, *poh*!	(Naamu)
	He said, "This will be sung about in Ma'an Sunjata's	
	praise song."	(Naamu)

[163] Fakoli's wife, Keleya Konkon (see l. 4621–30 and n. 151).

They sang, "Head-breaking Mari Jata."	(Na-amu)
5165 It was Fakoli who broke it.[164]	(Naamuu)
(You heard it?)	(Na-amu)
When Fakoli started to leave there,	(Naamu)
He was still angry, so he went back again.	(Naamu)
He went back and struck Sumaworo on a leg, *gbao!*	(Naamu)
5170 He broke his leg.	(Naamu)
He said, "This will be sung in Ma'an Sunjata's praise song."	(Naamu)
That is why it was sung, "Leg-breaking Mari Jata."	(Naamu)
It was Fakoli who did that.	(Naamuu)
He went back again and took his axe.	(Na-amu)
5175 He swung it and broke Sumaworo's arm.	(Naamu)
He said, "This will be sung in Ma'an Sunjata's praise song."	(Naamu)
It was sung, "Arm-breaking Mari Jata."	(Naamu)
Aheh! It was not Jata who broke it!	(Naamu)
It was Fakoli who broke it.	(Na-amuu)
5180 (You heard it?)	(Naamu)
After they did that,	(Naamu)
They returned home.	(Na-amuu)
Laughter came to Manden.	(Naamu)
Soso became part of it.	(Naamu)

[164] It is unusual for a *jeli* to describe the death of Sumaworo, as Tassey Condé does here. In many versions, Sumaworo flees to the mountain at Koulikoro where he disappears (e.g., Johnson 1986: 176; Conrad 1999b: 89). The Kouyaté and Diabaté *jeliw*, among others, are usually careful not to say that Sumaworo was slain by Sunjata, Fakoli, or anyone else. Such things are taken seriously in modern times, because Maninka and Bamana identify with the ancestors whose names they carry. This was recorded in a private performance in the narrator's own house, but in a public performance, giving details of a humiliating defeat (even one alleged to have occurred more than seven centuries ago) risks embarrassing any people in the audience who regard themselves as descendants of the defeated ancestor.

*[In omitted passages, the narrator describes how, following the defeat of
Sumaworo, the people of Soso dispersed and eventually settled in vari-
ous communities along the Atlantic coast. Meanwhile, Sunjata begins
to initiate reforms and organize the newly unified Mali Empire.]*

THE CAMPAIGN AGAINST JOLOFIN MANSA

5185	After the war had ended,	(Naamu)
	Ma'an Sunjata then said,	(Naamu)
	"My fathers and my brothers,	(Na-amu)
	Since the war has ended and the *mansaya* has come to us,	
	the Mansaré,	(Naamu)
	Let us send the horse-buyers to Senu.	(Naamu)
5190	Many horses of Manden have been killed by	
	Sumaworo.	(Na-amu)
	When we buy the horses,	(Naamu)
	Let us put the elders and warriors of Manden on	
	horses."	(Naamu)
	They sent the horse-buyers to Senu.	(Naamu)
	They went and bought the horses, hundreds of them.	(Naamu)
5195	They bought the horses and started home with them.	(Naamu)
	While they were bringing those horses,	(Na-amu)
	They came to the *jamana* of Jolofin Mansa.	(Naaaam')
	Jolofin Mansa took the horses away from the buyers.	(Naamu)
	He captured the horse-buyers and beheaded them,	(Naamu)
5200	Except for two men.	(Na-amu)
	Jolofin Mansa sent them to tell the Mande *mansa*	
	Ma'an Sunjata	(Naamu)
	That he knew Ma'an Sunjata had taken over the power,	(Naamu)
	That Sunjata had recently received the Mande *mansaya*.	(Naamu)
	But he said he knew the Mande to be people who	
	walked dogs,	(Naamu)

5205	That he did not know the Mande to be people who rode horses,	(Naaaam')
	That the Mande people should leave the horse-riding to others.	(Naamu)
	(You heard it?)	(Na-amu)
	The messengers came and told Ma'an Sunjata.	(Naamu)
	Ma'an Sunjata said, "Jolofin Mansa has invited me.	(Naamu)
5210	Jolofin Mansa has extended me an invitation.	(Na-amu)
	No one besides me will lead this campaign.	(Naaaam')
	I will lead this campaign myself,	(Naamu)
	To go against Jolofin Mansa."	(Naamu)
	His younger brother Manden Bori said, "Elder brother,	(Naamu)
5215	Are you going to lead us in that campaign?	(Naamu)
	Give me the command, and I will do the fighting."	(Naamu)
	Sunjata said to his younger brother Manden Bori,	
	"I am not giving you command of the army."	(Na-amu)
	Fakoli said, "Simbon, give me the army!"	(Naamuu)
5220	He said, "We will not stay here while you lead the army.	(Na-amu)
	Give the army to me, Fakoli, so I can go after Jolofin Mansa."	(Naamu)
	(You heard it?)	(Naamu)
	Simbon said,	(Na-amu)
	"I will not give you the army."	(Naamu)
5225	He said, "I will go myself."	(Naamu)
	While they were discussing this,	(Na-amu)
	Turama'an was digging his own grave.	(Naamu)
	Mamady Kouyaté!	(Naamu)
	Turama'an dug his grave.	(Na-amu)
5230	He cut some *tòrò* branches,	(Naamu)
	Laid them on it.	(Naamu)
	He had his shroud sewn.	(Naamu)
	He came and said to Ma'an Sunjata,	(Na-amu)
	"Simbon, if you do not give me the army, I will kill myself.	(Naamu)

5235	Would you leave us behind?	(Na-amu)
	And you lead the army to go after Jolofin Mansa?	(Naamu)
	Give me, Turama'an, the army.	(Naamu)
	If you do not give me the army,	(Naamu)
	If you go for Jolofin Mansa yourself,	(Naamu)
5240	You will lose me.	(Naamu)
	I will kill myself.	(Naamu)
	If I hear that you have taken the army to go for Jolofin Mansa,	
	I will kill myself."	(Naamu)
	"Ah," said Simbon, "Since you have said that, Turama'an,"	(Naamu)
5245	He said, "Your *dalilu* and my *dalilu* are tied together.	(Naamu)
	My mother was given to your fathers, who killed the buffalo of Dò ni Kiri.	(Naamu)
	If your father and my mother had gotten along,	(Na-amu)
	My mother would have stayed with your father.	(Naamu)
	Because my mother did not get along with your fathers,	(Naamu)
5250	Your fathers brought my mother to my father,	(Naamu)
	And I was born.	(Naamu)
	My younger brother Manden Bori was born,	(Naamu)
	And So'olon Jamori was born."	(Na-amu)
	(You heard it?)	(Naamu)
5255	He said, "My father took my younger siblings,	(Naamu)
	Took Nana Triban and Tenenbajan,	(Naamu)
	And gave them to your fathers,	
	To Danmansa Wulanni and Danmansa Wulanba.	(Naamu)
	You, Turama'an, are the son of that Danmansa Wulanni.	(Naamu)
5260	Considering what you have said,	
	You and I are equal in this war, and I will let you take the army."	(Naaaam')
	Sunjata gave Turama'an command of the army.	(Naamu)
	Turama'an prepared the army for war.	(Na-amu)
	They marched on Jolofin Mansa.	(Naamu)

5265	The campaign had begun.	(Na-amu)
	They arrived at Jolofin Mansa's land.	(Naamu)
	You know Jolofin Mansa,	(Naamu)
	He was one of the Mansaré.	(Na-amu)
	(You heard it?)	(Naamu)
5270	The Mansaré ancestor,	(Naamu)
	Latali Kalabi,	(Naamu)
	His son was Danmatali Kalabi,	(Naamu)
	Danmatali Kalabi,	(Naamu)
	His son was another Latali Kalabi.	(Naamu)
5275	This Latali sired Kalabi Doman and Kalabi Bomba.	(Naamu)
	(You heard it?)	(Na-amu)
	Kalabi Doman,	(Naamu)
	He sired Mamadi Kani.	(Naamu)
	Mamadi Kani sired Kani Simbon,	(Naamu)
5280	He sired Kani Nyogo Simbon,	(Naamu)
	He sired Kabala Simbon,	(Naamu)
	He sired Big Simbon Madi Tanyagati,	(Naamu)
	He sired M'balinene,	(Naamu)
	M'balinene sired Bele,	(Naamu)
5285	Bele sired Belebakon,	(Naamu)
	Belebakon sired Maghan Konfara,	(Naamu)
	Farako Manko Farakonken,	(Naamu)
	He sired Ma'an Sunjata.	(Naamu)
	Ah, Ma'an Sunjata was commander of the army.	(Na-amu)
5290	(You heard it?)	(Naamu)
	Kalabi Bomba,	(Na-amu)
	His descendant is Jolofin Mansa.	
	They all descended from the same person.	(Naamu)
	Turama'an went in the direction of Senegal.	(Naamu)
5295	They became known as "the people of Jolofin."	(Naamu)
	Jolofin na mò'òlu became Wolofo.[165]	(Naamu)
	Do you not hear people calling the Wolofo "little Mande people"?	(Na-amu)

[165] Maninka pronunciation attaches an extra vowel. The Wolof, who call their country Jolof (see previous line), are mainly in Senegal, and they speak a language that is not interintelligible with Manding languages.

They all came from Manden.   (Naaaam')

Turama'an marched against Jolofin Mansa.   (Naamu)
5300 He took the army of Manden and marched to
    Jolofin Mansa's land.   (Naamu)
He destroyed Jolofin Mansa's place like it was an
    old clay pot;   (Naamu)
He broke it like an old calabash.   (Naamu)
He captured those who were supposed to be captured,   (Naamu)
Killed those who were supposed to be killed.   (Naamu)
5305 Jolofin Mansa fled.   (Naamu)
Turama'an pursued him,   (Na-amu)
He pursued him.   (Naamu)
Jolofin Mansa knew his soldiers had been defeated,   (Naamu)
But he himself had not yet been captured.   (Na-amu)
5310 He fled.   (Naamu)
He went toward the big river.[166]   (Na-amu)
It was not known that he could transform himself into
    a crocodile.   (Naaaam')
He could live on land, he could live under water.   (Naamu)
Jolofin Mansa came to the big river.   (Na-amu)
5315 When he reached the place where his cave was,   (Naamu)
Jolofin Mansa plunged into the river.   (Naamu)
After plunging into the river,   (Na-amu)
He went into a cave.   (Naamu)
When he was in the cave,   (Naamu)
5320 He transformed himself into a crocodile and lay
    down there.   (Naamu)
Turama'an and his troops arrived.   (Na-amu)
They stood above the cave.   (Naamu)
They said, "Jolofin Mansa went in here."   (Na-amu)
The Manden men were good warriors,   (Naamu)
5325 But they were not used to water fighting.   (Naamu)
Have you understood that?   (Na-amu)

[166] The Senegal River.

For us to know that we had someone who could fight	
in the water,	(Naamu)
That was only discovered at the entrance to that cave.	(Naamu)
All the battle commanders came and stood above the	
entrance to the cave.	(Na-amu)
5330 Everybody carried a quiver and bow,	
Everybody wore a hunter's hat and shirt.	(Na-amu)
They went and stood there.	(Naamu)
Turama'an said, "He went in here."	(Naamu)
He said, "But let me tell you Mande people;	(Na-amu)
5335 When we fight this battle,	(Naamu)
If we destroy the war *mansa's* home without killing the	
war *mansa*,	
We have not won the battle.	(Naamuu)
Jolofin Mansa went in here,	(Na-amu)
He has transformed himself into a crocodile.	(Naaaam')
5340 Who will go after him?"	(Naamu)
Everybody kept quiet, *lele*!	(Na-amu)
(You heard it?)	(Naamu)
He asked, "Who will go after him?"	(Naamu)
Nobody spoke up.	(Naamu)
5345 He asked, "Who will follow this man?"	(Na-amu)
Oh, among those soldiers,	(Naamu)
The Diawara chief came out.	
His name was Tombonon Sitafa Diawara.	(Naamu)
Sitafa Diawara said, "Turama'an,"	(Naamu)
5350 He said, "Tell the Mande people,	(Na-amu)
I am not trying to prove my manhood.	(Naamu)
If such a thing should happen,	(Na-amu)
That we return to Simbon like that	(Naamu)
And say we have destroyed Jolofin Mansa's home,	(Naamu)
5355 But we did not capture him,	(Naamu)
Simbon will ask why we told him to stay home."	(Naaaam')
He said, "Tell the Mande people that if they agree,	(Naamu)
I, Sitafa Diawara, will go after Jolofin Mansa.	(Naamu)
I will go after him.	(Na-amu)

5360	But I am not trying to show off my manhood."	(Naaaam')
	That is why when you are a real man,	
	When you are among the *kamalenw*,	
	You should stay low to the ground.	(Naamu)
	The time for you to reveal the kind of man you are	(Naamu)
5365	Is when somebody challenges your group.	(Na-amu)
	Sitafa Diawara said, "I will go after him.	(Naamu)
	But you Mande people,	(Naamu)
	I will give you a sign,	(Na-amu)
	I will give you two signs,	(Naamu)
5370	When I go after him."	(Naamu)
	Meanwhile, Jolofin Mansa's crocodile wraith was lying	
	in the cave.	(Naamu)
	Its mouth was open wide.	(Naamu)
	The upper jaw extended to the top of the entrance,	
	The lower jaw extended to the bottom of the entrance.	(Naamu)
5375	Anybody who went after the crocodile would end up	
	in its stomach,	(Naamu)
	And when he was in its stomach, it would close its	
	mouth.	(Na-amu)
	Eh! There would be no need to chew.	(Naamu)
	(You heard it?)	(Naamu)
	Diawara said, "When I go down,	(Naamu)
5380	When I get there,	(Naamu)
	If the water bubbles and starts to churn,	(Naamu)
	If it begins to foam,	(Naamu)
	When it turns the color of blood,	(Na-amu)
	If you see a pelican coming from where the sun sets	(Naamu)
5385	To where it rises,	(Naamu)
	Manden should weep.	(Naamuu)
	You will know that Jolofin Mansa has defeated me.	(Naaaam')
	You should return to Manden in tears.	(Na-amu)
	But if I go down,	(Naamu)
5390	If the water bubbles and starts to churn,	(Naamu)
	If it begins to foam,	(Naamu)

When it turns the color of blood,   (Naamu)
If the pelican comes from where the sun rises   (Naamu)
To where it sets,   (Naamu)
5395 You Mande people,   (Naamu)
Be happy."   (Naamu)
He said, "It will be God's honor,
It will be your honor.   (Naamu)
Those are the signs I have given you."   (Naamuu)

5400 He put on his medicine clothes,   (Na-amu)
He took with him all his *dalilu*.   (Naamu)
He had a small knife that he fastened to his chest.   (Naamu)
The iron fish-spear of the Bozo,[167]   (Naamu)
With a short wooden handle,   (Naamu)
5405 He hung from his waist.   (Naamu)
He said to the warriors, "Excuse me.   (Naamu)
We may meet in this world,
We may meet in God's kingdom.   (Na-amu)
If I succeed, we will meet in this world.   (Naamu)
5410 I will come back and find you here.   (Naamu)
But if it overcomes me,   (Naamu)
We will meet in God's kingdom."   (Naamu)
He dove into the water.   (Naamu)
When he was under the water,   (Naamu)
5415 He entered the cave.   (Na-amu)
When he entered, he thought he was in the cave,
Not knowing he was in the crocodile's stomach.   (Naamuu)
The crocodile closed its mouth on him.   (Na-amu)

When the crocodile closed its mouth on him,   (Naamu)
5420 The hunter demonstrated his *dalilu*.   (Na-amu)
He was inside the crocodile, but he was alive.   (Naamu)
He was inside the crocodile as if he were in his own
    house.   (Naamu)

---

[167] An ethnic group of the Middle Niger, specializing in fishing and boating occu-
pations, mainly located between Sansanding and Lake Debo in Mali.

	He took his spear from his side.	(Naamu)
	He stabbed the crocodile here,	(Naamu)
5425	He stabbed it there.	(Naamu)
	When he did, *pu!*	(Naamu)
	The crocodile went *kututu*.	(Naamu)
	He would pull out the spear and stab it again.	(Naamu)
	The water bubbled.	(Naamuu)
5430	Blood came to the surface of the water.	(Naamu)
	As the water turned the color of blood,	(Naamu)
	He reached for the knife on his chest.	(Naamu)
	He sliced open the belly and went out through that hole.	(Naamuu)
	When he came out, he stayed under the water.	(Naamu)
5435	He twisted the front legs behind the crocodile and tied them together.	(Naamuu)
	While he was coming up with it,	(Na-amu)
	A pelican flew squawking from the east to the west.	(Naamu)
	Manden laughed.	(Na-amu)
	(You heard it?)	(Naamu)
5440	They pulled out the wraith.	(Naamu)
	They hauled it onto the bank, and Jolofin Mansa himself appeared.	(Naamu)
	He was captured and tied up.	(Naamu)
	They took him to the *mansa*.	(Naamuu)
	Turama'an was the commander at that battle.	(Naaaam')
5445	He brought Jolofin Mansa's treasure to Ma'an Sunjata.	(Naamu)
	Manden was at last free, and the war was over.	(Naamu)

EPILOGUE

After describing the defeat of Sumaworo and the successful campaign against Jolofin Mansa, some of the most knowledgeable *jeliw* include descriptions of a great assembly held at a large open space called Kurukanfuwa. They generally claim it was there that Sunjata laid the groundwork for administering the newly established Mali Empire, including the assignment of provincial governorships to his leading generals. Among those who mention the assembly at Kurukanfuwa is our narrator Tassey Condé, who presents it as the occasion for efforts to shape the social framework of Manding peoples. He claims that quarrels over who had rights to the services of *jeliw*, blacksmiths, leatherworkers, potters, and other occupational specialists were settled at Kurukanfuwa. In this bard's view, the solution was to assign a special social classification to the artists and craftsmen, who became collectively known as *nyamakalaw*, and to award their services to the most worthy and successful families of Manden.

Aside from the fact that Tassey Condé's basic narrative required six days to complete (more was added in subsequent interviews), it is unusual because it continues for several thousand lines after the fall of Sumaworo and Jolofin Mansa. Tassey revisits subjects mentioned earlier in the narrative and provides a wealth of additional details and explanations about them. A few such details appear in the "Introduction" and explanatory notes, such as the origins and occupation of Sumaworo's ancestors in the place called Folonengbe, and remarks about the absence of guns in the time of Sunjata. Subjects that did not find a place in the present book include details about the "original" five Islamic lineages of Manden and the towns where they settled, the iron-working communities of Negeboriya, Fakoli's genealogy and descendants, the Koroma lineage's dispersal and towns they founded, Manden's first pilgrims to Mecca, Manden Bori's descendants and where they settled, history of Sankaran, five branches of the Kulubali of Segu, leading families of Kouroussa and the Hamana region, Dò ni Kiri's war with Sawuru, early settlers in various regions to the south of Manden, Baté and Kankan history with the Nabé and Kaba as latecomers from Diafunu, the four *jamanaw* of Soso, the Soso people's diaspora, ancestry of the Magasouba of Siguiri and their *dalilu*, more on the history of the Kaba of Kankan, background on the Konaté of the *jamana* of Toron, and Kamanjan's famous meeting at Kalasa.

Follow-up interviews with Tassey Condé and the elders of Fadama elicited more discourse, revealing additional detailed information on a variety of subjects. The entire corpus of discourse on the Condé perception of the Manding peoples' history will be included in the complete, exhaustively annotated scholarly edition being prepared for publication.

GLOSSARY OF FREQUENTLY USED MANINKA TERMS

Note: The suffixes "*w*" and "*lu*" are alternatively used to signify the plural—e.g., *jeliw* or *jelilu*.

bala   Also known as *balafon*, the indigenous xylophone. Constructed of hardwood slats tied to a bamboo frame with small gourds attached below each slat for resonance. Played with wooden mallets, the heads of which are covered with liquid latex tapped from wild rubber trees.

balansan   In Manding lore, one of the trees that carries strong associations with genies and the spirit world.

dabali   A scheme or a plan. As a verb, to make something happen in a positive way—e.g., to repair; also, secret power sometimes used in negative ways—e.g., "the sorcerer will *dabali* him so he will not be able to walk."

dado   Dried hibiscus blossoms and/or leaves, used as a condiment in sauces.

dalilu   According to the context usually seen in oral tradition, magic, or occult power; more generally, any means used to achieve a goal, referring to secret power, whether supernatural or not. Someone might have the *dalilu* to bring rain, but also used in casual daily usage—e.g., "he has the *dalilu* to repair a car," or "I have no *dalilu* to interfere in that quarrel."

gbensen   An old unit of trade currency made of thick strands of iron wire bent into the shape of a cross.

jamana   Land, territory, province; in Maninka oral tradition: chiefdom, kingdom; Bamana syn. *kafu*.

jamu   Family name, patronymic, identity.

jeli   Occupationally defined bard (popularly and more broadly known as "griot"), born into the profession, specializing in speech including genealogies, proverbs, and extended oral narrative, also vocal and instrumental music.

jelimuso   Female bard (*muso* = "woman," "wife," "female"), specializing in praise-singing and vocalization of songs from the vast Mande repertoire.

jeliya   Condition of being a *jeli* or *jelimuso*.

kamalen   Male youth distinguished by two categories: *kamalennin* = adolescent; circumcised youth; vigorous young males 15–25 years of age; *kamalenkoro* = a mature male at the height of his power and ability, 25–40 years of age. The most physically capable social ranks, from which came the hunters, warriors, champion farmers, and long-distance traders.

karamogo   Teacher, scholar, wise man; as a proper noun, *Karamogo* is a term of respect for learned men, usually Muslim clerics.

kora   Largest of the calabash harps, with twenty-one strings.

kòwòro   A musical instrument also known as *dan*, consisting of an inverted open calabash with a neck for each of its six strings; technically known as a pentatonic pluriac.

maghan   See *mansa*.

mansa   Ruler, king, chief, lord, emperor (syn. *magha* or *maghan*).

mansaya   Kingship, royalty, the condition of being a ruler.

mori   In general, a Muslim cleric (Fr. *marabout*), but in oral tradition often referring to a seer or diviner who draws on spiritual connections with both the indigenous system of belief and Islam.

naamu   From the Arabic *na'am*. Most often used as a reply or comment by the *naamu*-sayer (*naamu namina*, or *naamutigiw* = *naamu* "owner"), who encourages the principal performer. There is no very accurate translation, though it is what people also say when they hear their name called, and it can be rendered as "yes," or "I hear you."

nege   "Iron"—syn. *nkarinyan*: a rhythm instrument consisting of a notched iron tube 7–8 inches long, held in one hand and scraped with a thin metal rod. It is often played to accompany the hunters' or youth harps.

nkoni   A type of traditional lute consisting of four to five strings attached to a single neck on a wooden, trough-shaped body covered with animal skin.

sunsun   An extremely hard wood called "false ebony" or "West African ebony."

MAJOR CHARACTERS

Abdu Karimi   Son of Abdu Serifu, the king of Morocco. Younger of the two brothers who hunted the Buffalo of Dò ni Kiri, and the one who actually killed it. Subsequently known by the praise name Danmansa Wulanni.

Abdu Kassimu   Son of Abdu Serifu, the king of Morocco. Elder of the two brothers who hunted the Buffalo of Dò ni Kiri. Subsequently known by the praise name Danmansa Wulanba.

Bala Fasali   Also known as Bala Fasaké, Fasséké, or other variants of that name. Son of Nyankuman Duga, the *jeli* of Sunjata's father. Destined to be the principal *jeli* of Sunjata, Bala was sent to Soso and acquired the traditional xylophone, or *bala*, from Sumaworo. With his father, he is recognized as an ancestor of the great bardic lineage known as Kouyaté.

Dankaran Tuman   Eldest son of Maghan Konaté of Konfara and Sansun Tuman (Sansuman) Bereté, rival stepbrother of Sunjata. He inherited the power from their father, plotted to kill Sunjata, and, as ruler of Manden while Sunjata was in exile, failed to protect his country from Soso invasion and occupation.

Danmansa Wulanba   Formerly known as Abdu Kassimu, elder of the two brothers from Morocco. After his younger brother killed the buffalo of Dò ni Kiri, he sang his praises and consequently became the legendary ancestor of the bardic lineage called Diabaté.

Danmansa Wulanni   Formerly known as Abdu Karimi, younger of the two brothers from Morocco. He killed the buffalo of Dò ni Kiri and became the legendary ancestor of the Tarawèlè (Traoré) lineage.

Dò Kamissa the Buffalo Woman   Stepsister of Donsamogo Diarra, the *mansa* of Dò ni Kiri. She was the elder sister of both Sunjata's mother, Sogolon Wulen Condé, and Fakoli's foster-mother, Tenenba Condé. One of the greatest sorceresses in Manding epic tradition, Kamissa is especially remembered for her ability to transform herself into a buffalo.

Donsamogo Diarra   Full name: Donsamò'ò Nyèmò'ò Diarra, *mansa* of Dò ni Kiri. He was the son of Ma'an Solonkan and the elder brother of Sekou, Mafadu, and Kiri Diarra, and the three sisters Dò Kamissa, Sogolon, and Tenenba Condé. Upon inheriting the power at Dò ni Kiri, he refused to share the father's legacy with Dò Kamissa.

Fakoli Koroma Son of Yerelenko Koroma, *mansa* of Negeboriya, and his second wife Kosiya Kanté, who was the sister of Sumaworo of Soso. As a distinguished son of both Soso and Negeboriya, Fakoli was the single most important military ally of Sunjata. He is also recalled as the greatest sorcerer of the male Manding ancestors, and as patriarch of many of the principal blacksmith lineages.

Faran Tunkara *Mansa* of Nema/Mema, who ruled from his capital of Kuntunya and hosted Sogolon Wulen Condé, her son Sunjata, and his siblings during their years of exile.

Jelimusoni Tunku Manyan Diawara One of nine *jelimusow* (female bards) married by Maghan Konfara, in his quest to find the mother of Sunjata, and the only one of that group said to have borne a child. She was among the four messengers who traveled to Nema/Mema in search of Sunjata. She was also one of the nine sorceresses bribed by Dankaran Tuman to assassinate Sunjata, and the one who warned him of the plot. She later provided the sorcery mare that Sunjata rode at the Battle of Dakajalan.

Jinna Maghan Lit. "Genie King," a ubiquitous supernatural being who can appear wherever important events occur involving genies.

Jolofin Mansa *Mansa* of the Jolof Kingdom of Senegal, who confiscated Sunjata's herd of horses and sent him an insulting message, and was later defeated by an army led by Turama'an Traoré.

Jonmusoni Manyan One of nine slave girls married by Maghan Konfara in his quest to find the mother of Sunjata, and the only one of that group who is said to have borne a child. She was among the four messengers who traveled to Nema/Mema in search of Sunjata.

Kamanjan Kamara Full name and title: Tabon Wana Faran Kamara (or Sibi Wana Faran Kamara). The most distinguished ancestor of the Kamara (also Camara) lineage, he was *mansa* of Sibi and Tabon, and a contemporary of Sunjata's father Maghan Konfara. He became an elderly brother-in-law to Sunjata when he married Kolonkan after she and her siblings returned from exile.

Kankejan Son of Danmansa Wulanba and Tenenbajan, who was a daughter of Maghan Konfara's younger brother. An ancestor of the Diabaté *jeliw*, he was one of Sunjata's important generals and fought at the Battle of Dakajalan.

Keleya Konkon The wife of Fakoli, who had been given to him by his uncle Sumaworo of Soso. When Sumaworo became aware of Keleya's great power as a sorceress, and after he quarreled with Fakoli, he reclaimed her from his nephew.

Kolonkan   Daughter of Maghan Konfara and Sogolon Wulen Condé, and sister of Sunjata. After she returned from exile with Sunjata, she was married to Kamanjan Kamara of Sibi and gave birth to a son, Fadibali.

Kosiya Kanté   Sister of Sumaworo Kanté, second wife of Mansa Yerelenko of Negeboriya, and mother of Fakoli. She sacrificed herself to Jinna Maghan, the genie chief, so her brother could acquire the Soso *bala*.

Maghan Konfara   Husband of Sogolon Wulen Condé, father of Sunjata, generally identified as an ancestor of the Konaté. Full name in this text: Farako Manko Farakonken; identified elsewhere as Naré Maghan Konaté and Naré Famagan, among other variants. He was *mansa* of Konfara, descendant of Latili Kalabi, Mamadi Kani, Kani Simbon, Kaninyo'o Simbon, Kabala Simbon, Big Simbon Madi Tanyagati, M'bali Nèènè, Bèlè, and son of Bèlèbakòn.

Manden Bori   Youngest son of Maghan Konfara and Sogolon Wulen Condé, brother of Sunjata, Kolonkan, and Jamori. He is the ancestor of the chiefly Keita families of the Hamana region of Guinea.

Manjan Bereté   Identified by a place name as Tombonon Manjan Bereté (cf. Sitafa Diawara). Brother of Sansun Tuman Bereté. One of Maghan Konfara's chief advisors, he is recalled as being the leading Muslim of his day. He was one of the four messengers who traveled to Nema/Mema to bring Sunjata back from exile.

Nana Triban   Daughter of Maghan Konfara and Sansun Tuman Bereté, half-sister of Sunjata. She was the wife of Danmansa Wulanni and mother of Turama'an Traoré.

Sansamba Sagado   Chief of the Somono boatmen. He ferried Sogolon and her children across the Niger River when they left Manden to go into exile.

Sansun Bereté   Full name: Sansun Tuman (Sansuma) Bereté. Sister of Tombonon Manjan Bereté, wife of Maghan Konfara, co-wife of Sogolon Wulen Condé, mother of Dankaran Tuman and Nana Triban.

Siriman Kanda Touré   One of Sunjata's important generals. He was one of the four messengers who journeyed to Nema/Mema in search of Sunjata, and he later fought at the Battle of Dakajalan.

Sitafa Diawara   Identified as Tombonon Sitafa Diawara. He was one of Sunjata's important generals and fought at the Battle of Dakajalan. Later, on the campaign against Jolofin Mansa, he was the hero who followed Jolofin Mansa's crocodile wraith into the underwater cave and emerged triumphant.

Sogolon Wulen Condé   Daughter of Ma'an Solonkan, *mansa* of Dò ni Kiri. She was a sister of both Dò Kamissa the Buffalo Woman and Tenenba

Condé. A formidable sorceress, she became the wife of Maghan Konfara and gave birth to Sunjata, Kolonkan, Jamori, and Manden Bori.

So'olon Jamori Second son of Maghan Konfara and Sogolon Wulen Condé. As the middle brother (some say he was a half-brother), he was younger than Sunjata and older than Manden Bori. He was killed in an ambush when he and his siblings were leaving Nema/Mema on their return journey from exile.

So'olon Kolonkan See *Kolonkan*.

Sumaworo Kanté Son of Bali Kanté, he was the *mansa* of Soso. He is associated with the origin of Manding stringed instruments, as well as the Soso *bala*, which he is said to have acquired from the genies. Taking advantage of the weakness of Dankaran Tuman, he conquered the formerly autonomous Mande chiefdoms and occupied them while Sunjata was in exile.

Sunjata Keita Also known as So'olon Jara (Sogolon's Lion), So'olon Ma'an, Ma'an Sunjata, Mari Jata, Danama Yirindi, Simbon, and other praise names. Son of Maghan Konfara and Sogolon Wulen Condé. He was leader of the army of Manden when it defeated Sumaworo and the army of Soso, and is generally credited as "founder" of the Mali Empire.

Tenenba Condé Also known as Soma Tenenba or Ma Tenenba. Daughter of Ma'an Solonkan, the *mansa* of Dò ni Kiri; sister of Dò Kamissa and Sogolon Wulen Condé. She was the first wife of Yerelenko, *mansa* of Negeboriya, co-wife of Kosiya Kanté, and foster mother of Fakoli.

Tenenbajan Konaté Daughter of a younger brother of Maghan Konfara. She was the wife of Danmansa Wulanba and the mother of Kankejan, who was an ancestor of the Diabaté *jeliw*.

Turama'an Traoré (Tarawele) Also Turamaghan, Tirmakan, and so on. Son of Danmansa Wulanni and Nana Triban. As one of Sunjata's most important generals, he fought at the Battle of Dakajalan, and after the defeat of Soso, he commanded the campaign against Jolofin Mansa.

Yerelenko Koroma *Mansa* of Negeboriya, which was probably the most important iron-producing region of Manden. His senior wife was Tenenba Condé of Dò ni Kiri. He became the brother-in-law of Sumaworo when he married Kosiya Kanté of Soso, who was the mother of his son Fakoli.

SUGGESTIONS FOR FURTHER READING

Austen, Ralph A., ed. *In Search of Sunjata: The Mande Epic as History, Literature, and Performance.* Bloomington and Indianapolis: Indiana University Press, 1999.

Barber, Karin, and P. F. de Moraes Farias, eds. *Discourse and Its Disguises: The Interpretation of African Oral Texts.* Birmingham, UK: Centre of West African Studies, University of Birmingham, 1989.

Belcher, Stephen. *Epic Traditions of Africa.* Bloomington and Indianapolis: Indiana University Press, 1999.

Brett-Smith, Sarah C. *The Making of Bamana Sculpture: Creativity and Gender.* Cambridge: Cambridge University Press, 1994.

Bulman, Stephen. "A School for Epic? The 'Ecole William Ponty' and the Evolution of the Sunjata Epic, 1913–c. 1960." In *Epic Adventures: Heroic Narrative in the Oral Performance Traditions of Four Continents,* edited by Jan Jansen and Henk M. J. Maier, 34–45. Mûnster, Germany: Lit Verlag, 2004.

———. "The Buffalo-Woman Tale: Political Imperatives and Narrative Constraints in the Sunjata Epic." In *Discourse and Its Disguises: The Interpretation of African Oral Texts,* edited by Karin Barber and P. F. de Moraes Farias, 171–88. Birmingham, UK: Centre of West African Studies, University of Birmingham, 1989.

Camara, Laye. *The Guardian of the Word.* Translated by James Kirkup. New York: Vintage Books, 1984 (first Eng. tr. 1980, Fr. ed. *Kouma Lafôlô Kouma,* 1978).

Charry, Eric. *Mande Music: Traditional and Modern Music of the Maninka and Mandinka of Western Africa.* Chicago and London: University of Chicago Press, 2000.

Colleyn, Jean-Paul, ed. *Bamana: The Art of Existence in Mali.* New York: Museum for African Art, 2001.

Conrad, David C. "Mooning Armies and Mothering Heroes: Female Power in Mande Epic Tradition." In *In Search of Sunjata: The Mande Epic as History, Literature, and Performance,* edited by Ralph A. Austen, 89–229. Bloomington and Indianapolis: Indiana University Press, 1999a.

————, ed. *Epic Ancestors of the Sunjata Era: Oral Tradition from the Maninka of Guinea*. Madison, WI: African Studies Program, University of Wisconsin, 1999b.

————. "A Town Called Dakajalan: The Sunjata Tradition and the Question of Ancient Mali's Capital." *Journal of African History* 35 (1994): 355–77.

————. "Searching for History in the Sunjata Epic: The Case of Fakoli." *History in Africa* 19 (1992): 147–200.

————. "Islam in the Oral Traditions of Mali: Bilali and Surakata." *Journal of African History* 26 (1985): 33–49.

Conrad, David C., and Barbara E. Frank, eds. *Status and Identity in West Africa: Nyamakalaw of Mande*. Bloomington and Indianapolis: Indiana University Press, 1995.

Hale, Thomas A. *Griots and Griottes: Masters of Words and Music*. Bloomington and Indianapolis: Indiana University Press, 1998.

Hoffman, Barbara G. *Griots at War: Conflict, Conciliation, and Caste in Mande*. Bloomington and Indianapolis: Indiana University Press, 2000.

Innes, Gordon, ed. *Sunjata: Three Mandinka Versions*. London: School of Oriental and African Studies, University of London, 1974.

Jansen, Jan, and Clemens Zobel, eds. *The Younger Brother in Mande: Kinship and Politics in West Africa*. Leiden, The Netherlands: Research School CNWS, 1996.

Janson, Marloes. "The Narration of the Sunjata Epic as a Gendered Activity." In *Epic Adventures: Heroic Narrative in the Oral Performance Traditions of Four Continents*, edited by Jan Jansen and Henk M. J. Maier, 81–88. Münster, Germany: Lit Verlag, 2004.

————. *The Best Hand is the Hand That Always Gives: Griottes and their Profession in Eastern Gambia*. Leiden, The Netherlands: Research School CNWS, 2002.

Johnson, John William, ed. *Son-Jara: The Mande Epic*. 3rd ed. Text by Fa-Digi Sisòkò. Bloomington and Indianapolis: Indiana University Press, 2003.

Johnson, John William, Thomas A. Hale, and Stephen Belcher, eds. *Oral Epics from Africa: Vibrant Voices from a Vast Continent*. Bloomington and Indianapolis: Indiana University Press, 1997.

Koné, Kassim. "When Male Becomes Female and Female Becomes Male in Mande." *Mande Studies* 4 (2002): 21–29.

Levtzion, Nehemia. *Ancient Ghana and Mali*. London: Methuen & Co., 1973.

Levtzion, Nehemia, and J.F.P. Hopkins, eds. *Corpus of Early Arabic Sources for West African History*. Cambridge: Cambridge University Press, 1981.

Levtzion, Nehemia, and Jay Spaulding, eds. *Medieval West Africa: Views from Arab Scholars and Merchants*. Princeton, NJ: Markus Wiener Publishers, 2003.

McIntosh, Roderick J. *The Peoples of the Middle Niger: The Island of Gold*. Malden, MA and Oxford: Blackwell Publishers, Ltd., 1998.

McNaughton, Patrick R. *The Mande Blacksmiths: Knowledge, Power, and Art in West Africa*. Bloomington and Indianapolis: Indiana University Press, 1988.

Niane, Djibril Tamsir. *Sundiata: An Epic of Old Mali*. Translated by G. D. Pickett. London: Longman, 1965.

Suso, Bamba. *Sunjata*, edited by Graham Furniss and Lucy Duran. London and New York: Penguin Books, 2000.

Vansina, Jan. *Oral Tradition as History*. Madison, WI: The University of Wisconsin Press, 1985.